WOMEN
OF THE
ENGLISH
RENAISSANCE
AND
REFORMATION

Recent Titles in
Contributions in Women's Studies

WOMEN
OF THE
ENGLISH
RENAISSANCE
AND
REFORMATION

Retha M. Warnicke

Contributions in Women's Studies, Number 38

GREENWOOD PRESS
Westport, Connecticut • London, England

Library of Congress Cataloging in Publication Data

Warnicke, Retha, M.
  Women of the English Renaissance and Reformation.

  (Contributions in women's studies, ISSN 0147-104X ;
no. 38)
  Bibliography: p.
  Includes index.
  1. Women—England—History—16th century. 2. Human-
ists—England—History—16th century. 3. Women—Educa-
tion—England—History—16th century. 4. Women—England
—Religious life—History—16th century. 5. Great
Britain—Social life and customs—16th century. 6. Great
Britain—History—Tudors, 1485-1603. I. Title.
II. Series.
HQ1596.W37   1983   305.4'0942   82-12180
ISBN 0-313-23611-9

Library of Congress Catalog Card Number: 82-12180
ISBN: 0-313-23611-9
ISSN: 0147-104X

First published in 1983

Greenwood Press
A division of Congressional Information Service, Inc.
88 Post Road West
Westport, Connecticut 06881

Printed in the United States of America

10 9 8 7 6 5 4 3 2 1

Copyright Acknowledgment

Psalm 134 is reprinted by permission of New York
University Press from *The Psalms of Sir Philip
Sidney and the Countess of Pembroke* edited by
J.C.A. Rathmell. Copyright © 1963 by John C.A.
Rathmell.

Contents

Acknowledgments

As this book grew out of my teaching experience at Arizona State University, where in 1972 I originated courses in women's history, I must thank my students, especially Judith Taylor, for inspiring my research efforts. I am also grateful for the helpful comments of four faculty members: Thomas Karnes, History Department Chair, Robert Bininger, Liberal Arts College Associate Dean, Beth Luey, Historical Editing Program, and Mary Rothschild, Women's Studies Director. In addition, three graduate students, Carol Martel, Vicki Hay, and Deborah Lantz, assisted me with the bibliography.

Professors Fredi Chiappelli and Jeanie Brink, the first Directors of the Arizona Center for Medieval and Renaissance Studies, gave me an opportunity to express some of this book's ideas at a conference in March, 1982. I am appreciative of their confidence in me and of the bibliographic help of two eminent scholars on the program, Arthur Kinney, University of Massachusetts at Amherst, and Jan Van Dorsten, Leiden University.

Special thanks must be extended to Marjorie Keniston McIntosh, University of Colorado at Boulder. Since our days as graduate students of Professor W. K. Jordan, Harvard University, she has been an inspiration to me. She read an early draft of this book, making numerous perceptive comments. (I take responsibility for all remaining errors.) Her own interest is the Cookes of Tudor England, and when she completes her work on their manor at Havering, she plans a study of the family's learned women.

My research, which was funded in part by a Faculty-In-Aid Grant of the Graduate College, Arizona State University, was begun at Hayden Library in Tempe, Arizona. I am grateful to the Microform and Inter-Library Loan staffs for their friendly cooperation. I must also thank the staffs of the British Library, the Institute of Historical Research, the University of London Library, the Northampton Public Library, and the Widener and Houghton Libraries, Harvard University, for their aid.

While Gwen Stowe, English Department, Arizona State University, did some of the initial typing, the major part was done by the staff of my husband Ronald's

Phoenix law firm. I extend my thanks to Joanne Bjorklund, Marion Scoville, Linda Breedlove, and Jackie Madison, but my greatest appreciation is reserved for Patti Lovelace, whose wizardry on a word processor made the completion of several drafts far less painful than I had anticipated.

My family has been a constant joy to me. One day in 1977 when I was searching for books to use in my Tudor Women course, my husband put a halt to my mounting frustration by challenging me to write a book about these women. This present volume is my response to that charge. Since I dedicated my biography of William Lambarde to him and to my son, Robert, it is proper that I dedicate this work to my daughter, Margaretha.

WOMEN
OF THE
ENGLISH
RENAISSANCE
AND
REFORMATION

1

Introduction

This book is about the women of the English Renaissance and Reformation, two great movements which brought enormous cultural change to Tudor society. Heralding new standards in education and new values in literature, a group of Christian humanists early in the reign of Henry VIII began to advocate instructing young men and women in classical languages. The humanists hoped to educate male students to become enlightened governors and female students to become erudite wives and mothers. When they gained control of the Church, many reformers began to express a similar interest in ancient scholarship and in educating women for marriage and motherhood. These theories on female education will be compared and contrasted to each other and to those of the Counter-Reformation Catholics, who journeyed to England in the Elizabethan period with the intention of restoring Roman authority. In addition to identifying the learned women of these movements, this book will focus on those who were religious activists. Since the two Tudor queens and most of their female competitors were not only classicists but were also participants in these religious disputes, the events surrounding their enthronement must necessarily form an integral part of this study. First, a note of caution: it is well to begin this investigation with the reminder that the majority of Tudor women lacked any academic training beyond elementary instruction in conversational English and in religious exercises. The accomplishments of the women humanists and reformers took place against a backdrop of stark illiteracy for most of their female contemporaries.

An instructive way to study these women is by the use of a generational model. In this book four different generations have been isolated for this purpose: the pre-Reformation, the Reformation, the mid-Elizabethan, and the Jacobean. The Jacobean generation, whose important female participants were born in the last two decades of the reign of Elizabeth, is included here because an analysis of Catholic reform and literary accomplishment would otherwise remain incomplete. The leading members of each generation will be identified and their interaction with the cultural changes will be reviewed. Attention will also focus on how each generation of women built upon the efforts and the suffering of their predecessors, rejecting or adopting earlier trends to suit their needs and the fashions of the time. For example, the mid-Elizabethan generation's rejection of the classical scholarship that had been popular with some of their aristocratic predecessors will be explored in detail.[1]

In fact, the unifying theme of this book will be an analysis of the English acceptance of classical training for women, a program of study advocated by Sir Thomas More. This topic will be traced through these four generations, beginning with a study of the women humanists of More's household school and ending with several Jacobean scholars, including Elizabeth, Lady Falkland; Lady Mary Wroth; and Elizabeth Jane Weston. To gain a better understanding of the variety of ways these women adopted More's educational and familial philosophies, it will be necessary to explore the impact of religious reform upon Christian humanism, the movement with which he has been associated. As from the beginning of this period royal leadership had a major influence on the new educational and religious concepts, the attitudes of the monarchs from Henry VIII through James I will also be examined.

The use of this generational model makes it possible to avoid the error committed by many writers of referring to these women as though they existed in a timeless historical vacuum. Ignoring chronological and comparative information, some, like Pearl Hogrefe in her recent study, *Tudor Women: Commoners and Queens,* have included all the female scholars of the entire century in a single discussion, assuming that their education was inspired by the same social aspirations. It is unreasonable to suggest that, because it had several learned women, Tudor society as a whole encouraged its gentlewomen to become well educated. Before arriving at this or any other determination, questions must be asked about who the women were and to which generation they belonged, where and how they were educated, why they received this instruction, and what they achieved. And these questions have to be asked in relationship to developments in men's education. By studying women within this context, conclusions reached about the significance of their scholarly excellence will have greater value.[2]

The use of this model also makes it possible to compare and contrast with some validity the accomplishments of the women of the various generations. Heretofore, several scholars, including Pearl Hogrefe, have argued that the first sixty years of the Tudor century, when several female classicists were trained, was a "golden age" for women. Others, like John Buxton, have preferred this epithet for the reign of Elizabeth because her glorious presence was an inspiration to many poets and authors.[3] The contention of this book is that none of the first three generations was responsible for as much creative activity as the fourth or Jacobean one. Chapter 10 will detail and analyze the activities of the women of this last generation, who not only composed original works in Latin and founded Latin schools for girls, but who also wrote original plays and prose fiction in English. It was only in the constitutional arena that the example of prior generations was apparently ignored when in 1603 James I received an enthusiastic welcome as the new monarch of England. Despite its jubilation, the political nation did not reject the basic right of women to reign and even chose to replace his male line with his female line in the early eighteenth century.

Outside the royalty gentlewomen were normally expected to remain at home caring for the needs of their families. The only wider community organizations in which they regularly participated were their parish churches, where their activities were usually restricted to worshipping under the leadership of male priests. Those women who rose to prominence by defying clerical leadership will receive particular attention in this book. In the 1530s Henry VIII suppressed the convents, which a few women had previously left home to join. The social dislocation and distress of these nuns will also be discussed in some detail. From the time of these dissolutions—except for a brief period in Queen Mary's reign—until Mary Ward established a London underground branch of the Institute of the Blessed Virgin Mary (a Jacobean foundation for the education of young girls), no convents existed in England. Throughout this period there was an urgent need for girls' schools but, as the reformers associated them with nunneries, support for them was virtually non-existent.

With the possible exception of Ward and the members of her Institute, the women of this century were not feminists. When they took advantage of greater opportunities for education or when they accepted martyrdom rather than attend church, they may well have unconsciously been creating unconventional role models for their sex, but they were not seeking to promote sexual equality. Neither they nor their male associates defended their actions on the basis of absolute equality on earth. While St. Paul, a New Testament writer favored by both the humanists and the reformers, had been willing to concede that there was no male or female in Christ Jesus and while Sir Thomas More could argue that women should be educated in the same manner as men, both assumed that women were the inferior sex and needed firm male governance.[4]

It may at first impression seem to be a misinterpretation of humanism to refer to More's students and other women classicists as humanists since they rarely wrote original scholarly treatises or functioned as public leaders. In fact, because they were expected to perform the special domestic roles of educating their children in ancient languages and reading with their husbands classical works which male humanists deemed proper for women with their extraordinary advantages, the word, humanist, defines them more correctly than any other term. They were indisputably instructed by standards and for purposes different than those of their female contemporaries. It is an argument of this book that for humanism, as for many other historical phenomena, definitions must sometimes be extended or enlarged to encompass women participants. It is for these reasons that the women classicists of the first and second generations, who were tutored by such scholars as Thomas Linacre and Roger Ascham, are called humanists. In the Elizabethan period, this definition, as used here, began to break down, for unlike their learned predecessors, the women of the third generation with the most noteworthy scholarly accomplishments were not classicists.

Before turning to this present generational study of Tudor women, it will be useful to give some information about late medieval English society. Approximately ninety percent of the people lived in the countryside where villeinage had almost disappeared from the manor. Clearly, the visitations of the bubonic plague and other communicable diseases, which had created a labor shortage by drastically reducing England's population, had accelerated the transformation of the manorial system from labor services to a money economy. For women, these economic changes meant only that although publicly many of them were being freed, privately they were still unfree. By marrying as society expected, women customarily passed from the lordship of their fathers to the lordship of their spouses, for the law treated wives, regardless of their social status, as *feme covert,* by which it was meant that they were their husbands' wards, unable alone to buy or sell property for their households, to initiate lawsuits, or to draw up wills.[5]

A majority of the increasingly free population of the countryside was composed of laborers, some of whom were perhaps the owners of small plots of land. After them on the social structure came the husbandmen, small farmers, and artisans; next were the tenant farmers and the yeomen. Above the farmers was the aristocracy, subdivided into the peerage and the gentlemen, the latter formed in part out of the feudal military ranks of the knights and the esquires. Left with few or no serfs and faced with paying the wages of free workers, the aristocracy resorted to leasing out the manor's demesne or home farm. A few of these landlords, along with other propertied individuals, also enclosed manorial land for the raising of sheep. Because members of the upper classes were increasingly set against each other, seeking financial gain and land acquisition through legal action, advantageous marriages, and control of the patronage of local government, many gentlemen found patrons or lords among the peerage in a clientage system for mutual support in their legal and political maneuvering.[6]

None of these men, from the ones in charge of small farms to those directing several estates, could easily do without a wife. As the writer Thomas Tusser later told his Tudor contemporaries, "To thrive one must wive." The wife's first duty, whether as a duchess or as a goodwoman, was housewifery, a task that was far more formidable than cleaning and dusting and keeping order. The women directed a small factory for the production and manufacture of most of the goods consumed at home: bread, butter, cheese, pottage, ale, candles, and clothing. The dairy and the poultry were their special concerns, for milk products and eggs were important sources of protein. Since they were also responsible for doctoring the farm's sick animals, the members of their household, and—if they were of the gentle classes—the entire population of the local village, they had to have salves, lotions, and other medicines replenished and available. Sometimes they had to assume control of the household in their husbands' absences and to protect the estate from violent attack by domestic and even foreign enemies. If their husbands owned much land, they frequently had to see to the leasing of farms, to deal with attorneys about legal problems, and to oversee the marketing of crops. Clearly a wife too old to bear children or even one who was childless remained an important part of the family's industry: "Housework was creative because without it society would have been hungry, naked, and without remedies against sickness."[7]

Although housework was also a major occupation of urban women, some had taken the opportunity to become traders. A labor shortage, created in part by the plague, seems to have opened up new kinds of employment for a few women in the towns. Many civic guilds maintained ordinances that permitted wives and daughters of their members to join the freedom, sometimes without formal apprenticeship, and encouraged the widows of their members to continue in the family business although their remarriage to a non-member might result in their expulsion from the guild. Some towns even had customs for treating married women as *feme sole,* the legal status of single women, to protect their husbands from the obligation of discharging their debts. The positive result was that these wives were able to gain personal control over their financial affairs and trans-actions, an important prerequisite to successful business ventures.[8]

Examples of women in urban employment abound, from those investing in the cloth trade to those working in domestic industry. They even dominated some occupations: the Brewers' Company had thirty-nine female members in 1419 and the Silkweavers' Company, an organized body of women composed of merchants' wives, petitioned the crown in 1455 for assistance against Italian competition. In the sixteenth century, the names of women began to disappear from the guild records, perhaps because of stricter regulations and the tremendous population growth that began about 1470. The employment needs of an increas-ingly large number of men would have been considered a sufficient reason to exclude women from many lucrative positions. Indeed, as early as 1461 the men of Bristol had complained about the competition of female weavers. There is also evidence that town economies of the early Tudor period went through "a period of considerable difficulty," particularly in the provinces where the demand for labor decreased. What is undisputed is that some occupations dominated by women in the fifteenth century, among them brewing and silkweaving, had become male strongholds by the seventeenth century.[9]

Even with their exclusion from some guilds, most urban women probably continued to assist their husbands in family businesses. Others were undoubtedly apprenticed to traditional occupations: spinning, embroidering, and the garnishing of cloth and wearing apparel with jewelry. The poorest women often had to work as fishwomen, hawkers of wares, menial servants, and prostitutes. Whatever the employment, women's wages were always lower than men's wages for comparable work.[10]

Urban women probably had less restricted routines than their country coun-terparts, for early sixteenth century visitors were amazed at their freedom. They charged that the women, whose husbands futilely pleaded with them to follow the more industrious examples of the German or Dutch women, left their house-hold chores to their servants while they paraded in their finery in the streets and chatted with their friends. These visitors must have been referring to the wealthiest merchants' wives, for it was also stated that the same idle women were given seats of honor at banquets. While unmarried girls of the propertied classes were much more closely confined, apprentices and lower-class women seem to have danced in the streets, to have played rather rough games, and to have drunk beer and ale with the men.[11]

Matrimonial laws reflected the prevailing financial and economic motivation for wedlock. Marriage was permitted at the age of seven although consummation was usually delayed until the girls were twelve and the boys were fourteen. While most couples waited until a much later age for the initial plight or betrothal, these rules legalizing juvenile marriages indicated that for many matrimony was primarily a business contract. The more valuable the dowry, the more favorable the social and financial alliance parents and their attorneys could arrange. Traditionally, the prospective bridegroom had agreed to provide his bride, in the event of her widowhood, with a dower that usually amounted to about one-third of the value of his estate, but in the late medieval period, he and his family were frequently guaranteeing her an annuity called a jointure instead. Held in trust, the jointure was an important legal and social advance for women. The conviction of a man for treason or a felony usually resulted in the forfeiture of all of his lands, including those to be set aside for the dower, often leaving his wife destitute, but the jointure property, which has been set up in a trust, was inviolate. In addition, women, at the age of fourteen rather than at twenty-one, the legal age for men, could inherit the family's estates if there were no brothers and if the estates had not been entailed to other relatives. Because these heiresses were eagerly sought as brides, they were occasionally kidnapped and forcibly married. In 1487 after these abductions (which were often of minor children) had increased because of the fierce competition for land and wealth, this practice was made a felony by parliamentary action.[12]

In a society in which land was the primary determinant of status, dowers, jointures, and the inheritance of property all gave an important economic role to wealthy women. But after their marriage, wives lost control of their estates to their husbands, who administered them for their spouses as though they were wards. While efforts were made to prevent husbands from alienating or losing their wives' property entirely, it is not clear how effective those attempts were. All of the women's personal possessions, including beds, jewelry, and apparel, remained under the control of their husbands.[13]

Viewing virginity as the superior human condition, the Church had disparaged marriages which tied women socially and financially to their husbands. A homily of the thirteenth century, for example, had warned young girls against marrying a "r n of clay" who would enslave them and force them into the "drudgery" ework. A good marriage, this author had admitted, could be a comfort, arned that such alliances were a rarity on earth. While the Church d matrimony, it offered no respectable alternatives for young women e few wealthy ones who could join convents.[14]

Unless she took the vows, a woman's economic security lay in marriage, as dependence upon a husband for support was usually preferable to living with hostile relatives. Even in the towns where there were opportunities to pursue careers, matrimony was encouraged by ordinances that prohibited women under the age of fifty from dwelling alone, leaving them with the options of becoming live-in domestics or of being imprisoned. Among the propertied classes, the only excuse for remaining single was the lack of a dowry, but the woman without one was scorned as useless. Social custom inevitably made it advisable for women outside nunneries to find husbands.[15]

The Church also recognized widows who took vows of chastity as votresses. Although some retired to convents, many remained in secular life, charged with the duties of visiting the sick and of saying prayers and devotions. As votresses, they were protected from unwanted suitors and from kidnappers, for no woman of wealth was otherwise allowed to stay unwed. Widows who needed extra income also took these vows as a way of promoting their appointment as deaconesses or endowment as anchoresses. A few husbands encouraged their wives to become votresses by providing special bequests for that purpose.[16]

Even though by the fifteenth century the Church had begun to exercise some control over marriage, hitherto viewed solely as a private contract, canon law still considered mutual vows without the presence of priests as binding and valid. There were two kinds of vows: 1) *de futuro,* a promise made in the future tense that could be broken unless consummation occurred after it was taken; and 2) *de praesenti,* a promise made in the present tense that constituted a binding agreement and could be dissolved only by death or by entrance into holy orders. These secret vows could cause the invalidation of a later Church-supervised wedding.

There was no divorce in the modern sense, only a legal separation, *a mensa et thoro,* that left the spouses still married, or annulment, *a vinculo,* that was relatively easy to obtain if the expenses of going to the Church courts could be met. Given enough time canon lawyers could almost always discover a case of consanguinity that extended even to spiritual relationships or a precontractual agreement to invalidate or annul a marriage. As most people expected to remain wedded for life, very few ever took the extreme expedient of seeking an annulment or legal separation. More often suitors in Church courts, in which marital disputes were litigated, sought to have their unions declared valid or to obtain redress for adultery or other conjugal lapses.[17]

One of the most important duties of wives was giving birth to the family heir. In a discussion of childbirth, Howard Wilcox Haggard noted that the art of caring for the pregnant woman in the medieval period may have been at its lowest level in history. Even the studied neglect of primitive people, he thought, was preferable to that of Christians who believed that because childbirth was the result of carnal sin, it had to be expiated in pain and sorrow. Unconcerned about the well-being of expectant mothers, those in charge of difficult deliveries sometimes attempted to create intrauterine baptismal tubes to administer the sacrament to the unborn infants and to perform Caesarean sections with surgical techniques that could only result in the mothers' death. Many women also died in normal childbirth because of the ignorance of midwives, for the first instructional book on this skill was not published in English until 1540. In the London parish of St. Botolph's between 1558 and 1626, for example, there was a maternal death rate of 23.5 per 1,000 deliveries. Indeed, as the population aged, the relative number of females to males began to decline largely as a result of childbirth fatalities.[18]

In part because of primitive ideas about contraception, an act that was in any event outlawed by the Church, women gave birth to a succession of babies. It was not uncommon for them to bear children every two years until the onset of their menopause. At a time when life expectancy may have been only thirty or thirty-five years, married women spent most of their lives in breeding, an activity deprecated by their Church. New mothers, until they were purified in a special religious ceremony, usually between thirty and forty days after childbirth, were considered unclean; they could not make bread, prepare food, or touch holy water. Because it was believed that even the Virgin Mary had needed absolution, Candlemas Day, celebrated annually on February 2, was recognized as a special Holy Day for the commemoration of her Purification.[19]

Aristocratic children were necessary to preserve intact the family property and to add to it through advantageous marriages. Born into a family setting Lawrence Stone has labeled "open lineage," these offspring were not valued for their individual characteristics or personalities. Much more important than parental-child relationships or other nuclear family ties was loyalty to the family's lineage and to its patron or lord. These infants for whom their mothers so frequently risked death often remained strangers to their parents, especially those of aristocratic birth. Handed over immediately to wetnurses who sometimes took them to their own more modest homes for about two years, the infants also suffered swaddling of their feet and hands for the first few months of their lives. It was not until they were weaned, an event occasionally signaled by the placing of wormwood on their nurses' breasts, that they were returned to their families for a few years.[20]

Through oral instruction at home, perhaps with the aid of local priests or of itinerant schoolmasters, all children were expected to memorize traditional Christian exercises, including the *Paternoster,* the *Ten Commandments,* the *Ave,* and the *Credo,* to learn the moral values of their society, and to be trained in vocational skills. For the aristocracy and perhaps some other propertied people, the vocational skills, along with other lessons, were taught in the households of patrons, for contemporaries generally thought that children would be spoiled or cockered by parental indulgence if their instruction took place in their own homes. Somewhat skeptical of this reasoning, a Venetian observer noted that he thought English parents preferred to have other people's children in their households because it was easier to treat them as servants than their own offspring. Usually, as a part of this clientage system, patrons were relied upon to arrange good marriages for the children who came to live with them.[21]

Both aristocratic boys and girls were taught the proper manners and skills for serving their lords at mealtime. Besides etiquette, they were usually given instruction in dancing, singing, playing a musical instrument, occasionally reading, and sometimes French conversation. Before going to a patron's home, a few children might also have spent a year or two at a nunnery school learning religious lessons and how to read English. In addition to these subjects, boys learned chivalric skills while girls were taught needlework, spinning, and other domestic arts and were lectured about chastity, plain dress, humility, silence, and abject submission to male authority. The fourteenth-century author of *The Book of the Knight of La Tour Landry,* printed in English in 1484 by William Caxton who recommended it as proper reading for all young girls, warned that women who were not quietly obedient to their husbands deserved bloody and devastating beatings.[22]

One of the most intriguing problems of medieval education is the question of how many people were taught to read. Scattered evidence has survived which supports the conclusion that in the late fifteenth century literacy was increasing. Most of this information is derived from references about Church-related activities. Heretics called Lollards, who advocated translating the scriptures into English, for example, were charged with vulgarizing the text to make it more readily accessible to literate laymen and women. Another evidence of book-learning is the existence of many English primers with Latin cues which were intended chiefly for women who wanted to understand the service. The statute passed in 1489 to alter the rules for benefit of clergy certainly recognized the change in male literacy. Traditionally, arrested felons who could read were treated as clerks and were transferred to Church courts, which meted out much more lenient punishments than did the royal courts. From 1489 it was required that laymen and those below the order of subdeacon, who passed the reading test once, be branded to prevent their taking advantage of this privilege again. Unfortunately, there is inadequate documentation for the projection of definitive percentages of how many men and women could actually read.[23]

Despite the inadequacy of the surviving evidence, it seems likely that increasing numbers of young men were being trained to write as well as to read. Traditionally it has been argued, in part on the evidence of the extant fifteenth-century Paston family letters, that both men and women of the lesser aristocracy were being taught to write. A recent exhaustive review of those manuscripts by Norman Davis has indicated that the women's letters, unlike those of the men, were dictated to scribes. One woman, Marjery Paston, did sign her name but with a "halting and uncontrolled hand." While most gentlewomen could not write, apparently a few wealthy noble and royal women, as for example, Margaret, Countess of Richmond, the mother of Henry VII, did have that skill. The Countess learned to read French, enough Latin to follow the service, and to write English.[24]

The medieval theory of women was "Janus-faced," for the Church taught that she was evil, the image of Eve, but also encouraged honoring the Virgin Mary and female saints. With the aristocratic promotion of the chivalric code that often identified ladies with purity, women found themselves "perpetually oscillating between a pit and pedestal." Outside the society of a few misogynist priests and monks and a very few aristocrats, it is difficult to estimate the impact, if any, of these contradictory images, but without question there was general agreement that women were inferior to men and that they owed their fathers and husbands absolute obedience: "Submission was the woman's way to her meal ticket."[25]

Undoubtedly there was affection between many husbands and wives that helped to mitigate the harshness of the system of submission and obedience, for the custom of arranged marriages did not preclude the development of strong personal attachments between spouses. Occasionally, a woman with a stronger personality than her husband's could even dominate family life, but the woman who had difficulty adjusting to marriage or who was beaten regularly had little institutional help, for the rights of her husband were firmly entrenched in custom and law. An excellent example of a husband's power if he chose to wield it can be found in the early Tudor period. In 1536 Elizabeth Hungerford wrote to Sir Thomas Cromwell, then Lord Privy Seal to Henry VIII, begging for protection from her husband who, because he had suspected her of infidelity, had kept her a prisoner in his castle for four years. No one had come to her rescue during that period even though knowledge of her imprisonment was well known in the adjoining village, for the common law generally supported the right of the husband to prevent his wife from leaving her home and family. A less outrageous example of husbandly mistreatment was preserved by the Saxon reformer, Johann Busch, in his report of a conversation between himself and the dying Duchess of Brunswick, who was, of course, not an Englishwoman; but her plea speaks for many silent wives of Christendom. To Busch's perplexity she seemed content to go to heaven and to leave behind her the "manifold delights" of a castle and good food. When questioned about her feelings, the Duchess replied:

> Beloved father, why should I not now go to Heaven? I have lived here in this castle like an anchoress in a cell. What delights or pleasures have I enjoyed here, save I made shift to show a happy face to my servants and to my maidens? I have a hard husband, as you know, who has scarce any care or inclination towards women. Have I not been in this castle even as it were in a cell?[26]

With this historical background in mind, it is now possible to turn to an examination of women and humanism in Tudor England.

NOTES

1. Professor Bernard Bailyn, Harvard University, has long organized his lecture materials on colonial America by this method. The Elizabethan generation has been the subject of two books: Anthony Esler, *The Aspiring Mind of the Elizabethan Younger Generation* (Durham, N.C., 1966); and Richard Helgerson, *The Elizabethan Prodigals* (Berkeley, Calif., 1976); Judith Taylor used this method to study French teaching con-

gregations in "From Proselytizing to Social Reform: Three Generations of French Female Teaching Congregations, 1600-1720," Ph.D. dissertation, Arizona State University, 1980.

2. Pearl Hogrefe, *Tudor Women: Commoners and Queens* (Ames, Ia. 1975), p. 97; the need for integrative history was argued persuasively by Natalie Davis in "Women's History in Transition: The European Case," *Feminist Studies,* III (1976), 83-103.

3. Myra Reynolds, *The Learned Lady in England, 1650-1760* (Reprint, 1964), p. 23; Pearl Hogrefe, p. 115; John Buxton, *Elizabethan Taste* (New York, 1965), p. 9.

4. Galatians 3:28; St. Thomas More, *A Dialogue of Comfort Against Tribulation,* ed. Louis L. Martz and Frank Manley, The Yale Edition of the Complete Works of St. Thomas More, vol. 12 (New Haven, 1976) pp. 78 and 80.

5. Ephraim Lipson, *The Economic History of England,* 3 vols., 2nd ed., (London, 1929), I, 84; Eileen Power, "The Position of Women," *The Legacy of the Middle Ages,* ed. C. G. Crump and E. F. Jacob (Oxford, 1926), p. 432; Year Book 21, Henry VII, quoted by Julia O'Faolain and Lauro Martines, eds., *Not in God's Image* (San Francisco, 1973), p. 146; see also F. Pollock and F. W. Maitland, *History of English Law,* 2 vols. (Cambridge, 1898), II, 403 ff.

6. For an excellent economic study, see M. M. Postan, *The Medieval Economy and Society: An Economic History of Britain, 1100-1500* (Berkeley, Calif. 1972).

7. Thomas Tusser, *Five Hundred Points of Good Husbandry,* quoted in Mildred Campbell, *The English Yeomen* (New Haven, 1942), p. 255; Doris Mary Stenton, *The English Woman in History* (New York, 1957), p. 98; L. B. Wright, "The Reading of Renaissance English Women," *Studies in Philology,* XXVIII (1931), 677; James Gairdner, ed., *The Paston Letters,* 6 vols. (New York, 1965), II, 72-73; Lucy Toulmin Smith, ed., *The Itinerary of John Leland,* 5 vols. (Carbondale, Ill., 1964), I, 203; for the quote about creative housework, see Susan G. Bell, ed., *Women from the Greeks to the French Revolution* (Belmont, Calif., 1973), p. 199.

8. A. Abram, "Women Traders in Medieval London," *Economic Journal,* XXVI (1916), 276; Rosemarie Thee Morewedge, ed., *The Role of Women in the Middle Ages* (Albany, N.Y., 1975), pp. 13-15; R. W. Chambers and Marjorie Daunt, *A Book of London English, 1384-1425* (Oxford, 1931), pp. 41-51 Toulmin Smith, *English Gilds,* Early English Text Society, vol. 40 (London, 1870), pp. civ and cxii; O. Jocelyn and Richard D. Denman, *English Apprenticeship and Child Labour* (London, 1912), p. 38.

9. Eileen Power and M. M. Postan, *Studies in English Trade in the Fifteenth Century* (New York, 1966), pp. 189 and 243; Sylvia Thrupp, *The Merchant Class of Medieval London* (Ann Arbor, Mich., 1968), p. 170; Charlotte M. Waters, *An Economic History of England, 1066-1874* (Reprint, 1961), pp. 141-142 and 205-206; Mariam K. Dale, "The London Silkwomen of the Fifteenth Century," *Economic History Review,* IV (1933), 324-335; Ephraim Lipson, I, 317-318; for the quote, see Peter Clark and Paul Slack, *English Towns in Transition, 1500-1700* (New York, 1976), pp. 12 and 101.

10. Alan D. Dyer, *The City of Worcester in the Sixteenth Century* (Leicester, 1973), p. 96; Levi Fox, "The Coventry Guilds and Trading Companies with Special Reference to the Position of Women," *Essays in Honour of Philip B. Chatwin* (Oxford, 1962), pp. 13-26.

11. Sir Walter Besant, *Tudor London* (London, 1904), pp. 271-274; William Brenchley Rye, ed., *England As Seen by Foreigners* (New York, 1967), pp. 7 and 75.

12. George Elliott Howard, *A History of Matrimonial Institutions,* 3 vols. (Reprint, 1964), I, 357; J. H. Baker, *An Introduction to English Legal History* (London, 1971), p. 146; John Bellamy, *The Tudor Law of Treason* (Buffalo, N.Y., 1979), p. 51; E. W.

Ives, " 'Agaynst taking Awaye of Women,' the Inception and Operation of the Abduction Act of 1487," *Wealth and Power in Tudor England: Essays Presented to S. T. Bindoff* (London, 1978), pp. 22 ff.

13. A. Abram, *English Life and Manners in the Later Middle Ages* (London, 1913), pp. 33-34; Paul Vinogradoff, "Customary Law," *The Legacy of the Middle Ages,* p. 296; William Noye, *A Treatise of the Principall Grounds and Maximes of the Lawes of this Kingdome* (London, 1641), p. 125.

14. Oswald Cockayne, ed., *Hali Meidenhad,* Early English Text Society, vol. 18 (London, 1922), pp. 7 and 37-38; Doris Mary Stenton, pp. 41 and 98.

15. A. Abram, p. 19.

16. Andrew Clark, *Lincoln Diocese Documents, 1450-1544,* Early English Text Society, vol. 149 (Reprint, 1971), pp. 19-21; John Bellamy, *Crime and Public Order in England in the Later Middle Ages* (Toronto, 1973), pp. 32 and 58; Henry Harrod, "On the Mantle and Ring of Widowhood," *Archaeologia,* XL (1866), 308.

17. Chilton Powell, *English Domestic Relations, 1487-1653* (Reprint, 1972), pp. 2-5; John Bellamy, *Crime and Public Order,* p. 155; H. R. Helmholz, *Marriage Litigation in Medieval England* (Cambridge, 1975), pp. 25-30.

18. Howard Wilcox Haggard, *Devils, Drugs and Doctors* (Evanston, Ill., 1929), pp. 3-4, 25, and 41; Thomas R. Forbes, "By What Disease or Casualty: The Changing Face of Death in London," *Journal of the History of Medicine and Allied Sciences,* XXXI (1976), 395-420.

19. Lawrence Stone, *The Family, Sex and Marriage in England, 1500-1800* (New York, 1977), p. 68; Leslie Clarkson, *Death, Disease and Famine in Pre-Industrial England* (New York, 1975), p. 8; Richard L. Greaves, *Society and Religion in Elizabethan England* (Minneapolis, 1981), pp. 235-238; Frances and Joseph Gies, *Women in the Middle Ages* (New York, 1978), p. 9; the first book on midwifery was by Eucharius Roesslin, *The birth of mankinde, otherwise named the Womans Booke* (London, 1540); Rosemarie Thee Morewedge, pp. 6-15.

20. Lawrence Stone, pp. 4-7 and 90-95; David Hunt, *Parents and Children in History* (New York, 1970), p. 186.

21. Thomas Whythorne, *Autobiography,* ed. James M. Osborn (London, 1962), p. 3; Charlotte Augusta Sneyd, trans., *A Relation or Rather A True Account of the Island of England . . . about the year 1500,* Camden Society, Vol. 37 (London, 1847), p. 25.

22. Clara McMahon, *Education in 15th Century England* (Baltimore, 1947), p. 123; a few towns also had elementary schools, but they were not frequented by the aristocracy; for grammar schools, see Chapters 2 and 3. Thomas Wright, ed., *The Book of the Knight of La Tour Landry,* Early English Text Society, Vol. 33 (London, 1868), p. 25.

23. J. W. Adamson, *The Illiterate Anglo-Saxon and Other Essays* (Cambridge, 1946), pp. 40-41; Felix Makower, *The Constitutional History and Constitution of the Church of England* (New York, 1895), pp. 403-414; Roger Schofield, "Measurement of Literacy in Pre-Industrial England," *Literacy in Traditional Societies* (Cambridge, 1968), pp. 315-317; see also David Cressy, *Literacy and the Social Order* (Cambridge, 1980), pp. 45 ff.

24. Norman Davis, ed., *Paston Letters and Papers of the Fifteenth Century,* 2 vols. (Oxford, 1971), I, xxxvii; Thomas Stapleton, *The Plumpton Correspondence,* Camden Society, Vol. 4 (London, 1839), pp. 188, 191, and 197; see William E. A. Axon, "The Lady Margaret as a Lover of Literature," *Library,* second series, VIII (1907), 34-41; see also Retha M. Warnicke, "The Lady Margaret, Countess of Richmond (d. 1509), as Seen by Bishop Fisher and Lord Morley," *Moreana,* XIX (June, 1982), 47-55; and Joel T.

Rosenthal, "Aristocratic Cultural Patronage and Book Requests, 1350–1500," *Bulletin of the John Rylands Library,* LXIV (1982), 522-548.

25. Eileen Power, p. 401; Julia O'Faolain, pp. xx-xxi.

26. John Gough Nichols, ed., *Chronicle of the Grey Friars of London,* Camden Society, vol. 53 (London, 1852), p. 101; William Alexander, *The History of Women from the Earliest Antiquity,* 3rd ed., 2 vols. (London, 1782), II, 511; Johann Busch, *Liber de Reformatione Monasteriorium* (1470-1475) quoted by Eileen Power, p. 415.

2

Women and Humanism in Early Tudor England

Among the most influential Christian humanists in early Tudor England were John Colet, William Grocyn, Thomas Linacre, Erasmus, and Thomas More.[1] Because of their belief that the ancient civilizations of Rome and Greece had developed a moral wisdom compatible with that of Christianity, these scholars encouraged the study of classical languages and literature. The interest they shared in replacing corrupt translations with the original language of the ancient texts had first gained support in Italy, but it was not primarily to the early Italian humanists, among them Petrarch, that most of them looked for guidance. The work of Giovanni Pico della Mirandola, who had died in 1494 at the age of thirty-one, and that of other Florentine humanists, which had focused on the philosophy of Plato, became a major inspiration to many of these scholars, who increasingly turned to Greek sources for their moral and critical ideas. More, himself, translated from Latin into English a life of Pico della Mirandola that was subsequently published. While generally admiring Plato, the Christian humanists disagreed among themselves about the study of other ancient writers. This disagreement reflected a difference of opinion held by the Church Fathers, St. Jerome and St. Augustine, as to how suitable the pagans were for Christian study. Erasmus and More adopted the enthusiastic approach of St. Jerome, who had admired a wide variety of these authors, while John Colet, who was personally devoted to Cicero, shared the hesitancy of St. Augustine about widespread reading of the pagans for fear that their ideas might lead to a corruption of Christian doctrine.[2]

Although sometimes in disagreement about which works to value, the Christian humanists were generally unanimous in scorning scholastic philosophy with its interest in discovering "eternal verities" by way of dialectical exercises. Instead, they "lined their intellectual heritage inextricably with contemporary problems," a natural result of their conviction that by relating ancient experiences to the issues of their day and by asking new questions of the classics, they could cure the ills of their society.[3] Their zeal focused on many aspects of life: an uneducated community that clung to its religious and secular superstitions; a Church that was an exacting landlord; an economic system that fostered poverty; laws that encouraged greed and failed to inhibit crime; a political system that bred warfare; and other practices that marred human affairs.

Looking to the youth of their day for the transmission of their ideas, the Christian humanists were particularly interested in transforming the educational system. In early medieval society, some schools had been endowed to train young men as clerks for the keeping of written records or for more prestigious Church office, while patrons and lords offered chivalric education in their homes to young warriors who went off to fight in knightly armor. By the late fifteenth century many of the warriors who belonged to an increasingly literate secular society were attending the endowed schools along with the clerks. At these schools they still learned medieval or Church Latin by the traditional oral methods, for the expansion of education to the lay public generally was not accompanied by a change in subject matter or in teaching methods.

A major goal of the humanists was the training of governors for society, thus changing the focus and intent of education from clerical to secular. Emphasizing grammar and the art of rhetoric, insisting on instruction in Augustan or classical Latin and Greek, and upholding rigorous standards of accuracy in the translations of ancient manuscripts, they believed that their students would be able to apply to contemporary affairs the analytical methods and the new knowledge gleaned from ancient philosophies. Because human nature was capable of improvement, they further argued, the new instruction with its emphasis upon virtue, piety, and wisdom would produce enlightened public and royal administrators. Secular institutions were to transmit this new scholarship and the new methods, a further challenge to the Church's monopoly on "schoolkeeping," already evident with the spread of lay literacy. Thus, when John Colet, himself in orders, founded the first humanist grammar school in England, he placed it under the direction of the Mercer's, the most prestigious of the London livery companies.[4]

A few of the humanists even encouraged women to learn the Latin and Greek languages. Because he established a school in his home for his three daughters, one son, and other youth, Thomas More is usually recognized as the first Englishman to extend humanist training to women. Fritz Caspari has said that these students, who learned how to analyze critically Greek and Latin manuscripts, formed the "most civilized group in the England of Henry VIII,"[5] a noteworthy distinction for a circle in which the best scholars were women. Among his instructional techniques, More suggested the use of double translations, a method of translation and retranslation, and insisted upon kind and gentle treatment of students, principles which followed in part the ancient work of Quintilian and the contemporary efforts of Erasmus and which foreshadowed the later work of Juan Luis Vives and Roger Ascham.

As More was the first English humanist to implement his pedagogical ideas for women, it will be helpful to analyze his beliefs about how education would affect their traditional roles as wives and mothers. His personal letters and his scholarly work, particularly the Utopia, will be utilized for this purpose. The attitudes toward the family and female education which were revealed in Utopian society will be compared and contrasted with those prevalent in early Tudor England. A study will also be made of More's household school and the academic promise of its outstanding scholars, Margaret Roper and Margaret Gigs. Finally, the views about women and marriage of John Colet, the founder of the first humanist grammar school in England, will be examined.

Edward Surtz, a modern editor of the *Utopia*, perhaps "the greatest literary monument in early humanism," has noted that More put a "surprising amount of himself" into the work and that "even his more personal relationships as wooer, husband, and father may find expression in Utopian views." Another historian, D. B. Fenton, has called *Utopia* "an urbanized extension of More's household." Thus, any thorough analysis of his attitude toward women's education must consider this work that has already been the subject of endless debate and controversy. The story is well known. One Raphael Hythlodaeus, a traveler, was said to have described a hitherto unknown society in the New World to Thomas More, who took notes and decided to have the story, which was essentially a narrative dialogue, published in 1516.[6]

Many critics, among them C. S. Lewis, believe that the *Utopia* was written as a satirical model for the revealing of human avarice without meaning to give "practical advice," and still another scholar, J. H. Hexter has concluded that he can find no evidence for treating it other than as a serious diagnosis of social ills. The *Utopia* was, in fact, an attack on pride, the "rote of all myschyfe." Since pride must be measured by people's relative economic prosperity, it not only causes them to accumulate possessions and power to dazzle others but also forces them into self-righteous satisfaction at the impoverishment of those less-fortunate individuals. To cure these ills, More had private property abolished and had members of an elite group of scholars elected as governors. Adapting his economic ideas and attitudes from his Christian experience and from Platonic studies, his support for an elite group necessarily precludes More from being a prophet of modern socialism or communism.[7]

One of the most controversial issues of Utopia was its communal society. More created a highly regulated economic system in which he eliminated poverty and provided essential goods by abolishing private property, all monetary systems, and idleness. For More (who had Raphael charge that in Europe almost all of the women existed without working and that even when they were found to be busy, their husbands were sleeping) the problem with European society was not just the pride that causes vast accumulations of property but also the idleness and underemployment which result in a scarcity of essential goods. The English aristocracy, Raphael also complained, had too many male attendants who were weakened by idleness or softened by almost "womanish occupations."[8]

In Utopia, a state of cities with an agricultural hinterland, the citizens had alternating agricultural and industrial tasks. All citizens, including the scholars, spent two years on a rotating basis on farms which were directed by permanent masters and mistresses with the help of serfs who were not members of the

citizenry. Since only a few paragraphs in the book were devoted to this countryside, it was probably included in the story only to indicate the source of
agricultural produce for the cities, which were the primary interest of the author.[9]

Besides their country skills, the Utopians learned crafts, but only the essential
ones, like wool-working, linen-making, masonry, metal-working, or carpentry.
Women as the "weaker sex" had the "lighter occupations," such as the working
of wool and flax, while men had the freedom to choose among the other crafts
and could learn more than one skill. More's decision to limit the women to these
"lighter" tasks reflected a tradition already well established in English society
that foreshadowed the passage of the Artificers' Act of 1563 with its requirement
that all unmarried Englishwomen between the ages of twelve and forty had to
occupy their time spinning. This employment became so common among single
women that since the seventeenth century the word spinster has been used to
describe an unmarried woman rather than one following an occupation.[10]

The laws and customs of Utopia encouraged monogamous marriages. Even
clothing was used to denote the sex and marital status of individuals, who, until
they were wed (women could not marry until they were eighteen years of age
and men until they were twenty-two years of age), had to refrain from sexual
intercourse, an "activity generative of children." Both participants in an act of
fornication as well as the master and mistress of the house in which the crime
was committed were severely punished, for it was assumed that without stringent
controls on sexual freedom, few would marry. In a list of pleasures, the Utopians
included sexual enjoyment with "discharge of the feces and the itching of some
part."[11]

Before Utopians married, they were permitted to view their prospective spouses
naked, but Raphael warned that though some might be attracted by physical
beauty, "no man's love is kept permanently except by virtue and obedience."
The viewings, it was explained, were held to prevent the hiding of foul deformities
that might "alienate a man's mind from his wife," although both sexes were
permitted sneak previews. After they were married, the wives left their own
households to move into those of their husbands. It was assumed that marriages
would endure for life, but when the spouses agreed on their incompatibility,
divorces could be obtained with the official consent of the Senate, a body of
elected officials. Each divorced partner could then choose a new mate, but those
who were convicted of adultery or of "intolerable offensiveness" could be divorced, could not remarry, were enslaved, and for a second offense were executed. The innocent spouses were permitted remarriage but could elect to remain
with the guilty partners in enslavement.[12]

Each household, which was limited to sixteen adults, was ruled by the eldest
male. Within that social framework, the wives were expected to wait upon their
husbands, a requirement that was consistent with Raphael's remark, as noted
here earlier, that male attendants in Europe did "womanish" work. Thirty of
these households combined to eat in a common dining area, but although there
were slaves to do some of the heavy work, women still were required to take

turns cooking the food, an arduous and strenuous task, for sixteenth-century cooking took place over an open fire in the wall that smoked, blazed, and caused great discomfort with its heat, popping grease, and soot all contributing to burned faces and cracked hands. When the food was prepared, it was served first to the "old men," the elders to whom much respect was shown and who sometimes permitted the "young men" to talk at the table.[13]

The women sat silently on the outside of the table so that if they became ill, as those who were breeding often did, they could go to the nurses' dining room without disturbing anyone. It was assumed that childbearing women had eating difficulties, as in yet another passage More had Raphael refer to pregnant women whose "vitiated tastes" made them think that pitch and tallow were as sweet as honey. The nurses, who were almost always the natural mothers of the infants, kept their offspring under five years of age in separate quarters, a nurturing role that was probably considered a full-time occupation. Those youth over the age of five apparently attended schools.[14]

It was the husband's duty to discipline or correct his wife when she was in error, an authority that extended even to religious matters. On the last day of the month before their usual departure to the Temple, wives fell down at the feet of their husbands to confess their errors so that if any quarrel had arisen in the family, it could then be settled. Interestingly, no provision for male confession was made. Although the priests, who were permitted to marry, were usually men, on occasion a widow of ripe years might hold that office.[15]

Priests and secular officeholders were elected from the company of scholars, a group that included those enlisted from childhood because of their intelligence and those admitted later because of their advanced learning. The scholars, who were of both sexes, were required to attend public lectures before breakfast and were exempted from manual labor in the towns, but they could be reduced back to workers if they became slothful in their pursuit of learning. Many men and women who were not scholars also devoted their leisure time to study. Those chosen as the governors of the commonwealth were sometimes referred to as "fathers" and as "men of learning." Since, by contrast, the references to suffrage specified people, apparently both sexes had the right to elect the governors, whose wives, it was noted, were given special places of honor at meals.[16]

Some critics might be inclined to argue that life was better for women in Utopia than in England, but, in comparison to men, women were at a far greater disadvantage in this society than in English towns, particularly London. All Utopians had to work six hours a day at a craft, but while the men spent their leisure hours in reasonable and enjoyable pursuits, their wives had to wait upon them, a responsibility Raphael left undefined but that presumably included hauling water, washing clothes, making up beds, sweeping and dusting, emptying chamber pots, and attending to various other personal needs. As there were no servants, the women also had to perform those same duties for themselves and possibly for their older children. In addition, on a rotating basis, they were required to cook over an open fire for large numbers of people. Decidedly, More prevented the idleness of women that he had defined as a major social problem when he planned the Utopian woman's workday.

It is not even possible to argue that the lives of female scholars were superior to those of propertied women in London. While Utopian scholars did not have to work at a craft, if they were slothful in the pursuit of learning, they might find themselves reduced back to workers, a daily threat that more seriously disadvantaged female scholars than their male counterparts. Since, unlike the men, all women had to spend their leisure hours in routine housekeeping and in occasional cooking, they would surely have been too exhausted to maintain the alertness needed for their scholarly endeavors. All married women who were fertile, even if they had the intelligence for scholarship, probably had to devote themselves exclusively to childbearing and childcare since mothers were apparently relegated to the nurses' quarters with their offspring for the child's first five years. It is not clear what other responsibilities or privileges the nurses had, although it is unlikely that their husbands were called upon to do the family's housework or any other "womanish" task.

No one surely can read one of Raphael's final eulogies without thinking that Utopia was meant primarily to be a place of comfort for men:

> For what can be greater riches for a man than to live with a joyful and peaceful mind, free of all worries—not troubled about his food or harassed by the querulous demands of his wife or fearing poverty for his son or worrying about his daughter's dowry and feeling secure about the livelihood and happiness of himself and his family. . . .[17]

A wife's demands, a daughter's marriage, a son's economic future, these were the problems of most propertied Englishmen, including More. In his Utopia they were solved but not in ways that women might choose, for the commonwealth was not a very comfortable place for them to live, although it can always be argued that those starving in a traditional society would welcome the assured sustenance in Utopia. Yet, because this society had slaves and serfs as well as citizens, a fair and realistic comparison might be limited to one between wealthy Londoners and Utopian citizens. Freed from the financial constraints which forced them to marry in England, these women were still expected to take spouses whose ascendancy over them was defined in social and religious terms, for husbands had been elevated from mere "meal tickets" to spiritual counselors and had in the process gained greater control over their wives' destinies.[18]

The whole point of this analysis of More's work is to explore his attitude toward women and family relationships in a setting he fantasized as nearly ideal. Clearly, he rejected Lawrence Stone's "open lineage" family, for the Utopians did not marry to gain economic advancement, to accumulate property, to give status to their lineage, or to please patrons and guardians. In fact, Utopian family life was in a transitional stage toward the model that Stone called the "restricted patriarchal nuclear family," and that he defined as a Protestant development dating from about 1530. In the patriarchal family, Stone argued that a "boundary awareness" emerged, reinforcing the power of the father and creating a greater closeness and loyalty among the members of the nuclear family.[19] Although the family lost its economic functions in More's Utopia, it survived as a unit with extremely close personal relationships among its nuclear members. First of all, it is noteworthy that Utopian mothers, who lived with their children for their first five years, were expected to suckle them, an act which could not only increase the infant survival rate but could also serve to encourage intense maternal concern for the children's welfare. Secondly, even though the eldest male of each household had governing status, the husbands' control over their wives in religious and domestic arrangements was strongly emphasized. While it was noted that wives were admonished to be submissive and obedient to their husbands, it was also expected that spouses would be mutually compatible even to the point of being physically attractive to each other.

On most critical issues, the family relationships of Utopian society reflected the opinions of English humanists and except for the absence of economic attributes, resembled Stone's patriarchal model. Many humanists denounced the system of wetnurses, advocated the education of children in the classics to better prepare them as governors of the kingdom, encouraged the family to assume some religious function such as family prayers and scripture reading, reinforced the husbands' emotional controls over their wives by warning against undue priestly influence, and maintained that marriage was not only for propagation and the avoidance of fornication but also for mutual comfort and support. In emphasizing the need for compatibility of spouses, English humanists adopted some of the ideas of fifteenth-century Italians like Leon Battista Alberti who had written tracts lauding the perfect matrimonial union. Sir Thomas Elyot and Juan Luis Vives, two friends of More, wrote similar treatises encouraging loving relationships between spouses whose reasons for marriage should include, they thought, enjoying each other's company, "the society and fellowship of life." Both also vigorously denounced housework, claiming that it was a duty fit only for women, as men would "dwell in a desert" rather than submit to such drudgery.[20]

The relationships of More to the members of his family are of paramount interest in light of the ideas about marriage advocated by his humanist friends and tentatively outlined by him in the *Utopia*. Although as a young man, More had yearned to become a monk, he had been unable to "master his desire for a wife." At the age of twenty-six, he chose to marry Jane Colt, a daughter of John Colt of Netherall, Essex. Because More had sought an undeveloped woman whom he could educate to his tastes, he had first preferred a younger sister of Jane, but had ultimately decided that he could not embarrass the Colt family by choosing the younger girl.[21]

With the conviction that to be proper companions, wives should be learned, Thomas became Jane's tutor, but her education had not made much progress before she became involved in the duties of motherhood. Married in late 1504, she died about six years later, leaving four children for her husband to rear. One month after her burial, Thomas wed Alice Middleton, a London Mercer's widow who was six years his senior. As he had married a mature woman, Thomas undoubtedly did not intend to mold her intellectual interests according to humanist standards. Certainly, she was not "too old" to learn Latin as R. W. Chambers has suggested, but she probably did not have time in her busy schedule of directing the household and caring for her new husband's children for prolonged study of the classics.[22]

To some extent Thomas' view of matrimony fluctuated between that of his friend John Colet, the Churchman who argued fiercely in favor of chastity, and that of Erasmas, Vives and Elyot, who promoted matrimony in their writings. Having married despite his own desires to suppress his natural longings, Thomas had tried to justify his decision by creating a humanist union with Jane. There was to be a meeting of intellects as well as baser emotions between him and his wife, forming in the process the kind of marriage lauded by the Italian humanists. When his attempt to implement these theories had ended with Jane's death in 1511, he apparently married Alice Middleton primarily because he needed someone to care for his motherless children. It was through his daughters, who were to be educated as perfect wives in his home rather than in the household of a patron, that he hoped to effect his ideas about the ideal union of man and woman.[23]

The most perfect woman of Thomas' acquaintance was undoubtedly his eldest daughter, Margaret, who became an excellent classical scholar. Unfortunately, most of the records of her life are in letters written by others, especially her father, an inadequate source of information that has led E. E. Reynolds, her modern biographer, to lament that Thomas' personality has so overshadowed hers that it is difficult to resurrect her as a person in her own right.[24]

As women of the wealthy classes were sometimes literate, it was not because Margaret and her sisters were educated that they were unique but because they were instructed as humanists. In his household school Thomas had all of his children, three girls and one boy, and other dependent youths, taught Latin, Greek, rhetoric, philosophy, theology, logic, mathematics, and astronomy. While they may also have learned French, the most popular language at court, no evidence has survived of their training in that language. Since a humanist education for men had not then gained acceptance in England, More's decision to offer that instruction to his daughters was considered extraordinary. It was in a 1518 letter to William Gonell, a tutor to his children, that Thomas explained his reasons for extending classical instruction to women. According to this letter, his approach was essentially a utilitarian one in which the educational goals were the preparing of men for public employment and women for maternal and wifely service. A learned woman, he argued, could be a guide to her children in their education and a delight to her husband who would gladly desert other men's company to share in her erudite conversations. This study would also teach women "piety towards God, charity to all, and Christian humility."[25]

Equal education was not necessarily based on equal intelligence. In his letter to Gonell, after first stating that both sexes had the same nature that separates

humanity from the beasts, More also admitted that the brains of women might
be weaker than those of man.

> If it be true that the soil of women's brain be bad, and more likely to bear
> bracken than corn (and on this account many keep women from study), I
> think . . . on the same grounds a women's wit is to be cultivated all the
> more diligently, so that nature's defect may be redressed by industry.[26]

One of those defects, according to him, was that women talked excessively. In
a letter to Margaret warning her against idleness, he asked her to write to him
in Latin every day even when she had nothing to report, a task that he thought
should not be too difficult since girls were "chatterboxes" who could always
think of something to say about nothing. After Margaret had married William
Roper and had become pregnant, her father wrote that he hoped God would give
her a child like herself in everything but sex, but on second thought, he went
on to add that it would be all right if the baby were a girl as long as she made
up for the "inferiority of her sex" by zeal in learning.[27]

Even after her marriage her father continued to advise Margaret on domestic
relations and on her education. In one letter, keeping faith with his belief that
wives should be submissive, he reminded her that he had been accustomed to
urge her to "yield in everything" to her husband. In another letter he exhorted
her to devote herself to medical science and sacred literature so that she might
have a healthy soul in a healthy body but he also hoped, he said, that she could
still spend some time on "humane letters and liberal studies." Later, after he
first warned her that she could never hope for an adequate reward for her advanced
education, he cautioned her to avoid with modesty public praise, for he and her
husband were as large a circle of readers as she needed. Despite this admonition,
he, himself, could not refrain from sharing her work with others. After both
Reginald Pole, later Archbishop of Canterbury, and John Veysey, Bishop of
Exeter, had expressed surprise at the excellence of Margaret's Latin letters,
Thomas boasted to them that it would be impossible to find a man who could
compose in Latin as eloquently as she. Another friend, John Leland, the antiquary,
concurred with this assessment of Margaret's ability. In an epigram he wrote in
praise of her and her sisters, he said:

> Then blush, ye Men if you neglect to trace
> Those heights of learning, which the Females Grace.[28]

Partly because he was impressed by Margaret's scholarly abilities, Erasmus,
too, supported women's education. In 1523 he dedicated one of his works to
her and sent her new baby a kiss. The next year she translated from Latin into
English his work, *A devout treatise upon the Pater Noster,* which, despite her
father's earlier admonition against seeking fame, was published. In his introduction to the work, Richard Hyrde, one of her former tutors, defended the

education of women and extolled the scholarship of Margaret, whose marriage, he assured his readers, was without equal in its felicity because she and her husband could take great delight in each others' learning.[29]

Margaret wrote poetry, corrected a passage from a corrupt manuscript of St. Cyprian, disputed before Henry VIII with her sisters, translated Eusebius from the Greek, wrote on the Four Last Things, an effort which her father thought was better than his own on the subject, composed an oration answering one by Quintilian, and penned many Latin letters. Of all of these efforts only some of her letters and her translation of Erasmus' work have survived. Pearl Hogrefe has suggested that she might have done more had it not been for the religious controversy of her day, but the truth is that in 1524 she had already exceeded even her father's view of the proper bounds of women's activity.[30]

After her publication, she had eight years left to her before her family fell into disgrace with her father's resignation as Lord Chancellor in 1532, but during that time she devoted herself to her husband and children. Although the baby born in 1523 to Margaret died, she did have five surviving children, two boys and three girls, for whom she attempted, but failed, to secure Roger Ascham as tutor. By her death in 1544, at the age of forty, she had seen that her children were given training similar to her own, thus completing the humanist goals for a well-educated woman.[31]

She was the perfect female humanist: a devoted daughter, a virtuous and obedient wife, an educator of her children, and a esteemed scholar, but to modern historians who are more interested in her as a humanist than as the daughter of a celebrated martyr or the wife of an important author, her history is mingled with frustration as well as joy because of the loss of her unused potential and the destruction of most of her written work. By the customs of her day, even her one fortuitous publication should never have been permitted, for two decades had passed since the last Englishwoman (and only the second one to do so), the Countess of Richmond, mother to Henry VII, had been able to read her own work in print. After Margaret Roper's effort in 1524, more than twenty years elapsed before another Englishwoman, who, like the Countess, was a member of the royal family, again had her work published. Despite the restrictions under which Thomas set out to educate his daughters, among them limiting narrowly the circle of people who could enjoy their scholarly works, Margaret's ability was so extraordinary and so obvious to those who knew her, including the foremost intellects of Europe, that even though she was merely the daughter of a knight, one of her translations reached print for many to read. What a splendid scholar she was.[32]

After praising her family for having her work published, it must also be pointed out that her translation would have had some value even if it had been poorly done because it was an English version of Erasmus' original thoughts on the *Pater Noster*. Apparently, the publication of Margaret's Latin version of a Greek work or even of an original classical composition was never considered, for Latin was the language of an international clique of scholars, who were not the readers her English translation was expected to reach. Works in the vernacular, like hers, were written for the perusal of men and women unschooled in Latin. English, itself, was not a language highly respected by European scholars, among them Erasmus who despite his lengthy sojourns in the kingdom, refused to learn it or even by the courtiers of Henry VIII who thought a knowledge of French absolutely essential to a cultured person. It was not until 1550 that any Englishwoman published a work in Latin.[33]

The More household school included many other young women besides Margaret, among them her two sisters, a stepsister, her father's ward, and the daughter of her nurse, Margaret Gigs. Although all of these women were probably given humanist instruction, the only other student known to have become a remarkable scholar was Margaret Gigs. Apparently, she loved and respected her foster father, Thomas, who often asked her to read the scriptures at mealtime and to act as his almoner. She became fluent in Greek, an achievement that Vives praised, and had special aptitudes for mathematics and medicine, interests she shared with her husband, John Clement, a former tutor in the More household. After studying to be a physician at Louvain, John gained appointment in 1528 as a court physician, perhaps with the recommendation of Thomas. After their marriage the Clements maintained their friendship with More, who was actually a guest at their home in April, 1534, when he received the summons to be questioned about his unwillingness to take the royal oath of succession, the first step toward his execution. Because it was well known that she and Margaret Roper were loyal to More's memory, collecting his manuscripts and buying his body, anyone who had been in their company was subject to governmental interrogation. Finally, in 1549 the Clements and their children, who were all given humanist instruction, fled into exile. With Mary's succession, John and Margaret returned to England but were forced to flee again during the reign of Elizabeth and died abroad.[34]

Most of the early English humanists were interested in education. While More established a household school, his friend John Colet with the advice of Erasmus endowed St. Paul's School, a public institution where among other young men, John Clement had been educated. Although the impact of St. Paul's on education in Tudor England will be explored in Chapter 3, it will be useful here to investigate Colet's attitudes toward women and marriage, which are significant because he was the founder of the first humanist grammar school and because his advice and guidance were important to both More and Erasmus, who claimed that Colet was first among humanists.[35]

When Colet returned to England from studying in Italy, he made his reputation by lecturing on St. Paul's Epistles at Oxford University, quickly becoming so popular that at Michaelmas Term, 1496, the entire academic community turned out to hear his Latin oratory. The Italian humanists had introduced the concept of anachronism: the past was different from the present. With that concept in mind, Colet rejected allegorical interpretations and placed the Epistles in their historical setting to determine what St. Paul, for whom he had "almost personal affection," had meant to say when he wrote them. Using humanist methods, he further analyzed the language and grammar of the texts to evoke their direct meaning, thereby avoiding dialectical implications. Because it has statements about both women and marriage, the First Epistle to the Corinthians is particularly relevant to this study on Tudor women. Man was superior to woman, St. Paul told the Corinthians, for as Christ was the head of man, so was man the head of woman. Created as a helpmeet to man, she was ordered to remain silent in the churches, waiting until her return home to seek religious guidance from her husband.[36] The salvation of Christian women, it would seem, like that of Utopian women, depended upon their mate's spiritual leadership.

Three of the most renowned Christian humanists in England differed in their attitudes toward marriage. Using the anachronistic approach, Erasmus was willing to suggest that since his own day was different from that of St. Paul's, perhaps even priests ought to be permitted to live in holy matrimony. Those arguments may have influenced More to permit clerical marriage in *Utopia,* but he personally supported priestly celibacy, while advocating lay marriages based on humanist philosophy. Colet's attitude went beyond anything that can be ascribed to St. Paul or any other early Church Father, except perhaps for St. Jerome. Colet went so far as to argue that since Christ the bridegroom had come to his bride, the Church, and had fulfilled the "truth of spiritual marriage," matrimony ought to be abolished. Christianity could continue to grow by converting the heathens until "all mankind, holy alike in mind and body, would come to an end in this state of sanctity, only to rise again as one to God, and live eternally." For him God was chastity, itself.[37]

As most of the early Christian humanists were in clerical orders, except for More, there continued in early English humanism a bias against marriage. That bias could be and often was translated into prejudicial attitudes toward women generally, for there had long been a tradition in Christianity against marriage and the female sex. This tradition had found its most extreme expression in the writing of St. Jerome, who believed that sex was dirty in a literal sense, but it had even been discussed at Church Councils, including one convened at Macon in A.D. 585 at which the men had seriously considered the question: "Does woman possess a soul?"[38]

The universal male problem was that if women were truly inferior beings, it would be difficult intellectually to rationalize matrimony with them, for had not St. Paul said, "he which is joined to a harlot is one body"?[39] The Christian humanists, among them Thomas More, who promoted women's education, found a resolution to that problem. Although unhappy with his own sexual weakness, More had argued that while they were inferior beings, women could excel in scholarship, thereby achieving intellectual equality or near equality with men. Together male and female humanists made the perfect marriage: a Margaret and William Roper discussing St. Cyprian or a Margaret and John Clement pouring over old Galen manuscripts. But even as some were lauding this new concept of marital union others continued to denounce holy matrimony, for both ideas, contradictory in nature, belonged to early English humanism.

NOTES

1. For information about Henry VII's patronage of humanists, see William Nelson, *John Skelton, Laureate* (New York, 1939), pp. 7-14; M. J. Tucker, "Life at Henry VII's Court," *History Today,* XIX (1969), 325-331; and Gordon Kipling, "Henry VII and the Origins of Tudor Patronage," *Patronage in the Renaissance,* ed. Guy Fitch Lytle and Stephen Orgel (Princeton, 1981), pp. 117-164.

2. C. S. Lewis, *English Literature in the Sixteenth Century Excluding Drama* (Oxford, 1954), pp. 2-57; Roberto Weiss, *The Spread of Italian Humanism* (London, 1964), p. 52; Henry B. Lathrop, *Translations from the Classics into English from Caxton to Chapman, 1477-1620* (Reprint, 1967), p. 31; E. Harris Harbison, *The Christian Scholar in the Age of the Reformation* (New York, 1956), pp. 7-66; Leland Miles, *John Colet and the Platonic Tradition* (London, 1961), pp. viii and 30.

3. F. J. Levy, *Tudor Historical Thought* (San Marino, Calif., 1967), p. 9; Arthur B. Ferguson, "Circumstances and a Sense of History in Tudor England: The Coming of the Historical Revolution," *Medieval and Renaissance Studies,* ed. John M. Headley (Chapel Hill, N.C., 1967), p. 176.

4. Joan Simon, *Education and Society in Tudor England* (Cambridge, 1966), pp. 60-65; Myron Gilmore, *The World of Humanism, 1453-1517* (New York, 1952), p. 204.

5. Fritz Caspari, *Humanism and the Social Order in Tudor England* (Chicago, 1954), p. 120.

6. Ibid., p. 45; St. Thomas More, *Utopia,* ed. Edward Surtz (New Haven, 1964), p. viii; D. B. Fenton, "England and Europe: Utopia and Its Aftermath," *Transactions of the Royal Historical Society,* XXV (1975), 122; see also Judith P. Jones and Sherianne Seilers Seibel, "Thomas More's Feminism: To Reform or Re-Form." *Quincentennial Essays in St. Thomas More: Selected Papers from the Thomas More College Conference* (Boone, N.C., 1978), pp. 67-77.

7. C. S. Lewis, pp. 166-170; J. H. Hexter, *More's Utopia* (Princeton, 1952), pp. 63 and 83; *Utopia,* pp. 77-150; for the quote, see Sir Thomas Elyot, trans., *A swete and devoute sermon of mortalitie of man by Saint Cyprian. The rules of a Christian lyfe by Picus erle of Mirandula,* (London, 1539); Fritz Caspari, p. 15.

8. *Utopia,* pp. 24 and 71.

9. Ibid., p. 61.

10. Ibid., p. 69.

11. Ibid., pp. 118 and 125.

12. Ibid., pp. 69, 99, and 109; later Leland related a story he found in the Earl of Rutland's book about a man who permitted King Arthur to view his three daughters naked for the purpose of choosing one as his wife. It is likely that More knew of this story. Lucy Toulmin Smith, *The Itinerary of John Leland,* 5 vols. (Carbondale, Ill., 1964), V, 148.

13. *Utopia,* pp. 77-81; G. E. and K. R. Fussell, *The English Country Woman* A.D. *1500-1900* (Reprint, 1971), pp. 23-24.

14. *Utopia,* pp. 79-80, 98, and 140.

15. Ibid., pp. 82, 112, 132-134, 139-143.

16. Ibid., pp. 67, 70-73, 89, 103, 114, and 139.

17. Ibid., p. 147.

18. Julia O'Faolain and Lauro Martines, eds., *Not in God's Image* (San Francisco, 1973) pp. xx-xxi.

19. Lawrence Stone, *The Family, Sex and Marriage in England, 1500-1800* (New York, 1977), pp. 123-218.

20. Erasmus, *A ryght Frutefull epystle in laude and prayse of matrymony*, trans. R. Tavernour (London, c. 1530); William Harrington, *Comendations of Matrimony* (London, 1528); Sir Thomas Elyot, *Defence of Good Women* (London, 1545); Juan Luis Vives, *Office and Duties of a Husband* (London, 1553); for a discussion of these treatises, see John K. Yost, "The Value of Married Life for the Social Order in the Early English Renaissance," *Societas*, IV (1976), 25-39; Margaret Roper, *A devout treatise upon the Pater Noster* (London, 1524), letter of introduction by Richard Hyrde.

21. P. S. Allen and H. M. Allen, *Sir Thomas More. Selections From his English Works and From the Lives by Erasmus and Roper* (Oxford, 1924), p. 5; St. Thomas More, *A Dialogue of Comfort against Tribulation*, ed. Louis L. Martz and Frank Manley, The Yale Edition of the Complete Works of St. Thomas More, vol. 12 (New Haven, 1976), p. 430; William Roper, "The Life of Sir Thomas More," *Two Early Tudor Lives*, ed. Richard S. Sylvester and Davis P. Harding (New Haven, 1962), pp. 198-199.

22. R. W. Chambers, *Thomas More* (Reprint, 1973), p. 111; *Utopia*, p. 79; generally scholars have suggested that Alice was a garrulous, shrewish woman, but there is no contemporary evidence to suggest that she was other than pious, diligent, and obedient to her husband. See Retha M. Warnicke, "The Making of a Shrew: The Legendary History of Alice More," *Rendezvous*, XV (1980), 25-37.

23. See later in this chapter for some comments about Colet's views on marriage.

24. E. E. Reynolds, *Margaret Roper* (London, 1960), p. ix.

25. For a list of the other possible female students, see Pearl Hogrefe, *Tudor Women: Commoners and Queens* (Ames, Ia., 1975), p. 100; E. E. Reynolds, pp. 15-26; the statement about leaving men's company for his wife's erudite conversation can be found in More's epigram, "To Candidas: How to Choose A Wife," quoted in Pearl Hogrefe, *The Sir Thomas More Circle* (Urbana, Ill., 1959), p. 216; there were, of course, many classical allusions to motherhood. See Betty S. Travitsky, "The New Mother of the English Renaissance," Ph.D. dissertation, St. John's University, 1976.

26. E. E. Reynolds, p. 17; *The Correspondence of Sir Thomas More*, ed. Elizabeth F. Rogers (Princeton, 1947), p. 122.

27. Ibid., pp. 21 and 36.

28. Ibid., pp. 28-35; Pearl Hogrefe, *The Circle*, p. 206; for Leland's epigram, see George Ballard, *Memoirs of British Ladies* (London, 1752), p. 35.

29. Erasmus, *The Colloquies*, trans. Craig R. Thompson (Chicago, 1965), pp. 219-223; and *Letters and Papers of Henry VIII*, III-ii, No. 1527; E. E. Reynolds, pp. 37-38; John A. Gee, "Margaret Roper's English Version of Erasmus' Precato Dominica and the Apprenticeship behind Early Tudor Translation," *Review of English Studies*, XIII (1937), 257-271.

30. E. E. Reynolds, *Margaret Roper* pp. 35-41; and *The Field is Won: The Life and Death of St. Thomas More* (Milwaukee, 1968), p. 174; Pearl Hogrefe, *The Circle*, pp. 145 and 207; and *Tudor Women*, p. 105; *Letters and Papers*, IV-iii, No. 5806.

31. C. S. Lewis, p. 179.

32. In 1504 the Countess published her translation of the fourth book of *Imitatio Christi*. In 1522 her translation, *The mirroure of golde for the Synfull soule,* appeared posthumously. The other earlier publications were by Dame Juliana Berners and by Margery Kempe. The Kempe work was published posthumously.

33. Three Seymour women published Latin poetry. See Chapter 6.

34. R. W. Chambers, pp. 179-186; Pearl Hogrefe, *The Circle,* p. 237; a story More preserved in print may have referred to Gig's ability. Apparently in 1520 when the doctors were unable to diagnose his illness, a young woman friend had found its description in Galen. Gigs has traditionally been identified as that woman. See St. Thomas More, *A Dialogue,* pp. cxl and 90; Elizabeth S. Bier, "Education of English Women under the Stuarts," M.A. thesis, University of California at Berkeley, 1926; A. W. Reed, *Early Tudor Drama* (London, 1926), p. 89.

35. Fritz Caspari, pp. 36 and 45; P. Albert Duhamel, "The Oxford Lectures of John Colet," *Journal of the History of Ideas,* XIV (1953), 510.

36. John Colet, *An Exposition of St. Paul's First Epistle to the Corinthians,* ed. J. H. Lupton (London, 1874), p. 112; P. Albert Duhamel, p. 493; Frederick Seebohm, *The Oxford Reformers* (London, 1911), p. 78; F. J. Levy, pp. ix and 42.

37. Following the example of many other scholars, I have included Erasmus, the Dutch scholar, here because of his close friendship with More and Colet; John Colet, *An Exposition,* pp. xxxi and 90-94. J. H. Lupton, *A Life of John Colet, D.D.* (London, 1909), p. 263; some scholars have suggested that Colet's hostility toward marriage decreased in his later life, but while it is true that he permitted the teachers in his grammar school to be married, he insisted that the vergers at the Cathedral remain "chaste and undefiled." See E. W. Hunt, *Dean Colet and his Theology* (London, 1956), p. 55; and J. H. Lupton, p. 263; it can be surmised that some of Colet's prejudice against matrimony arose from personal experience. His mother, to whom he was devoted, had twenty-two children, all of whom except for himself, the eldest, died before they reached adulthood. Blessed with a strong constitution, Dame Christian Colet outlived her husband and her surviving son. See Mary MacKenzie, *Dame Christian Colet,* (Cambridge, 1923).

38. Paul Johnson, *A History of Christianity* (New York, 1977), pp. 110-111; George Elliott Howard, *A History of Matrimonial Institutions,* 3 vols. (Reprint, 1964), I, 331.

39. First Corinthians 6:16.

3

The Pre-Reformation Generation

Many of London's citizens and even its visitors must have heard stories of Thomas More's household school where several young women, including his own three daughters, were given the same classical education as his son, John. This news must have been startling, for although aristocratic women had often shared in the intellectual training of the laymen of their class, they had usually not learned to write English and their knowledge of Church Latin had been confined to rote memorization of religious devotions. A few noble women, among them, Margaret, Countess of Richmond, had been able to write English and French, but More's plan, by contrast, went far beyond even her educational program in advocating that both sexes learn to translate classical texts, to create original compositions in the ancient tongues, and to correct faulty and corrupted versions similar to the one of St. Cyprian that Margaret Roper had successfully amended.

Despite an enthusiastic statement of Erasmus in 1521 that there was scarcely an English nobleman who was not providing his children with humanist instruction, the kingdom had almost no female classicists outside More's household. In his use of the word, children, Erasmus had probably intended to include only the male sex, for later he admitted to Catherine of Aragon that it was rare to find a lady at court reading the scriptures, which were then usually available only in Latin. After the Queen's death, when Henry Parker, Lord Morley, complimented the classical skills of her daughter, Princess Mary, he noted that a knowledge of Latin was rare for the "woman sex."[1]

It will be helpful to an understanding of the extent and quality of women's education in the pre-Reformation years to determine the academic accomplishments of the women who were reputed to be well educated. Following a review of the instruction of Elizabeth Withypoll, a bourgeois woman with Latin skills, a survey will be made of the training of the women of the royal family. The education of Henry VIII's first wife, Catherine of Aragon, their daughter, Mary, and his sisters and their female children, will be examined to determine how it was influenced by the philosophy of More and his Spanish friend, Juan Luis

Vives. Equally important to this investigation will be a survey of the activities of the court humanists, Sir Thomas Wyatt and Henry Howard, Earl of Surrey, who were favored by Anne Boleyn, the King's second wife, by Margaret Douglas, his niece, and by Mary, Duchess of Richmond, his daughter-in-law. Finally, the success of Sir Thomas Elyot and John Colet in disseminating their ideas to the male aristocracy will be contrasted with that of Juan Luis Vives and Sir Thomas More in popularizing their program of study among gentlewomen.

Since Christian humanism was at first primarily an urban phenomenon in England, it is interesting that there was another London family besides that of More with a learned daughter. Born in 1510 to a wealthy merchant and alderman, Elizabeth Withypoll, who died in 1537 after giving birth to four children in her five-year marriage to Emanuel Lucar, a merchant tailor, is known to have been well educated because her husband had a record of her accomplishments engraved on her tombstone. Able to read and to write in Latin, Spanish, English, and Italian, but not French, the language of the cultured at court, she also excelled in practical subjects which few women were taught such as accounting and arithmetic.[2]

It was not unusual for trading families to be fluent in several languages. By the sixteenth century there was a growing realization of the value in international transactions of both writing and Latin, the language of merchants as well as scholars and diplomats. Of the vernacular tongues that Lucar knew, Spanish was the one most likely to be associated with trade, for in early Tudor England that language was primarily used by cloth exporters to Spain. Although the arrival of Catherine of Aragon did generate an interest in Spanish literature, those who studied her native tongue were usually not scholars. It is possible that Lucar was educated as a humanist with her younger brother, Edmund, whose scholarship won the praise of Thomas Lupset, a friend of Erasmus and More, but she did not know Greek as would be expected for someone with this instruction. Since she was an exceptionally well-educated woman of her class and historical period, the enthusiasm of her husband in recognizing her skills on her tombstone is understandable, but it would be distorting this evidence to argue that she was a classicist. More likely, she learned Latin from a perusal of religious service books and mercantile accounts.[3]

As the only other women about whom there is sufficient information to suggest that they might have been humanists were associated with the court and the royal family, it is necessary to examine the cultural leadership of Catherine of Aragon and Anne Boleyn, two wives of Henry VIII with reputations as refined, intelligent women. That these consorts joined the King in his promotion of humanism is important for even with court endorsement the new educational theories did not easily spread beyond London to the aristocracy.

When Margaret Roper was learning to read ancient texts, the Queen of England was Catherine of Aragon. In fifteenth-century Spain where both the court and the Church had been influenced enough by its many cultural links to Italy to promote the study of classical literature, its monarchs, Isabella and Ferdinand, had chosen to provide Catherine and her three sisters, all of whom were ultimately to become queens, with a rigorous training. The Princesses studied drawing, music, sewing, embroidery, weaving, spinning, baking, and handwriting. In addition, they learned to read in Latin the Christian poets, Prudentius and Juvenus; the Church Fathers, Ambrose, Augustine, Gregory, and Jerome; some of the ancient sages, particularly Seneca; and the law, both civil and canon. Sympathetic scholars, like Garrett Mattingly, have warmly praised Catherine's training, but her education was somewhat limited. Unlike More's children, she was not taught logic, mathematics, astronomy, or Greek, the language that was the key to the new studies. By her sixteenth birthday she had also not learned any vernacular language except Castilian, although she had made some effort to learn French.[4]

There is no evidence that Catherine, whose favorite pastime was needlework, personally fostered classical translations or any other study except devotional ones until after her marriage to Henry VIII and the birth of their daughter, Mary, in 1516. It would be a mistake, as some have done, to give the Queen full credit for promoting the humanist instruction of the Princess, her one child to survive infancy. From the evidence it can be deduced that Henry, who was lauded as the patron of humanism from his succession to the throne, took a personal interest in the education of Mary, his only legitimate child at that time. Shortly after 1519 the celebrated scholar Thomas Linacre won appointment as the King's physician and as the tutor of the young Princess. Even though Catherine was acquainted with Linacre, who had been the resident Latin teacher for her first husband, Arthur, Prince of Wales, it was Henry and not she who had acted as his patron. Linacre became the recipient of two rectories by royal gift after he dedicated two books to the King. He also wrote a Latin grammar, *Rudimenta grammatices,* for Mary that was published in English with a Latin dedication to her, extolling her genius for learning. As the King seems to have had his servant, Thomas, Cardinal Wolsey, choose most of Mary's other attendants, the Cardinal may also have been given responsibility for the appointment of her tutors. Certainly, Henry, himself, regularly signed the instructions for her household.[5]

There is no reason to believe that he ignored the education of the daughter he recognized as his heir when he permitted her to assume the title of Princess of Wales, especially since there is evidence of his concern for the instruction of his other children. In 1525 after consulting with More and other scholars about the curriculum of his natural son, Henry Fitzroy, Duke of Richmond and Somerset, the King chose as his schoolmaster John Palsgrave. Later Henry was to provide a similar classical education for his daughter Elizabeth.[6]

Furthermore, it was the King as well as his first wife, Catherine of Aragon, who after the death of Linacre welcomed the guidance of Vives in Mary's instruction. Born in 1492 Vives had first studied with Antonio de Lebrijia and Arias, a scholar of European reputation in Spain, and then had gone to the University of Paris where he had associated with its Spanish section. By 1519 he had developed a close friendship with Erasmus and had been introduced to More. In an attempt to seek royal favor in England, he had dedicated his 1522 edition of St. Augustine's *De Civitate Dei* to Henry VIII and was subsequently invited by Wolsey to take a lectureship at Oxford University. After Vives dedicated to Catherine in 1523 *De Institutione Foeminae Christianae,* the leading theoretical manual on women's education in the sixteenth century, and published in 1524 *De Ratione studii puerilis,* a Latin study plan for her daughter, the Queen joined the King in requesting he become the tutor of Mary, whose instructor, Linacre, had just died.[7]

The *De Institutione Foeminae Christianae* was translated into English by Richard Hyrde, who credited More with assisting him in the project. Hyrde's introduction to the work, entitled *A Very frutefull and pleasant boke called the Instruction of a Christian Woman,* followed the example set in his earlier preface to Margaret Roper's version of the *Pater Noster* in extolling the classical training of women. Although its publication date is uncertain, it was probably printed in 1529.[8]

It was divided into three books, the first about the single years of a young woman's life, the second about her marriage, and the third about widowhood. In the first book, Vives suggested that infants ought to be nursed by their natural mothers and very early segregated by sex. Once they had reached the age of five years, he continued, the girls should be given either learned women tutors or happily married, aged male teachers who were to instruct them in their academic lessons, in their practical work, and in how to preserve their chastity. The girls were to study vernacular speech but were warned against becoming too talkative for they must always remember to be seen and not heard. They were also to read some of the early Church Fathers, and Christian poets, a few other classical authors, from whom they were expected to copy out chaste and prudent sentences, and parts of the Old and New Testaments in their original languages. The tutors were admonished to evaluate the students' abilities carefully because some would proceed faster than others and a few girls might even advance more quickly than some boys. When they were not studying, the girls were expected to keep busy with domestic chores, for idleness always bred vice.

The section on chastity included far more warnings about what young women should not do than constructive suggestions about what they could do, for despite his radical ideas about their academic preparation, Vives maintained the traditional prejudices about female character and behavior. Young women, he thought, were frail, naive, and easily deceived, weaknesses which led him to give them an assortment of protective orders. They should not think evil thoughts, should avoid hot and spicy foods, should fast frequently to quench "the heate of youth," should not drink ale, beer, or small wine which could injure their stomachs, should refrain from painting their faces, from wearing jewelry and velvet, and from dancing, and should never be alone or in a crowd of people where their chastity might be jeopardized. As they reached maturity, they should concentrate on remaining chaste and leave matrimonial matters to their parents, for as their sex was easily corrupted, it might be too tempting for them to dwell upon married intimacy. As brides they should be obedient, pleasant, gentle, submissive, and sweet spoken to their husbands. It was even more unbefitting for them as married women to go into the streets than it was as virgins, for the wife's place was in the home, keeping house, and pleasing her husband.

A complete reading of the *Instruction* indicates that its author believed women should be educated for the same reasons that More had advanced, to heighten their ability to please their husbands and to educate their children. Despite his suggestion that some women might advance more quickly than some men, Vives clearly did not advocate an equal education for both sexes. Gone from his plan were many difficult subjects, such as astronomy and mathematics, which More had extended to women.[9] Vives' students were sheltered, protected, and limited in their intellectual growth. In his school a Margaret Roper or especially a Margaret Gigs would never have developed, for their intellectual curiosity would have been choked off at infancy. By contrast, More first let his students grow in spirit and in intelligence before limiting their knowledge and ability to domestic purposes.

In other treatises on education, Vives advocated, like More, the use of double translations, records of which the students kept in two notebooks, one with a Latin translation of an English passage and the other with a retranslation into English. The students were also to maintain a dictionary of words and phrases in a third notebook. His techniques foreshadowed the work of Roger Ascham and that of the other great Elizabethan schoolmaster, Richard Mulcaster, who promoted the use of the vernacular in training and warned against too much haste in teaching.[10]

In the program of study for Mary, *De Ratione studii puerilis*, Vives suggested that girls should learn to speak as well as to write Latin and that they could become acquainted with grammar best through reading. There were sections on the teaching of pronunciation and the parts of speech, skills he thought would "exercise" the memory. For moral training he recommended the reading of the New Testament every morning and evening. He may even have spent a few months in 1527 instructing the Princess in Latin, but by then the divorce controversy between her parents was raging, and after publicly taking the Queen's side, Vives was first imprisoned and then permitted to flee to the continent never again to return to England.[11]

Garrett Mattingly has suggested that in addition to encouraging Vives, Catherine set up a school for her daughter and other women at court, but there is no extant evidence of it. From the early 1520's when the young Princess was given her own household, she rarely saw her parents except at Christmas and Easter. Despite their separation, the Queen maintained a personal interest in Mary's education. The year after Vives wrote the plan of study, Catherine admonished the Princess to write letters to her in Latin and also sent her two Latin books. Later, when a new tutor was appointed, Catherine apologized to Mary for her tardiness in corresponding and said that "as for your writing in Lattin, I am glad that you shall chaunge frome me to maister Federston [Featherstone]." From the context of her letter, it can be concluded that Catherine had been correcting her daughter's Latin letters, a responsibility she was then pleased to relinguish to the tutor. There is no suggestion that the Queen, who also asked Mary to send to her the Latin work corrected by Featherstone, had appointed the new instructor.[12]

Partly because Mary's literary interests were confined almost exclusively to works of piety and the scriptures, her intellectual and cultural interests have been given perfunctory treatment. It is well known, for instance, that her sister, Elizabeth, loved music but it has gone unnoticed that at least one of Mary's contemporaries also considered her "singularly accomplished" in music. While she did not view linguistic training as an enjoyable exercise in itself like Elizabeth, who prided herself on her mastery of languages, Mary may well have surpassed her as a Latin scholar. She read the *Utopia* and the works of Erasmus in their original tongue, and translated a Latin prayer of St. Thomas Aquinas that was included in the Primer of 1545. In the last years of Henry VIII's reign, Lord Morley referred to her great Latin skills in the prefaces of some manuscripts, still extant, which he presented to her as New Year's gifts. He thought that her translation of St. Thomas Aquinas was so fine "so neare to the Laten" that he copied it in the books of his wife and children to remind them that she "beinge the moste noblest Kinge's daughter" was "a myrroure to followe." Shortly thereafter, her last stepmother, Katherine Parr, asked her to translate one of Erasmus' Latin Paraphrases on the New Testament as part of a publication project to make them available in English.[13]

At the beginning of Henry VIII's reign the vernacular language most popular at court was French. Indeed, before Catherine of Aragon arrived in England, members of the Tudor family had requested that she be instructed in that language to provide her with a means of communication with them. At least competent in French, her daughter, Mary, was honored by one of the most celebrated French tutors in England, Giles Duwes, when he dedicated his book on that language to her, the third of four publications presented to her in the reign of her father.[14]

Besides these two languages, she was "well grounded" in Greek, and could understand Castilian and Italian.[15] While she probably lacked fluency in Greek because of its difficulty, she may have failed to excel in Italian because of lack of interest. Sir Thomas Wyatt, the poet who introduced Petrarch's love sonnets to England, along with most of the other court humanists who were experimenting with Italian literary forms, was associated with Anne Boleyn and her Howard relatives. Irrevocably alienated from that Queen and her circle, Mary remained an apostle of Christian humanism with its hostility toward the chivalric tradition, its celebration of the classical languages as the ones most capable of serious literary expression, and its belief that education was a vehicle by which women could aid their husband and children in their paths toward greater intellectual and spiritual felicity.

Two other royal families to which scholars might reasonably look for women trained as humanists were those of the two sisters of Henry VIII. By 1524 when Vives was printing his guidelines for the education of their niece, the Princess Mary, both of these sisters had daughters who could easily have been instructed by his directions. The younger sister Mary born in 1495 or 1496, had married Charles Brandon, Duke of Suffolk, in 1515 after the death of her first husband, Louis XII, King of France. Even though she had been instructed by her brother's last tutor, William Hone, and had received French lessons from the celebrated scholars John Palsgrave and Giles Duwes, she was not a classicist and it is questionable whether she provided this training for her daughters, Frances, born one year after the Princess Mary, and Eleanor born in the 1520s. Unfortunately, information about her children's education is so scarce that very little is known even of the instruction of the family's heir, Henry, other than that he too was tutored in the French language.[16]

As she was a particularly close friend of her brother and his consort, Catherine of Aragon, who named the royal princess after her, it would not be unreasonable to assume that the French Queen had patterned her daughters' education after that of her niece. In particular, it might be supposed that the elder child, Frances, the wife of Henry Grey, Marquess of Dorset, had been given instruction similar to that of her first cousin, the Princess, since two of her daughters by Dorset were classicists. Admittedly incomplete, the contemporary evidence seems to indicate that the Marchioness was less interested in scholarship than in hunting stags.[17]

The other sister of Henry VIII was Margaret, born in 1489 and married in 1503 to James IV, King of Scotland. By her second husband, Archibald Douglas, sixth Earl of Angus, the Queen of Scotland conceived a daughter, her namesake Margaret, who was born in England in 1515, the year before the birth of Princess Mary. The Queen, herself, has often been described as "uncultured," even though she patronized at least two Scottish poets, owned books which she is known to have read, had better handwriting skills than her younger sister, and was a skilled dancer and musician. Since the evidence is overwhelming that she neglected her children's education, there is no reason to believe that her daughter, who was in attendance at the English court from about 1530, was a classicist although she was among those who favored the court humanists during the years when Anne Boleyn was Queen.[18]

While the piety of Catherine of Aragon had prompted Vives, Erasmus, and other Christian humanists to praise her as a learned woman, her successor, Anne, was the inspiration of the court humanists who looked to the works of Petrarch, the Italian scholar often recognized as the first great humanist, as their prototype. Ironically, the English poet Thomas Wyatt, who introduced the Petrarchan sonnet to England, was, himself, a link between the first two wives of Henry VIII. In poetry unpublished in his lifetime and therefore impossible to date, he told of his unrequited passion for a woman usually identified as Anne, but he also wrote a more somber work for Catherine of Aragon. In 1527 Catherine asked him to translate a treatise of Petrarch on ill fortune but finding the labor "tedious," he had instead translated for her as a New Year's gift Guillaume Bude's Latin version of Plutarch's work, entitled in English, *Quyete of mynde*.[19]

Probably born in 1501, the first of two daughters of Sir Thomas Boleyn and

Elizabeth Howard, who was a child of Thomas, second Duke of Norfolk, Anne was not a classicist, but as she had spent fifteen months at the court of Margaret of Austria and several years at that of Francis I, King of France, she had become an accomplished French conversationalist. Indeed, one extant French poem from 1533 praises her as a distinguished linguist. She had a reputation as a cultured woman, is the disputed author of some poems and a song, was a good vocalist and dancer, played the lute well, and planned at least one masque for Henry VIII.[20]

It may well be that sometime between 1528 and 1533 Wyatt, also a married man, was in competition with Henry VIII for her affection. Surely, in 1527, when Catherine asked Wyatt for a translation, several months after the issue of the divorce had first been seriously raised, he was not then reputed to be Anne's lover. It is more reasonable to view him as an interpreter of the Petrarchan convention in English to describe poetic longing for an unattainable love than as a real competitor for Anne's affection. Wyatt, in honoring Anne, whose family had long been well known to him, was expressing the idea of love that was the "literary survival of the chivalric age," a noble ideal of Platonic love for women and of deep permanent suffering passion for their would-be lovers.[21]

Wyatt and other poets of the English court, who formed part of a cultured circle, were "scholar-soldier-courtiers," combining arms and letters in a "welding of medieval knight to Renaissance humanist."[22] Less interested in relating religion to politics than More, they turned to the vernacular tongues for their expression, thereby helping to make Italian fashionable. Unlike the Christian humanists, they generally remained ignorant of Greek although they, too, were interested in preserving accurate Latin texts. Wyatt, who introduced many Italian literary forms besides the Petrarchan sonnet, was a graduate of the humanist college of St. John's, Cambridge.

It has been difficult to identify the court humanists because their works remained undated and unascribed unless they were translations. Apparently, many of them were relatives of Anne Boleyn. Her brother, George, who wrote poetry and who also translated from Petrarch and Dante Alighieri, was married to Jane, the daughter of Lord Morley, himself a noted translator of Latin and Italian works. There were also the numerous Howard connections. Among them was Mary Howard, the only female relative of Anne at court who may have been a humanist. She was the child of Thomas, third Duke of Norfolk, and of Elizabeth Stafford, daughter of the third Duke of Buckingham. Neither of Mary's parents has been celebrated for supporting humanism although her father did appoint John Clerke, a friend of Richard Pace, as the tutor of her elder brother, Henry, Earl of Surrey, the celebrated poet. The tradition is that Mary, born in 1519, was educated as a classicist with her brother, a conclusion based primarily on evidence of her association with others who were learned. As the Spanish ambassador in 1530 and 1531 probably correctly suspected Norfolk of seeking a marriage between his son, Surrey, and Mary, the Princess of Wales, it is entirely possible that in hopes of a royal marriage for his own daughter the Duke had provided her with an advanced education. Those like Norfolk, with great pride in their lineage, might offer classical instruction to their daughters as a deliberate policy to associate them through their education with members of the royal family. Although the Duke's granddaughters were unquestionably trained as classicists, there is no extant contemporary evidence that his daughter Mary had been similarly educated.[23]

By the early 1530s, Mary and Surrey had joined the circle of Anne Boleyn and were participating in important royal ceremonies, including her ennoblement as Marquess of Pembroke in 1532, her coronation in 1533, and the christening of her only surviving child, Elizabeth, in 1533. Indeed, the year of Anne's coronation the futures of both of her Howard cousins seemed full of promise. After Anne's child was born, Mary was permitted to marry the King's natural son, the Duke of Richmond, a youthful partnership that was never consummated. Her brother, Surrey, who had been the companion of Richmond for some time, continued residing with him after the marriage while she remained at court where, along with Margaret Douglas, the King's niece, and Mary Shelton, Queen Anne's cousin, she favored humanists.[24]

Admirers of English literature are grateful that the Duchess of Richmond and her friends, Douglas and Shelton, collected in a volume known as the Devonshire Manuscript 184 poems, primarily of Wyatt, but several of Antony Lee, husband to Wyatt's sister; a few of Thomas Howard, brother to the third Duke of Norfolk; of Margaret Douglas; of Mary Shelton; of Surrey and of many other anonymous authors. The Wyatt pieces are valuable because some of them represent verses which would otherwise have been lost while others are the earliest versions of poems extant in other collections. It is unfortunate that only one of the pieces in the Devonshire Manuscript can be identified as that of Surrey. Although a disciple of Wyatt, whose son was a friend of his, Surrey, the introducer of the blank verse to English, was considered by many Elizabethans to have been the greatest poet since Geoffrey Chaucer. Like his mentor Wyatt, Surrey wrote of an unfulfilled love, honoring Geraldine Fitzgerald, daughter to Gerald, ninth Earl of Kildare, whom he may have first met when she was only nine years old. Perhaps his work is not widely represented in the Devonshire Manuscript because by the time of his greatest creativity it had passed out of the custody of his sister, who is credited with preserving in it his piece, "Oh happy dames."[25]

The Norfolk family's social and political position was threatened in 1536 by several ominous events: the execution of Queen Anne and the subsequent marriage of Henry VIII to Jane Seymour, the consumptive death of the Duke of Richmond, and a marriage scandal. That year Henry VIII was somewhat startled to discover that his niece, Margaret Douglas, had been secretly involved with Thomas Howard, a brother of the third Duke of Norfolk, and that she had been assisted in her clandestine romance by the Duchess of Richmond. When it was learned that the two lovers had exchanged *de praesenti* marriage vows, they were separated and imprisoned in the Tower where Howard, who was suspected of coveting the crown, died in October, 1537. Douglas, herself, was ultimately returned to favor at court where in 1540 she became a lady-in-waiting to the King's fourth wife, Anne of Cleves. After Henry married for a fifth time that year, Douglas formed a romantic liaison with Sir Charles Howard, the impoverished brother of the King's newest wife, Katherine, herself a granddaughter of the second Duke of Norfolk. Banished again from court, Douglas was sent to live with her friend the Duchess of Richmond, at which time she may have assumed permanent control of the Devonshire Manuscript, adding to it poems about her passion for her first Howard lover, Thomas. Finally, after her marriage to Charles Stuart, Earl of Lennox, in 1544, Margaret made the volume available to their son, Henry, Lord Darnley, who added a few pieces to it.[26]

In the meantime the fortunes of the Norfolk family, too, had risen and fallen. Restored to prominence with the royal marriage to their young relative, Katherine Howard, the third Duke of Norfolk and his children shared in her disgrace when she was executed for adultery in 1542. The decline in their influence was further exacerbated by the impulsive actions of Surrey, who was angered by the growing importance of the Seymours. Their power was based largely on their status as uncles to the King's only legitimate male child, Prince Edward, born in 1537 to Queen Jane Seymour. Proud of his lineage that could be traced back to Edward III on both his paternal and maternal sides, Surrey challenged the Seymours' position at court, in the process destroying any chance his widowed sister might have had, as their father had hoped, for a prestigious marriage alliance with them. To highlight the superiority of his lineage, Surrey even quartered the royal arms incorrectly on his shield, an action that led to his and his father's arrest in 1546. While Surrey was executed for treason, the King's death in January, 1547 led to a reprieve for Norfolk, who remained a prisoner until the reign of Mary. In the interval, the Duchess of Richmond supervised the classical education of Surrey's three daughters and two sons and promoted Protestantism through her support of both John Foxe, the future martyrologist, and John Bale, sometime Bishop of Ossory.[27]

Before the appearance of Vives' *Instruction* in 1529 and of Elyot's *The Book Named the Governour* in 1531, undisputed evidence of Englishwomen schooled in the classics exists for only two families: More's with at least four young women and the King's with only Princess Mary. It is possible, but not likely, that a few other women quietly struggled with classical Latin in their homes without winning recognition as scholars or without leaving any record of their activities. Three reasons can be proposed for this indisputably limited acceptance of More's ideas. First, he was not able to convince his personal associates to imitate his educational experiment. Many of his closest friends, including Reginald Pole, Thomas Linacre, William Grocyn, and Erasmus, who were the most likely to be impressed enough by their firsthand knowledge of Margaret Roper's abilities to attempt a similar program, had no legitimate progeny to instruct, as they were all churchmen. Even some of his married friends who were enthusiastic about women's education, among them Sir Thomas Elyot and Juan Vives, could not emulate his efforts because they were childless.[28]

In addition, there were two other major reasons for the unwillingness of the English to adopt advanced education for women: the failure of the humanists to convince the aristocracy of the usefulness of such training and their belief that it should be offered in households. While many English people read Hyrde's translation of Vives' *Instruction,* most remained unpersuaded that the program of study advocated by Vives would be desirable for their daughters. In contrast, Elyot's treatise, published in 1531 with a dedication to Henry VIII, had an impressive role in the popularization of this education for gentlemen.

A mixture of ancient pedagogical techniques, of Italian courtier literature, and of contemporary humanist theories on education, the *Governour* was divided into three books, the first of which is the most interesting for it outlines a program of study for young boys. All men, because they might use unclean and rough language, Elyot argued, should be banished from the nursery where women instructors should introduce the boys to Latin vocabulary. When their charges reached seven years of age, the nurses should be replaced by male tutors who were to have the boys begin reading Greek authors in a pleasant, instructional atmosphere. By the age of seventeen the students should be studying moral philosophy and reading Greek and Latin histories, Aristotle, Cicero, parts of the Old Testament and even Erasmus. The intent of the *Governour,* the "first substantial prose work of its kind in modern English," was to publicize the arguments of the humanists that the aristocracy should turn from warfare, hunting, hawking, and estate management to public administration. In fact, Elyot wrote a practical training manual in which he was able to adapt the ideals of the humanists to the needs of the English aristocracy.[29]

Elyot's book was far more successful as a plan for educating men than the translation of Vives had been as a model for instructing women largely because of the difference in the social customs of the two sexes. There was no prevailing tradition of secondary education for women as there was for men. The humanists had only to persuade the male population, in greater numbers to be sure, to switch from medieval to classical Latin and to add Greek to the program of study. For women the task was far more difficult. First, More and Vives had to combat a general bias against advanced female education and secondly, they had to convince society to accept their version of the proper instruction of women. Humanists failed in their attempts to change the traditional pattern of women's education because, with few exceptions, they were unable to persuade parents seeking wives for their sons to adopt classical training as a major criterion in the selection process. While insisting upon restructuring the relationships of the nuclear family, humanism simultaneously reinforced entrenched social commitments to the institution of marriage. The primary duty of the parents and patrons of young women remained that of obtaining husbands for them, a responsibility for which economic standing and social position continued to be the determining factors.

Although Elyot's work did contribute to the popularizing of humanism, it was not the key to the educational transformation that occurred in England, for, almost twenty years before the publication of the *Governour*, boys had been receiving this instruction at St. Paul's School, endowed by John Colet in 1512. Before turning to a study of this foundation, a brief description of traditional secondary institutions will be helpful to an understanding of the reasons for the triumph in them of the humanist curriculum. By the fifteenth century some young men had begun to attend secondary schools, collectively called grammar schools, for training in lay professions. The majority of these facilities had been associated with religious institutions such as monasteries, but some independents among them Winchester in 1387 and Eton in 1441 had also been founded. Regardless of their origins, their Latin instruction, which was usually based on the text of Donatus, a fourth-century Roman schoolmaster, was oral and traditional and was characterized by the Christian humanists as inferior.[30]

As humanism gained adherents among the Tudor aristocracy and at court where a royal government was conscious of its growing need for learned men to staff its administrative and diplomatic machinery, the question that had to be worked out was where the new instruction would take place. A combination of events helped to ensure that it would occur outside households in public grammar schools which came to adopt humanist standards. The first important development was John Colet's school, St. Paul's, completed in 1512 with an endowment that was part of the founder's mercantile inheritance. It had places for 153 boys and three masters, with William Lily, an accomplished Greek and Latin scholar who had studied with More, as the first highmaster. The boys were assigned a new text that, although known as *Lily's Grammar*, was actually a compilation of the efforts of Lily, Erasmus, and Colet.[31]

From the 1530's the number of humanist schools increased dramatically. Elyot's call in the *Governour* for aristocratic education caught the imagination of the wealthy classes, who began to endow schools after the model of St. Paul's. Generally, neither the independent schools, like Eton, nor the new humanist institutions were affected by the dissolution statutes of Henry VIII and Edward VI, which destroyed monasteries and other religious societies, as well as the schools that they had controlled. Both of these monarchs not only refounded or reconstituted the religious secondary schools under secular control, but they also fostered uniformity by requiring all grammar schools, regardless of their foundation dates or associations, to use *Lily's Grammar*.[32]

As large numbers of gentlemen enrolled in these institutions to study classical Latin and to struggle with the colloquial Greek of the New Testament, and perhaps a little Hebrew, they left their sisters and other female relatives at home without opportunities for similar training. For women the popularity of the grammar schools was an unfortunate development. Unless the education of young men continued to be conducted at home where humanist tutors could be made available to both sexes, aristocratic parents were unlikely to provide this instruction for their daughters. With classical teachers already present in the household, there was a remote possibility that some parents or guardians might deem it convenient or even desirable to permit the girls to share the lessons of their brothers. But as even in those households with Greek and Latin scholars very few women were trained as classicists, the major factor in dictating the level of female education remained the absence of secondary schools especially for them.[33]

Although Vives and More had promoted household training for girls in England, they might have approved of humanist instruction for women in nunneries, an experiment that could not be tested because, along with other religious societies Henry VIII destroyed the convents. While it is true that at the dissolution most nuns knew only enough Latin to follow services and probably could not even write English, some, as for example at Syon Monastery, were lauded for their learning. Had these nunneries not been suppressed, it is possible that a few of them could have been reorganized as secondary schools for women. Clearly a monarch who could enforce humanist standards on all grammar schools could have, had he been concerned or interested, provided some female educational facilities.[34]

With the disappearance of nunneries and their traditional elementary schools, households remained the only viable places for the instruction of women. This approach was not realistic because it did nothing to alleviate a newly emerging academic chasm between the sexes, for in the fifteenth century, except in practical training, the education of aristocratic men and women had been similar. At that time they had shared the same literary heritage, learning to read English, a little French, and some Church Latin. The Tudor grammar schools offered the young men a different cultural heritage: Cicero and other classical authors became familiar names to them, even if their philosophy was not always comprehended, while except in translation these ancients remained mysterious figures for women. It was not the early humanists who presided over the development of this intellectual dichotomy. In Chapter 5 of this book, the attitudes of the Protestants toward women's education will be investigated to ascertain why it was that they also neglected to establish these schools for girls.

NOTES

1. *Calendar of the Letters and Papers of Henry VIII,* III-ii, No. 1527 and IV-ii, No. 4000; Henry, Lord Morley, *Forty-Six Lives,* ed. Hubert G. Wright, Early English Text Society (London, 1943), p. 173.

2. G. C. Smith, "The Family of Withypoll, " *Walthamstow Antiquarian Society Official Publications* (1936), No. 34, p. 3; for the eulogy see George Ballard, *Memoirs of British Ladies* (London, 1752), p. 36; William Barker did not mention Lucar in his list of women renowned for their learning. See his *The Nobility of Women,* ed. Richard Warwick Bond (London, 1904), pp. 153-157.

3. Paul M. Kennedy, *The Rise and Fall of British Naval Mastery* (New York, 1976), p. 21; John Garrett Underhill, *Spanish Literature in the England of the Tudors* (New York, 1899), p. 56; Renaldo C. Simonini, *Italian Scholarship in Renaissance England* (Reprint, 1969), pp. 13-18.

4. Pearl Hogrefe, *The Sir Thomas More Circle* (Urbana, Ill., 1959), p. 214; Arthur Tilley, "Greek Studies in England in the Sixteenth Century," *English Historical Review,*

LIII (1938), 229; Myron P. Gilmore, *The World of Humanism, 1453-1517* (New York, 1952), p. 209; Mary A. E. Green, *Letters of Royal and Illustrious Ladies of Great Britain,* 3 vols. (London, 1846), I, 121; Garrett Mattingly, *Catherine of Aragon* (Boston, 1941), pp. 9 and 36-37; for evidence that she attempted French, see *Calendar of State Papers Spanish,* I, 254.

5. Linacre may have written a grammar for her as early as 1519. See D.F.S. Thomson, "Linacre's Latin Grammars," *Linacre Studies,* ed. Francis Maddeson, Margaret Pelling, and Charles Webster (Oxford, 1977), p. 26; John Noble Johnson, *The Life of Linacre* (London, 1835), p. 182; *State Papers of Henry VIII,* I, 20; Sir Frederick Madden, *The Privy Purse Expenses of the Princess Mary, daughter of King Henry the Eighth afterwards Queen Mary* (London, 1831), p. xli.

6. *Letters and Papers of Henry VIII,* IV-iii, No. 5806; John Palsgrave, *The Comedy of Acolastus,* ed. P. L. Carver, Early English Text Society, No. 202 (London, 1937), p. xxiv; see Chapter 4 for a discussion of her status as heir apparent.

7. The newest biographer of Vives found no evidence that Catherine commissioned the Latin Study Plan. See Carlos G. Norena, *Juan Luis Vives* (The Hague, 1970), pp. 18 ff.

8. Foster Watson, *Vives and the Renascence Education of Women* (New York, 1912), pp. 137-161; there were four earlier works on women's education in English: "The ancren Riwle," a manuscript of about 1250; "How the Good Wiif Taughte hir Doughter, written about 1430; "The Myroure of oure Ladye" by Thomas Gascoign of the fifteenth century; and "The Garmond of Gude Ladies" by Robert Henryson de Dunfermline, written about 1500.

9. William H. Woodward, *Studies in Education During the Age of the Renaissance* (New York, 1967), p. 190.

10. Foster Watson, *Vives: On Education* (Cambridge, 1913), pp. xxxiv, xxxvii, and xlvi.

11. Foster Watson, *Vives and the Renascence,* pp. 137-161; and G. A. Norena, "Juan Luis Vives and Henry VIII," *Renaissance and Reformation* XII (1976), 85-88.

12. For the household school, see Garrett Mattingly, pp. 183-188; for their separation, see Sir Frederick Madden, p. xxix; for Catherine's letters, see *Letters and Papers of Henry VIII,* IV-i, No. 1519; John Noble Johnson, p. 233; and Cotton Ms. Vespasian F. xiii, art. 91, f. 140, British Library; Vives suggested that Catherine had appointed a tutor. See Foster Watson, *Vives and the Renascence,* pp. 8-16 and 137-161.

13. Hilda Prescott, *Mary Tudor* (New York, 1953), p. 98; D. M. Loades, *The Reign of Mary Tudor* (New York, 1979), p. 8; Henry, Lord Morley, p. 173; for her English prayers, see John Strype, *Ecclesiastical Memorials,* 3 vols. (Oxford, 1822), III-ii, 144-145, and 550.

14. Giles Duwes, *An Introductory for to Learn to Read, To Pronounce, and To Speak French,* ed. R. C. Alston (Menston, England, 1972); Jasper Ridley, *The Life and Times of Mary Tudor* (London, 1973), pp. 12-31.

15. *Calendar of State Papers Venetian,* IV, 450 and V, 288. While the Venetian Ambassador suggested Mary could speak Spanish, the Spanish Ambassador reported she could only understand it. See *Calendar of State Papers Spanish,* XIII, 12; she may have learned to speak a little Italian. See Jasper Ridley, p. 31.

16. Mary A. E. Green, *Letters,* I, 171-193; Henry S. Bennett, *English Books and Readers, 1475-1557* (Cambridge, 1952), p. 95; Nicholas Orme, *English Schools in the Middle Ages* (London, 1973), p. 28; Richard Davey, *The Sisters of Jane Grey* (New York, 1912), p. 59.

17. Roger Ascham, *The Schoolmaster*, ed. Lawrence V. Ryan (Ithaca, N.Y., 1967), p. 36; Mary A. E. Green, *Letters*, III, 244.

18. Ida Woodward, *Five English Consorts of Foreign Princes* (London, 1911), p. 5; the poets were William Dunbar and Gavin Douglas; Caroline Bingham, *The Stewart Kingdom of Scotland, 1371-1603* (New York, 1974), p. 160; *Letters and Papers of Henry VIII*, IV-1, No. 1033 and No. 1224; Nancy Harvey, *The Thistle and the Rose* (New York, 1969), p. 55; Mary A. E. Green, *Lives of the Princesses of England from the Norman Conquest*, 6 vols. (London, 1857), IV, 68.

19. Henry B. Lathrop, *Translations from Classics into English from Caxton to Chapman, 1477-1620* (Reprint, 1967), p. 39.

20. For a recent study of Anne that lays to rest arguments about her age and the quality of her cultural accomplishments, see Hugh Paget, "The Youth of Anne Boleyn," *Bulletin of the Institute of Historical Research*, LIV (1981), 162-170; Kathleen Lambley, *The Teaching and Cultivation of the French Language in England During the Tudor and Stuart Times* (Manchester, 1920), p. 7; Charlotte Kohler, "The Elizabethan Woman of Letters," Ph.D. dissertation, University of Virginia, 1936, pp. 57-60; Edward E. Lowinsky, "A Music book for Anne Boleyn," *Florilegium Historiale: Essays Presented to Wallace K. Ferguson*, ed. J. G. Rowe and W. H. Stockdale (Toronto, 1971), pp. 186-190; L. Alfreda Hill, *The Tudors in French Drama*, (Baltimore, 1932), p. 2; the Rev. Alexander Dyce, *Specimens of British Poetesses* (London, 1828), p. 7.

21. Lewis Einstein, *The Italian Renaissance in England* (New York, 1902), p. 322.

22. Alexander M. Kinghorn, *The Chorus of History* (New York, 1971), pp. 251-264.

23. William S. Childe-Pemberton, *Elizabeth Blount and Henry the Eighth* (London, 1913), pp. 108-110; for specimens of the court poets, see Edward Hyder Rollins, *Tottel's Miscellany*, 2 vols. (London, 1928-1929), I and II; Alexander M. Kinghorn, p. 78; Edwin Casady, *Henry Howard, Earl of Surrey* (New York, 1966), pp. 17 and 56-57; A. K. Foxwell, *A Study of Sir Thomas Wyatt's Poems* (New York, 1964), p. 129; *Calendar of State Papers Spanish*, IV-i, pp. 367-368, 711, 721, and 790; Norfolk denied that he had sought the royal marriage for his daughter. See Mary A. E. Green, *Letters*, II, 373.

24. Philip Sergeant, *The Life of Anne Boleyn* (New York, 1914), pp. 167, 193, and 195; Thomas Millis, *The Catalogue of honor* (London, 1610), p. 42; Elizabeth Ogilvy Benger, *Memoirs of the Life of Anne Boleyn* (Philadelphia, 1822), pp. 312-315; Mary Shelton was the daughter of Sir John and Anne Boleyn, sister of Anne's father; for a later reference to Mary Shelton see *State Papers of Henry VIII*, VII, 7.

25. Raymond Southall, *The Courtly Maker: An Essay on the Poetry of Wyatt and His Contemporaries* (Oxford, 1964), pp. 171-175; Patricia Thomson, *Wyatt, the Critical Heritage* (London, 1974), pp. 90-95; A. K. Foxwell, pp. 18 and 126-129; Richard Harrier, *The Canon of Sir Thomas Wyatt's Poetry* (Cambridge, Mass., 1975), p. 26; Professor Raymond Southall of the University of Wallongong recently informed me that he has new evidence about the collectors of the Devonshire Manuscript. It had formerly been assumed that the Duchess preserved the Wyatt pieces instead of the poem of her brother.

26. Mary A. E. Green, *Letters*, II, 294; *Letters and Papers of Henry VIII*, VII, Appendix No. 13, XI, No. 48; XIII-ii, No. 622; XI, No. 147; and XVI, No. 1331.

27. Neville Williams, *Thomas Howard, Fourth Duke of Norfolk* (New York, 1964), p. 19; *Letters and Papers of Henry VIII*, XXI-ii, No. 1548; Surrey had incorrectly quartered the royal arms by placing them in the first instead of the second quarter; Henry Howard, *Indications of Memorials, paintings and engravings of the Howard Family* (London, 1834), Appendix IX; Gerald Brenan and Edward P. Statham, *The House of Howard*, 2 vols. (New York, 1907), II, 422.

28. Two other women who might have been trained in the classics were: Dionysia, the daughter of William Lily, the first headmaster of St. Paul's School, and the wife of schoolmaster, John Rightwise; and Gertrude Blount, a daughter of William Blount, fourth Lord Mountjoy, and the wife of Henry Courtney, Marquess of Exeter. Neither had a contemporary reputation for learning. See William Barker, pp. 153-157.

29. Sir Thomas Elyot, *The Book Named the Governour*, ed. John M. Major (New York, 1969), pp. 3 and 63-100; James Bowen, *A History of Western Education*, 3 vols. (New York, 1975), II, 401; Antonia McLean, *Humanism and the Rise of Science in Tudor England* (New York, 1969), p. 61.

30. David Cressy, *Education in Tudor and Stuart England* (New York, 1975), p. 3; Foster Watson, *The old Grammer Schools* (London, 1868), pp. 7 and 11.

31. J. H. Lupton, *A Life of John Colet, D.D.* (London, 1909), pp. 164-171; J. H. Lupton, *An Exposition of St. Paul's First Epistle to the Corinthians* (London, 1874), p. xlviii; William H. Woodward, p. 109; Foster Watson, *The Grammer Schools*, pp. 245-250.

32. David Cressy, pp. 5-9; W. K. Jordan, *The Charities of London* (New York, 1960), pp. 210-211.

33. A few grammar schools did admit girls, but only to read English. See Herbert C. Schultz, "The Teaching of Handwriting in Tudor and Stuart Times." *Huntington Library Quarterly*, VI (1943), 408; for the victory of humanist education, see Lawrence Stone, "Educational Revolution in England, 1560-1640," *Past and Present*, XXVIII (1964), 41-80; see Chapter 9 for a discussion of Mary Ward's schools.

34. Erasmus was opposed to educating the young in religious houses as he knew them. See W. H. Woodward, *Desiderius Erasmus: Concerning the Aim and Method of Education* (Reprint, 1971), p. 83; Vives did suggest elementary schools in the town of Bruges, but only for the paupers. See F. R. Salter, *Some Early Tracts on Poor Relief* (London, 1926), p. 18; for evidence of the literacy at nunneries, see Chapter 5; for a reference to Syon, see *The Manuscripts of his grace the Duke of Portland*, H.M.C., fifteenth report, pt. 4 (London, 1897) IV, 307.

4

Queens Regnant and the Royal Supremacy, 1525–1587

In the sixteenth century Mary and Elizabeth Tudor became queens regnant because there were no serious male claimants. Their most important competitors were the female descendants of their father's two sisters, Margaret, Queen of Scotland, and Mary, Queen of France. It is one of the ironies of the Tudor age that Henry VIII's daughters both successfully inherited the crown despite his colossal efforts to continue his dynasty with male heirs. His six marriages and a schism from the Holy Roman Catholic Church were wasted dynastically when his teenage son, Edward VI, died in 1553, leaving a succession disputed among his half-sisters and his female cousins.

The question of whether or not a woman could succeed was not seriously debated in the early Tudor period, for it was generally assumed that the kingdom would be plunged into civil or foreign war if the attempt were made. While it was common knowledge that a few countries such as Castile had accepted queens regnant, no such precedent had been established in England. The most celebrated woman prevented from reigning because of her sex was the Empress Matilda, Henry I's only surviving legitimate child, who had made valiant but futile efforts in 1135 to prevent her first cousin, Stephen, the son of her father's sister, from becoming monarch in her stead. The claim of the Empress was so discounted that at the end of his reign, Stephen had been able to recognize as his heir, her son, Henry of Anjou, who became king during her lifetime.

Until the sixteenth century no other woman attempted to succeed to the throne. In fact, the most important rule governing the monarchy in the late medieval period seems to have been that of primogeniture, since between 1216 and 1377 each ruler was succeeded by his eldest surviving male child or that child's eldest male issue. It was a precedent Henry Bolingbroke discarded in 1399 when he deposed his childless first cousin, Richard II, in a palace revolution that heralded many future power struggles. Bolingbroke, the grandson of Edward III by his *fourth* son, John of Gaunt, Duke of Lancaster, was able to seize the throne only by ignoring a potentially better candidate, his cousin, Edmund Mortimer, an eight-year-old descendant of the *third* son of Edward III. The weakness of

Mortimer's claim was that it had to be traced back through his grandmother, for the last man to ascend to the throne on the basis of a woman's royal status had been Matilda's son, Henry of Anjou, in 1154.

In this Chapter a brief survey of the subsequent dynastic struggles leading to the Tudor succession will first be made. Next, after a review of the crises that led Henry VIII to repudiate his first wife and to execute the second one, the succession problems of the reigns of his son, Edward VI, and his daughter, Mary, both of whom remained childless, will be investigated and related to contemporary religious strife. After the death of Henry VIII, the issue of whether a woman could succeed to the throne generally became subordinated to questions of religious belief. Attention will focus in this analysis on the efforts of the Protestant Grey family to challenge first the authority of Mary and later that of her sister, Elizabeth. Finally, a study will be made of the Scottish designs on the throne of Elizabeth and of the Protestant and Catholic abhorence for the royal supremacy in the Church of England, especially when it was exercised by a woman.

In the decade of the 1450s, Richard, Duke of York, the heir of the Mortimer family, challenged Henry VI, the last Lancastrian monarch for control of the kingdom. The resulting dynastic disputes were won by York's heir, who was crowned Edward IV. During his reign and that of his brother, Richard III, Margaret, Dowager Countess of Richmond, the senior descendant of John of Gaunt's alliance with Katherine Swynford, was left with the best Lancastrian claim in England. She took advantage of the intra-Yorkist disputes which resulted from Richard III's seizure of the throne of his brother's children to conspire on behalf of her exiled son, Henry Tudor. In 1485 her efforts, and those of his friends, were rewarded when he was crowned King of England.

She apparently never considered seizing the throne for herself. This was a wise decision because the English aristocracy would have hesitated to elevate to the kingship her third husband, Thomas, Lord Stanley, whom all would have expected to rule on her behalf, and, further, because such a claim would have lacked the political support gained by the marriage of her son Henry, to Elizabeth of York, the eldest daughter of Edward IV. By long custom and the most immediate example of the Countess, who did not die until 1509, a few weeks after the succession of her grandson, Henry VIII, women did not succeed to the English throne.

In 1485 Henry Tudor claimed the crown by combat, ignoring questions about his hereditary right. As a descendant of Gaunt's marriage to Swynford, there was a taint of illegitimacy on the birth of his ancestors. Named Beaufort, they had been born before the marriage of their parents, and questions had long been raised about whether or not their legitimate status, set out in a parliamentary statute of Richard II, carried with it a claim to the throne. By seizing the crown, Henry answered those questions affirmatively, and by marrying Elizabeth of York, he hoped to unite in his offspring the dynastic claims of York and Lancaster. The subsequent birth of an heir, Arthur, was spoiled by that son's tragic death in 1502, just a few months after his teenage marriage to Catherine of Aragon. Despite this terrible loss, at Henry VII's death in 1509, the succession seemed secure in his seventeen-year-old son, Henry VIII, who became the husband of his brother's widow, Catherine, then twenty-four years old.

During the next few years, a Tudor succession crisis developed because only one child of Catherine and Henry VIII, a daughter, Mary, born in 1516, survived. By early 1525 Henry had to admit defeat on two dynastic fronts. It had become apparent that his forty-year-old wife, who had not had a pregnancy since 1518, was no longer capable of giving birth to a surviving male child. Concerned about the future of his daughter, Henry had also been unsuccessful in securing her marriage, for Charles V, the Holy Roman Emperor, to whom she had been betrothed, jilted her for an adult Portuguese princess. The alliance with Charles V, a Habsburg nephew of Catherine of Aragon, had undoubtedly been an important part of Henry's plan to allay one of the major fears concerning a queen regnant. If Mary as queen married a foreign prince instead of an English subject, a choice most of her regal predecessors had made, it was feared that England might be absorbed by the country of her spouse, who would, as her husband, become the *de facto* ruler of the kingdom. Since the Holy Roman Empire encompassed many semi-autonomous provinces, there had been reason to believe that with Mary and Charles as monarchs, England would be permitted to retain its distinct governmental institutions. By this marriage Henry probably also hoped to enhance the political and social future of his descendants by making it possible for them to be elected Holy Roman Emperors.[1]

In the midst of these disappointments, in June, 1525, in a public ceremony, he chose to have his six-year-old illegitimate son, Henry Fitzroy, ennobled as Duke of Richmond and Somerset and recognized as the premier duke in the kingdom. Since both Edward IV and Henry VII were represented in England by natural sons without similar ennoblement, Fitzroy's elevation was an extraordinary action. The choice of titles, one Richmond, formerly belonging to Henry VII, and the other, Somerset, formerly belonging to the head of the Beaufort line, has caused most scholars to view the event as part of some deliberate scheme to give the young boy social and political precedence over Princess Mary.[2]

It is more likely that Henry hoped to give his son a status that would attract suitable brides from among the continental royalty, for when a review is made of Mary's position during the same year, it is impossible to conclude that their father planned to have Richmond recognized as heir apparent instead of her. She was addressed as the Princess of Wales, the office and title that had been conferred upon the royal child next in line to the throne since the reign of Edward I. While there is no extant record of her formal investiture, she was sent to Ludlow, the customary place of habitation for the holder of that office. Since her birth Mary had been styled Princess, the first daughter of the English line to have that title in her own right and not by virtue of her husband's status, a departure from the normal almost as startling as that of bestowing ducal honors upon Fitzroy. Later, when she was declared illegitimate and her Welsh title was transferred to her infant half-sister, Elizabeth, not to Richmond, their royal father characterized his elder daughter's refusal to relinquish her title of Princess as an attempt to usurp her younger sister's position as "heir apparent."[3]

It is possible to suggest that Henry approached the issue of the succession from both traditional and radical viewpoints. The traditional solution depended upon his begetting a surviving legitimate male child, a challenge that he had hitherto attempted without success and to which he ultimately returned when he determined to have his first marriage annulled. In 1525, with the sending of Mary to the Welsh Marches, he had for the moment committed himself to recognizing his daughter as heir apparent, a decision perhaps motivated by his desire to warn all possible pretenders to the throne that he expected to be succeeded by a child of his begetting, even if she were a female. By securing her position as Princess of Wales, the King may also have hoped to make the recently jilted daughter a more attractive candidate on the royal marriage market. Clearly, despite his high social elevation, Richmond did not take precedence over anyone with the status of Prince or Princess, or, as the Letters Patent stipulated, over any future legitimate child of the King with the title of duke.

By 1527 Henry had returned to the traditional solution for an heir with a scheme to annul his marriage with Catherine and to have a son by a new wife. As a queen had never ruled in England, he may genuinely have doubted his ability to prepare the kingdom for his daughter's succession. The need for a son, this obsessive interest in the sex of the infants in the nursery, permeated all of English society, for the goal of the propertied classes was the begetting of a male child to carry on and enlarge their family lines and fortunes. From the fourteenth century, at least, the family line and its inheritance had been the main preoccupation of the aristocracy, who anxiously added estates to their holdings through arranged marriage and royal favors, an economic and political domesticity Lawrence Stone has defined as "open lineage." Although changes in family life were gradually occurring, the parents in early Tudor England continued to hold the traditional attitude that marriage was important primarily for social and financial gain. The inheritance that Henry hoped to preserve and enlarge upon was, of course, a kingdom, but his diplomatic ploys among his European peers and their ambassadors can be viewed as exercises on a grander scale of the daily negotiations among the English aristocracy and their attorneys for the future of their lines. With their country estates and their kingdoms to preserve, both Henry VIII and his subjects were fundamentally agreed that their task was much simpler and more effective in its results if the chess piece that they were using in their moves for the survival of their posterity was a legitimate male heir.[4]

The public challenge to the status of his daughter ignored the constitutional question of whether a woman could be queen regnant and focused, instead, on the religious issue of whether her parents' marriage was valid. A contemporary chronicler of the reign and a staunch supporter of the King, Edward Hall, suggested that Charles V had spurned Mary Tudor because of her youth and her birth, as she had been begotten by her father on his brother's wife. A later chronicler had Henry VIII charge that Mary was not his "lawful daughter" and had him express concern about the "mischief" that might occur at his death if his "true heyre" was not known. These statements appealed to the verse in the Book of Leviticus which warned men against the taking of their brothers' wives, but it had usually been extended only to wives of consummated marriages, an issue that had been raised at the time of Catherine's betrothal to Henry. In 1505 the dispensation of Julius II, permitting her to marry Henry, had provided for the possibility that the union with her first husband, Arthur, had been consummated. Thus, in 1527, Henry's grounds for the annulment were that no one, not even Popes, could dispense with the Biblical prohibition against the taking of a brother's wife when the union had been consummated as in the case of Catherine and Arthur.[5]

Even though the Queen had not been pregnant since 1518, Henry presumably did not seek a divorce until 1527 when he was infatuated with Anne Boleyn, a gentlewoman often described as the catalyst for his actions. Who first suggested that the best resolution of the succession crisis was a divorce from Catherine and marriage to Anne is unknown, but divorce was not as extraordinary a solution to a marital problem among the royalty, as among the population as a whole, for in fact, both of Henry's sisters had been personally affected by them. His elder sister, Margaret, the Queen Dowager of Scotland, and her second husband, the Earl of Angus, had been involved in well-publicized marital problems for years, and it had long been English policy to effect their reconciliation. As early as 1521, for example, Wolsey had sent a plea to Rome arguing against the Papal confirmation of a divorce between them. Nevertheless, the long-expected decree of Pope Clement VII invalidating the marriage because of a precontract by Angus was finally made on March 11, 1527, but news of it did not arrive in Scotland until December. Shortly thereafter, the Queen Dowager publicly confirmed that Henry Stewart, Lord of Methven, had become her third husband. If it had ever occurred to Henry VIII to accept seriously his sister's suggestion in 1525 that James V, her son by her first husband, wed the Princess Mary to settle the succession question for both countries, her obsession with ending her marriage to Angus must certainly have prevented any serious attempt to implement the proposal.[6]

In 1527 both of Henry's sisters had marital appeals pending before Clement VII, Margaret for an invalidation and Mary for approval. The French Queen's husband, the Duke of Suffolk, had been married to two women before his wedding to her; one wife, Anne Browne, had died, making him a widower, but the other, Margaret Mortimer, had separated from him after an annulment. When Mortimer decided to challenge the validity of that annulment and therefore the marriage to the French Queen, Wolsey was able to obtain a special bull from Clement in May, 1528 annulling the Mortimer marriage and thus confirming the one with the French Queen.[7]

While in 1527 and 1528 his sisters were obtaining favorable rulings from Clement VII, Henry VIII also was planning a marital action. He probably expected a quick and easy end to his annulment proceedings because his grounds had a good basis in canon law, the Levitical warning against taking a brother's wife. Whatever the validity of the legal issues and the theological arguments offered by Wolsey and other royal agents, the final Papal decision was based upon political considerations. While Catherine fought her husband's design through diplomatic channels and legal appeals to Rome, the army of her nephew, Charles V, occupied that city in 1527. Between that defeat and 1532, Clement VII hedged and delayed, fearing the reactions of both Charles and Henry, but when he finally gave his ruling that the royal marriage was valid, events were already underway in England that were to lead to the denunciation of Papal power.

The gentlewoman some blamed for the annulment proceedings was probably twenty-five in 1526, the year the King apparently began to plan his future around his desire for her. As a child, Anne had resided at the courts of Margaret of Austria and Francis I. While in France, Anne had met Margaret of Navarre, the sister of Francis I and the wife of Henri d'Albret, the King of Navarre. A learned woman, knowledgeable in Italian, perhaps Greek, and German, Margaret's greatest passion was for Church reform. Later English reformers, who have been eager to praise Anne as the mother of Queen Elizabeth, have argued that because of Margaret's influence, Anne returned to England in January, 1522 as a Protestant. It is more likely that her celebrated support for Church reform was a reaction to the refusal of Clement VII to permit a favorable decree in the royal divorce. She probably was, as has been claimed, the first person to draw to the King's attention William Tyndale's work, *The Obedience of the Christian Man,* in which it was argued that the Papacy had usurped the position of the Godly prince as head of the Christian community. Although she was pleased with Tyndal's statements denouncing Papal power, she surely was not appreciative of his well-known arguments against the royal divorce. Anne, herself, apparently made some futile efforts to preserve Catesby Monastery in Northamptonshire when it was threatened by dissolution and her father acted as one of the inquisitors of the esteemed Protestant martyr, John Frith. That she aided those who denied Papal power and that she read the scriptures in the vernacular do not constitute sufficient evidence to characterize her as a Protestant, but she should not be viewed as irreligious either. Even the Imperial Ambassador charged her with Lutheranism and at least two different reformers dedicated works to her.[8]

After he decided to divorce Catherine, Henry kept promises of marriage to Anne alive by granting honors and presents to her and to the members of her family. When her father was ennobled as Earl of Wiltshire in 1529, she and her sister obtained the right to be addressed as Dames Anne and Mary Rochford while her brother became the new Viscount Rochford. After he sensed political victory in the late summer of 1532 when the death of William Warham left the office of Archbishop of Canterbury vacant and available for a more sympathetic, indeed, heretical, churchman, Thomas Cranmer, Henry paid what can be interpreted to be the material price of Anne's submission. He granted her an income of £1,000 per year and a marquisate in her own right to devolve upon her heirs

without the usual requirement of legitimacy. This was an extraordinary invest-
ment, for the bestowal of peerage on a woman, as distinct from her supportive
status as a wife or as a daughter, was almost without precedent, the sole previous
example having been Henry's grant in 1514 of her family's title of Salisbury to
the Yorkist Lady Margaret Pole, daughter to George, Duke of Clarence.[9]

The new Marquess of Pembroke conceived and at the end of January, 1533,
she and the King were secretly wed, a step subsequently validated by a decree
of Archbishop Cranmer which, by authorization of the Statute of Appeals, annulled the first royal marriage. In the final victory, the decision was made at
first to ignore the Roman Curia and then in 1534, the year after the Boleyn
marriage, to usurp Papal power altogether by virtue of the Statute of Supremacy
that recognized the King rather than the Pontiff as the Supreme Head of the
English Church. The most reasonable explanation for the King's decision to seek
an annulment is that the example of his sisters' similar suits came at a time when
his need for a male heir coincided with the availability of an agreeable, suitable
mate who had strong political support at court. If Catherine had been delivered
of one surviving male child, there surely would have been no divorce action.[10]

After their marriage, when Anne, like Catherine, failed to give birth to the
desired son, the friends of the Princess Mary and others, including Thomas
Cromwell, conspired with the relatives of Jane Seymour, a maid of honor, to
force Anne's disgrace. With her miscarriage in January, 1536, the same month
coincidentally of Catherine's death, Anne's life was forfeited. She was convicted
of treason for commiting adultery, a charge that her judges, including her own
father, permitted although there was no legal precedent for suggesting that the
adultery of a queen consort, even if it could be proved, was an act of treason.
Shortly after her execution, her daughter was declared illegitimate as the result
of yet another divorce hearing presided over by Cranmer in which Anne's marriage
to the King was annulled.[11]

Following Anne's death, Jane Seymour became Queen but died in 1537 shortly
after giving birth to Edward, the long-awaited son. Despite his marriages to three
other women, Henry failed to beget any more children. Near the end of his life,
he showed his gratitude to his third wife by making arrangements to be buried
at her side at Windsor, his final reward to her for his son's birth. With his death
in January, 1547, his nine-year-old heir Edward succeeded to the throne under
the guidance of a Council dominated by his uncle, Edward Seymour, Duke of
Somerset, who assumed the position of Lord Protector. Tutored by Richard Cox,
John Cheke and other religious reformers, the young King wanted to be succeeded
by a Protestant when he discovered that he was critically ill. He agreed to the
scheme of John Dudley, Duke of Northumberland, who had supplanted his
Seymour relatives in the Council, to alter the succession as it had been established
by his royal father.[12]

In 1543 Henry VIII had signed his Third Succession Act, settling the crown
first on Edward and his heirs lawfully begotten, then on any of the King's future
lawfully begotten children and their heirs, next on his daughters, Mary and

Elizabeth and their heirs lawfully begotten, respectively. Even though they remained illegitimate and would lose precedence to any future lawfully begotten children of the King, male or female, Henry VIII gave his daughters an important place in the settlement. The statute also empowered him to set the conditions whereby they could inherit and to limit the succession in more detail, stipulations which he made in his will dated December 30, 1546. He ordered that if Mary and Elizabeth married without the consent of Edward's Regency Council, they would lose their claim to the throne. By thus limiting the choice of their husbands, who it was thought would actually govern for them, Henry could justify permitting his daughters to inherit, thereby preserving his dynasty in the event of the death of his young son without issue. Further, he ignored the descendants of his elder sister, Margaret, who was represented in Scotland by her four-year-old granddaughter, Queen Mary, an omission that probably reflected Henry's desire to win the child as a bride for his young son. Edward's government would presumably have a stronger bargaining position in implementing the already-negotiated marriage treaty if the Scots had to recognize, by way of Henry's will, that their Queen could gain the English throne only by this marriage. Finally, he designated the Suffolk children, the descendants of his younger sister, the French Queen, next in line after his own children and their issue.[13]

It was this settlement of the crown that Northumberland proposed to change upon learning that Edward was terminally ill. Since the Princess Mary had remained a Catholic and the Princess Elizabeth was elusive about her personal religious beliefs, Northumberland turned to the Suffolk line, favored by Henry VIII, to find an heir. Henry Grey, Duke of Suffolk, and his wife, Frances, the daughter of Henry VIII's younger sister, had reared their three daughters as Protestants and were willing to accommodate Northumberland.

Ultimately, two different documents were drawn up to effect the proposed alteration of the settlement. The second, the Letters Patent, the basis of the final public statement, are more important, but the "devise," a preliminary draft in the King's handwriting, is more interesting because of its attitudes toward the succession of women. The "devise" proposed to grant the crown to the legitimate male heirs of the Duchess of Suffolk, if she had any before his death. After them, the crown was to descend to the legitimate male heirs of her daughters, first Jane, next Katherine, and then Mary. In an attempt to avoid a queen regnant, Northumberland had essentially provided that a male child of Jane and her new husband, his son, Guildford Dudley, would succeed to the throne. This preliminary draft was extraordinarily optimistic for while the doctors had given Edward only about three months to live, Jane and Guildford needed about nine months to produce the desired child, who, if it survived, would have to be male to qualify under these arrangements.[14]

Despite the warnings of a few reluctant associates that an executive decree could not amend the Henrician statute, Northumberland persisted in changing the order by a second document, the Letters Patent of Edward, in which it was conceded that the heir would have to be a female. Of the reasons for altering the succession, the most interesting was the charge that the Princesses might marry aliens who would subvert the laws of England. This argument was important because it was one of the major prejudices against queens regnant. As recently as March, 1549, the celebrated Protestant, Hugh Latimer, had reminded the King in a sermon at court of the dangers involved in permitting the succession of his sisters who might turn to foreigners for husbands.[15]

The Letters Patent also set forth the reasons for naming the Suffolk line as heirs: Jane, Katherine, and Mary Grey were "naural born here within the realm," the excuse for excluding the Scottish line, and were good Protestants. Then came the order of succession. The crown was to descend to the legitimate male children of the Duchess of Suffolk born before Edward's death and then to her daughters: Jane and her male heirs, Katherine and her male heirs, and Mary and her male heirs. By designating the succession to Jane and her sons, Northumberland did what he could to ensure that she would not be succeeded by a woman, but if she had no male children, her heir would be her sister rather than her daughter.[16] Although this challenge to the claims of Edward's sisters focused principally on the religious issue rather than on the feasibility of a queen regnant, it evidenced far more hostility toward women rulers than the final succession decisions of Henry VIII, whose foremost concern had been the continuation of his dynasty.

When Edward died on July 6, 1553 of acute pulmonary tuberculosis, the Council kept the news secret to aid the succession of Jane and Guildford. Born the same year as the young King, Jane had been well educated in the classics as preparation for a royal alliance. First, her parents had futilely hoped to arrange her marriage with King Edward and when that scheme had failed, they had readily agreed to the succession alterations and to her wedding with Guildford Dudley. It is apparent from the evidence that Jane was a reluctant participant in and a victim of her parents' ambitious plans. When she had at first refused to marry Guildford, she was forced into submission and when she objected in July, 1553 that the crown actually belonged to Edward's sister, Mary, she was pressured into accepting it for herself. And finally, when her forces lost, Jane willingly surrendered and asked to be sent home, but she spent the remainder of her short life in the Tower as a royal prisoner, while her mother and her father were set free.[17]

In 1553 Mary's forces won a victory that was a "triumph of the principle of legitimism, and an almost reverential trust" in the succession statute and will of Henry VIII. While many of the political nation may have been dreading an experiment with a queen regnant, they had paid little heed to sermons by Protestants like Nicholas Ridley, Bishop of London, who argued for the exclusion of both Mary and Elizabeth. When given an alternative between a daughter of Henry VIII and a great-granddaughter of Henry VII, they chose the one favored by parliamentary statute. Mary became monarch by popular choice and because the Tudor family had run out of males to challenge her.[18]

Within six months of her succession, she was faced with a serious rebellion because of her marriage contract with Philip of Spain. Fearing Spanish influence, some dissidents planned four separate revolts to begin in March, 1554, but because of prerevelations and other organizational difficulties, the conspirators were forced to act before the end of January. Of the four revolts, two are particularly interesting: the one in Leicestershire, even though it was a dismal failure, because it was led by the Duke of Suffolk, and the other in Kent, organized by Sir Thomas Wyatt, son of the poetic admirer of Anne Boleyn, because it almost succeeded. The motives and goals of the conspirators have long been debated and discussed. Except for Suffolk, most of the rebels claimed to be loyal Catholics, but it is unlikely that they were concerned with doctrinal matters, for despite the charge by one contemporary chronicler that Wyatt was also a heretic, the conspiracy was "secular and anti-clerical" rather than Protestant.[19]

It was against the Spanish match that they rebelled, but they realized early in their plans that the only way it could be defeated was to dethrone Mary. Clearly, in her case, the fear that Edward VI had voiced in his Letters Patent about his half-sisters' marrying alien princes had come true. In deciding to support Elizabeth as a replacement for her sister, the conspirators planned to avoid a similar marital crisis by providing her with a Yorkist husband, Edward Courtney, Earl of Devon, a descendant of Edward IV. When the conspiracy failed, some who had not been personally involved were punished. Although Elizabeth had remained aloof and distant from all treasonable activities after learning of the plans, she was imprisoned in the Tower to be released only after no evidence could be discovered against her. Jane, by contrast, was totally innocent, for the rebels had not planned to "enthrone" her a second time, but along with her husband and her father, she was executed in 1554, "a spectacular and pointless sacrifice."[20]

One of the brightest young women in Tudor England, Jane had studied many languages, among them Latin and Greek, and had corresponded in the classical tongues with Protestant divines on the Continent. Roger Ascham, the tutor of Elizabeth, wrote of a visit he made to Jane's home, Bradgate Hall, in Leicestershire in 1550, about three years before she became involved in the conspiracy of Edward VI and Northumberland. Ascham had discovered her there alone, he said, reading Plato's *Phaedon* in Greek while her family was away hunting. In her conversation with him, Jane had explained that studying with her kind and gentle tutor, John Aylmer, the future Bishop of London, was the only refuge she had from the harshness and physical cruelty of her parents. It may well be that Ascham arrived at her home just after a particularly bitter confrontation with her family because she apparently worked in tandem with her father to further the Protestant cause and supported her mother in time of illness.[21]

It was not unusual for Tudor parents to use physical abuse in the discipline of their children, although it does seem remarkably cruel in the case of Jane, who has been sanctified by Protestant writers, among them Ascham. The ultimate cruelty of her parents was their ambitious scheming that led to her death, but it was their failure and not their goals that have caused their plans to be so maligned. Given the context of religious and dynastic politics, the aims of the Suffolks, if not their inexpert and naive efforts to implement them, were not out of line.

Their contemporaries would have considered it most extraordinary if Lord and Lady Suffolk had refused to participate in the plans of the young King. Other noble and royal figures with more distant claims than Jane would continue to challenge the will of Henry VIII.

Elizabeth was to learn two valuable lessons from her sister's reign: not only were innocent royal claimants often the rallying point for rebellion but king consorts, particularly foreign ones, were extremely unpopular. While there was no precedent for that office in England, Philip of Spain, by virtue of the marriage treaties, had adopted the regal title even though Mary could not obtain for him a coronation ceremony because of the fear that it might symbolize the transference of her power to him as an anointed monarch. Since even the announcement of the marriage had caused a rebellion, it was not surprising that Parliament passed a statute in the spring of 1554, just before the wedding, with a provision specifically confirming that a queen regnant had all the powers possessed by former kings of England. Ironically, it was the widespread perception of a woman's weakness and her subservience to her husband that gave rise to a statute recognizing the constitutional validity of a queen regnant and confirming her royal power.[22]

After Mary died childless, leaving the crown somewhat reluctantly to her sister, Elizabeth, the most compelling issue in the country was which claimant would win designation as royal successor until the new Queen married and gave birth to an heir. Although some looked to Henry Hastings, third Earl of Huntingdon, a representative of the Yorkist family, the most seriously considered pretenders were female descendants of the first Tudor monarch. By virtue of Henry VIII's will, Jane Grey's two sisters continued to have important places in the succession although initially some Protestants did support the candidacy of their mother, the Duchess of Suffolk, until her demise in 1559. The older sister, Katherine, who had been a maid of honor at the court of Queen Mary where she had become acquainted with devout Catholics and with Spanish diplomats, was briefly favored by Philip II of Spain as a possible Catholic challenger to Elizabeth and as a Spanish alternative to the French-backed pretender, Mary, Queen of Scots.

Continuing as maid of honor at the court of Elizabeth, Katherine soon lost the support of Philip II because of her decision to wed a Protestant, Edward Seymour, Earl of Hertford, the eldest son of the deceased Duke of Somerset, the former Lord Protector and uncle of Edward VI. Hertford's sister, Jane Seymour, also a maid of honor to Elizabeth and a friend of Katherine, helped them to arrange a secret wedding, a union that was finally discovered because of the young bride's pregnancy. Traditionally, it has been their intense mutual love that writers have emphasized, but it cannot have hindered Hertford's desire to become her husband that many Protestants favored naming Katherine as Elizabeth's heir. Her succession would have made him king of England.

Elizabeth's hostile reaction to their clandestine marriage was rather predictable, especially as Katherine may have earlier promised the Queen not to marry without her consent. Suspecting a conspiracy against her throne, she had the Earl and his new Countess separated and imprisoned, but after the birth of their son in 1561, Hertford regained access to Katherine, and she was delivered of yet another son in 1563. Because his sister, Jane Seymour, had died and the clergyman, along with all of the documentary evidence of their marriage, had disappeared, the two were unable to prove that they had wed and that their two sons were legitimate. Placed under more stringent supervision, Katherine remained separated from her husband until her early demise in 1568 of tuberculosis. After Elizabeth's death, the officiating clergyman miraculously reappeared to substantiate their story, and ultimately the descendants of their sons were able to claim the honors and the titles of their paternal ancestors.[23]

As the wife of Hertford, Katherine had become a respectable Protestant alternative to Elizabeth, causing the Queen to fear that some zealous reformers might ignore the illegality of the Letters Patent of Edward VI which had placed the Grey sisters before the Queen in the line of succession. Those eager for further Church reform might prefer a Hertford/Grey alliance that had already produced two sons to a virgin Queen who displayed a deplorably lukewarm and even hostile attitude to some of the reformed doctrine. Her fears seemed to have been confirmed by the events of 1563 when John Hales, Clerk of the Hanaper, in collaboration with Hertford's stepfather, Francis Newdigate, and some other Protestants, wrote a work entitled, "A Declaration of the Succession of the Crown Imperial of England." In the tract Hales defended the legality of the Hertford marriage and proposed that the Countess be named successor to the throne. Support for Katherine's position seems to have been found among other factions as well. Even Thomas Howard, fourth Duke of Norfolk, secretly considered marrying a daughter of his to her elder son. As Elizabeth had no personal reason to favor the Seymour or Grey families, who had caused her much anguish and some fear for her safety in the reign of Edward VI, she remained suspicious of the political implications of the marriage.[24]

To complicate matters further, in the summer of 1565, Mary, the younger Grey sister, also found herself in trouble because of a clandestine wedding. Only about four feet tall, Mary was ridiculed when she married Thomas Keyes, who was over six and one-half feet tall and who as a serjeant-porter was far below her in social rank. As the Queen was not prepared to welcome the birth of any more male claimants to the throne, she had Keyes imprisoned and had Mary placed under house arrest. Released after her husband's death in early 1571, Mary remained single and childless, and apparently supported the extreme Protestant cause, for when she died in 1578 she left in her library copies of several works by Protestant divines, including John Knox and Thomas Cartwright.[25]

In addition to English claimants, there were candidates abroad who were eager to supplant Elizabeth. Despite Spanish hostility, the most acceptable Catholic pretender on the continent was a member of the French royalty. The wife of the Dauphin, Mary, Queen of Scots, was the granddaughter of Margaret, the elder sister of Henry VIII, and her first husband, James IV, King of Scotland. In 1542 as an infant, Mary had succeeded her father, James V, to the Scottish throne, and at the age of five, had been shipped to France while her mother, Mary of Guise, remained in Edinburgh as regent. At the French court Mary had been well educated, had become fluent in several languages, and had married the Dauphin. Ambitious for his dynasty, her father-in-law, Henry II, King of France, had proclaimed her ruler of England and had her assume the English royal arms at the death of Mary Tudor in November, 1558. As Elizabeth was illegitimate, the French argued, Mary Stuart ought to be recognized as monarch of England.[26]

With his father's death in 1559, Mary's husband succeeded to the throne but died in 1560 after reigning for little more than a year. She subsequently decided to return to Scotland, but even before her departure from France, she encountered diplomatic difficulties with England because of her decision not to ratify the newly negotiated Treaty of Edinburgh until Elizabeth recognized her as heir apparent. Since the English Queen steadfastly refused to name a successor, an impasse developed between the two monarchs on that issue. Once back in Scotland, Mary married her cousin, Henry, Lord Darnley, who, as the son of Margaret Douglas and her husband, the Earl of Lennox, was also the grandchild of Henry VIII's elder sister, Margaret, but by her second husband, the Earl of Angus. This marriage had serious implications for the English succession as it was not Darnley's new wife but his mother, the Countess of Lennox, an English resident, whom many of the kingdom considered the best Catholic alternative to Elizabeth as monarch.

It was because the Countess of Lennox had been born in England that some Catholics preferred her candidacy to that of her Scottish-born daughter-in-law, Mary. But there were others who charged that Lennox ought to be barred from the succession because her parents' annulment had made her technically illegitimate by English law. Since in Scotland where the divorce had been granted, both domestic and canon law held that children were lawfully begotten if their parents in good conscience believed that at the time of their marriage their unions were valid, Lennox had never been formally declared illegitimate. The claims of the Countess to the English throne as well as some mutual personal bitterness with Elizabeth, had led to her brief imprisonment early in the reign. Her second incarceration occurred after the marriage of the Scottish Queen to her son, Lord Darnley, when he was on a trip to Scotland ostensibly to visit his father. Since she had been grooming Darnley as a Roman Catholic alternative to Elizabeth, her son's marriage to Mary Stuart met with her approval although she most certainly must have regretted this alliance when he was later assassinated. Ultimately, her grandson, James, the child of Mary and Darnley, did succeed to the English throne despite the will of Henry VIII and the Letters Patent of Edward VI.[27]

The events in Scotland following the birth of the prince do not need to be related in detail. After Mary's estranged husband, Darnley, was killed, she forfeited much of her support by marrying his murderer in a Protestant ceremony. When she was subsequently forced to abdicate in favor of her son, she inexplicably sought assistance in England, where she gained only lifelong imprisonment, a captivity of nineteen years during which she was the subject and conspirator in several plots. Replacing the Countess of Lennox as the best Catholic claimant in England, Mary tried to win political support by arranging a marriage with the fourth Duke of Norfolk, a Protestant with strong Catholic connections. After this scheme failed, she remained in prison while her would-be bridegroom, like his father, Surrey the poet, was executed for permitting his noble pride to cloud his political judgment. In the final conspiracy, the Babington Plot of 1586, Mary was to be crowned queen of England after the assassination of Elizabeth that was to coincide with an invasion from abroad and a Catholic uprising at home. With great reluctance the English Queen permitted her cousin to be convicted of treason, a price for meddling with an insecure Tudor succession that had already been paid by many of the royal blood far more innocent than she.

From 1553, when Edward VI died, to 1587, the year of Mary's execution, the major Protestant and Catholic claimants were women. Lacking a viable male candidate, political and religious pressure groups were forced to support the woman whose views were most compatible with their aspirations. For reformers this alliance was at best an uncomfortable one because the monarch of England was not only head of the kingdom but also head of the Protestant Church. Their begrudging acceptance of a female ruler is evident by a pamphlet war over the merits of queens regnant that occurred during the reigns of Elizabeth and Mary.

Just before Mary Tudor's demise in 1558, John Knox, the future Presbyterian leader of Scotland, became so outraged at the burning of Protestants in England that he authored a treatise against female monarchs. His immediate excuse for writing this masterpiece of invective, *The First Blast of the Trumpet Against the Monstrous Regiment of Women,* was the reign of Mary Tudor, whom he characterized as a "wicked woman, yea . . . a traiteresse and bastard" but he extended his attack to all female rulers. They were not, he argued, to be tolerated for three basic reasons: they were repugnant to the laws of nature; they were contrary to divine will; and they were a subversion of good order and justice. While they were by nature weak, frail, impatient, and feeble, women had by divine law been created to serve and not to rule, for Eve had been evicted from the Garden of Eden with two curses: one to bear children in pain and sorrow and the other to live in subjection to man. Pointing out that a man with his head out of place on his body is called a monster, Knox argued that a commonwealth with a woman as head, who appoints the officers of law and justice, was also a monster. There were, he admitted, some women, like Deborah, a great prophetess and judge, who had played important roles in Old Testament times but they were only exceptions to the rule. Finally, he admonished Godly men to refrain from serving queens regnant and from defending them against those whom God had called to suppress their "monstrous rule."[28]

Knox decided not to write more blasts as he had intended because of his discovery that his *First Blast* had offended many Protestants more because of its political implications than because of their disagreement with its view of women. As Mary was ill when it was published in 1558, many reformers were looking forward eagerly to the succession of her sister whom they began to fear would be hostile to the Protestant cause because of the strident tone of the *First Blast*. Its message had angered Elizabeth, for when she succeeded in November, 1558, she refused to grant Knox a visa to enter her kingdom, an action that he challenged. In two letters he wrote to the new Queen, he contended that she had no reason to be angry with him because he had not written the treatise specifically about her rule, an assurance that did not immediately mollify Elizabeth although she did later support his reform efforts in Scotland. While his call to Godly men to refuse to defend their female monarchs against insurrection had not been pointedly directed against her, there was always the chance it might encourage others with royal ambitions to rebel against her authority.[29]

Earlier in 1558, the same year the *First Blast* appeared, Christopher Goodman had published similar arguments in *How Superior Powers Oght to be Obeyd of Their Subjects*. In it Goodman pointed out somewhat incorrectly that since Englishwomen could not be peers, justices, sheriffs, or bailiffs, surely they should not be queens regnant. He reacted to the reign of Mary by arguing that even if "she were no bastarde, but the Kinges daughter as lawfullie begotten as was her sister, [Elizabeth] that Godlie Lady [and] meke Lamb, voyde of all Spanish pride and strange bloude," still the "crowne belongeth only by God's worde, to the heyres males." Elizabeth knew this work as well as that of Knox and must have been rather vocal in her denunciations of both, for early in 1559, her secretary, Sir William Cecil wrote, "Of all others, Knoxes name, if it be not Goodmans, is most odiouse here."[30]

The arguments of the *First Blast*, the best known of the tracts against women rulers, did not go unanswered, for John Aylmer, the former tutor of Jane Grey, printed a reply in 1559. He began his treatise, *An Harborowe for faithful and trewe Subjectes against the late blowne Blaste, concerning the Government of Women*, by charging Knox with showing too much zeal in his reaction to Mary's cruelties against English Protestants. It was evident, Aylmer said, that as God often worked through the weaknesses of people, he could effect some secret purpose through the fraility of a female ruler. In response to the contention of Knox that St. Paul had forbidden a woman to govern, Aylmer made a distinction between temporal and spiritual rule, denying that women had been excluded from the former, for after all, St. Paul had said that women were to manage households, which were nothing more than little commonwealths. It would be well, Aylmer suggested, not to "grate upon the woordes" of this Saint too much, for women surely could govern by divine will.[31]

Aylmer still had one remaining objection to overcome, for, as he admitted, in England the royal supremacy, which had been recognized first in the reign of Henry VIII with the repudiation of Papal power, gave the monarch administrative authority over spiritual matters. Again Aylmer could find a distinction, this one between the "doer" and the supervisor, for Moses, the ruler, he reminded his readers, had been given the oversight of Aaron, the priest, but had not, himself, functioned as a cleric. This was an extremely delicate distinction but one Aylmer hoped he had made to the satisfaction of his Protestant readers, who believed as he did, that women were barred from the eccelsiastical functions of teaching and preaching. Indeed, traditionally women had not even been permitted to approach the altar or to stand within the chancel of the church. That this treatise was less than an enthusiastic defense of Elizabeth's supremacy in the Church and state may be one reason why the author had to wait almost twenty years before his elevation to a bishopric.[32]

These arguments were not convincing to many Catholics and extreme Protestants, who not only abhorred the concept of the lay supremacy but who were also horrified at the thought of a woman functioning in that office. In fact, the original supremacy had been different from that which Aylmer described in his treatise, for like a lay bishop, Henry VIII had exercised legal powers with a "semi-ecclesiastical element" that had included judging heretics. Elizabeth's father had claimed that his headship, which encompassed the authority to declare the law of the Church of England, had been an "intrinsic part of the Kingship," a right that Popes had usurped and that his Parliaments recognized and enforced but did not confer upon him.[33]

During the reigns of Mary and Edward, Parliaments had participated in the exercise of the royal supremacy, a constitutional change that Elizabeth was forced to recognize although after the passage of the Acts of Uniformity and Supremacy in 1559, she attempted to limit further legislative interference in religious matters. Some of her efforts in 1559 had been directed toward accommodating Catholics by softening the Protestant prayer service with the retention of ceremonies and vestments which many of the reformers viewed as Popish. It is thought that in an attempt to win over conservative Protestants and Catholics, who were reluctant to accept the lay supremacy, she also decided to adopt the title of Supreme Governor, rather than the one of Supreme Head that had been held by her predecessors. There is no doubt that her office was markedly less eccelsiastical than her father's, for as one Erastian apologist, John Jewel, Bishop of Salisbury, wrote, the Queen had adopted the title of Governor to limit her rule to "jurisdictional matters."[34] Conservative on other Church issues such as clerical celibacy, Elizabeth may have personally agreed with the rejection of semi-ecclesiastical roles for women monarchs.

In the reign of the second Tudor Queen, the English people became accustomed to defending the legality of the female succession. When Sir Thomas Smith, an outstanding Elizabethan author, wrote his political tract *De Republica Anglorum,* published in 1583, he first maintained that women "can beare no rule" but then he continued "except it be in such cases as the authoritie is annexed to the blood and progene as the crown." In England, he asserted, the royal succession had only blood, but not sex or age, limitations. Otherwise, he said, women did not "mingle with public affairs," for they were by nature weak and fearful, and easily forced into obedience and submission by men with their superior strength and courage.[35]

Tudor legitimacy had prevailed even though it had incorporated the succession of women to the throne. English scholars soon began to superimpose this constitutional right upon an earlier age when fixed rules had not yet been delineated. Most of the Tudor chroniclers of the Norman period charged that "unjustly and contrary to his oath made to Mawd [Matilda] the Empresse, daughter to King Henry, he [King Stephen] took on him the Crowne of England." One antiquary, William Lambarde, even scorned the "Estate of the Realm" that would not be subject to a woman.[36] The reigns of Elizabeth and Mary had so changed the English constitutional climate that dynastic history was written with the Tudor assumption that blood, not sex and age, ought to determine succession rights.

Even in the midst of this victory for women, one Elizabethan scholar, William Camden, viewed Empress Matilda only as a daughter of King Henry, a wife of another King Henry, and the mother of yet a third King Henry when he wrote about her tomb at Reading:

> Great born, match'd greater, greatest
>   brought to bed.
> Here Henry's Daughter, Wife and
>   Mother's laid.[37]

She could be counted, Camden continued, as "greatest and most happy in her issue." In this enthusiastic eulogy, he neglected to state that she could have been queen regnant, but then, her dynastic claims were inappropriate to the sense of his couplet—that female greatness is an extension of the achievements and reputation of their male relatives, especially their children. Matilda was memorable because of her relationship to three kings named Henry not because she had made a valiant effort to become queen of England.

NOTES

1. P. S. Crowson, *Tudor Foreign Policy* (New York, 1973), p. 84; *Calendar of the Letters and Papers of Henry VIII,* IV-i, No. 1409; for a discussion of the various reasons Henry had to raise Fitzroy to noble status, see Michael Joseph Lichnar, "Henry VIII's Bastard: Henry Fitzroy, Duke of Richmond," Ph.D. dissertation, Northwestern University, 1977, pp. 33-175.

2. Richard B. Wernham, *Before the Armada: The Growth of English Foreign Policy, 1485-1558* (London, 1966), p. 111; in 1523 Arthur Plantagent, Viscount Lisle, the illegitimate son of Edward IV had received his peerage when his former wife inherited the title of her brother John Grey, Viscount Lisle. See *Letters and Papers of Henry VIII,* III-ii, No. 2979; for the illegitimate children of Henry VII, see David Williams, "The Welsh Tudors: The Family of Henry VII," *History Today,* IV (1954), 84.

3. *Letters and Papers of Henry VIII,* IV-i, No. 1577 and VI, No. 1186; Mary A. E. Green, *Lives of the Princesses of England from the Norman Conquest,* 6 vols. (London,

1857), I, 1-2; the Countess of Richmond as the mother of the King was addressed as princess. When she was betrothed to the Prince of Castile, Mary, later the French Queen, was also styled princess; Chapuys wrote in 1536 that it was Cardinal Wolsey who was responsible for Mary's (the daughter of Henry VIII) obtaining the title of Princess of Wales. See *Calendar of State Papers Spanish,* V-ii, 221; Caroline A. J. Skeel, *The Council in the Marches of Wales* (London, 1904), p. 49; *Letters and Papers of Henry VIII,* IV-i, No. 1431; *Calendar of State Papers Venetian,* IV, 455.

   4. Lawrence Stone, *The Family, Sex and Marriage in England, 1500-1800* (New York, 1977), pp. 5, 42, 91, and 101; G. A. Holmes, *The Estates of the Higher Nobility in 14th Century England* (Cambridge, 1957), p. 47; Henry VIII, himself, referred to his failure to increase his "father's inheritance." See *Calendar of State Papers Spanish,* III-ii, 28.

   5. Edward Hall, *Henry VIII,* Intro. Charles Whibley, 2 vols. (London, 1904), II, 64, 96, and 143. Charles V would never have made this charge against his aunt's marriage; Richard Grafton, *Grafton's Chronicle or A Chronicle at Large, and Meere History of the Affayres of England and Kinges of the Same* . . . (London, 1569), p. 1176; after 1337 the common law held a child illegitimate if the parents discovered an impediment to their marriage and then separated. See F. Pollock and F. W. Maitland, *History of English Law,* 2 vols. (Cambridge, 1895), II, 377, note 3; in any case the common law of England had never recognized the legitimacy of children of invalid marriages for purposes of inheritance. See F. M. Powicke and C. R. Cheney, *Councils and Synods with other Documents Relating to the English Church,* 2 vols. (Oxford, 1964), II-i, 198 and Arthur Smith, *Church and State in the Middle Ages* (Oxford, 1913), p. 99; for a discussion of Leviticus and the legal arguments involved, see J. J. Scarisbrick, *Henry VIII* (Los Angeles, 1968), pp. 163-197; and Henry Ansgar Kelly, *The Matrimonial Trials of Henry VIII* (Stanford, Calif., 1976).

   6. *Letters and Papers of Henry VIII,* III-ii, No. 1762; IV-1, No. 1725; VI-i, No. 1111 and No. 1446; Mary A. E. Green, *Letters of Royal and Illustrious Ladies of Great Britain,* 3 vols. (London, 1846), II, 9; Ida Woodward, *Five English Consorts of Foreign Princes* (London, 1911), pp. 57-58; Caroline Bingham, *The Stewart Kingdom of Scotland, 1371-1603* (New York, 1974), pp. 156-157; Richard Glen Eaves, *Henry VIII's Scottish Diplomacy, 1513-1524* (New York, 1971), p. 163; Agnes Strickland, *Lives of the Queens of Scotland,* 8 vols. (Edinburgh, 1886), I, 229.

   7. Richard Davey, *The Nine Days' Queen* (London, 1909), pp. 7-11.

   8. Hugh Paget, "The Youth of Anne Boleyn," *Bulletin of the Institute of Historical Research,* LIV (1981) 162-170; for an example of the praise of Anne for her Protestantism, see John Aylmer, *An Harborowe for faithfull and trewe Subjectes against the late blowne Blaste, concerning the Government of Women* (Strassburg, 1559); Henry Ellis, *Original Letters Illustrative of English History Including Numerous Royal Letters,* 4 vols. (London, 1846), II, 245 and III, 50; James Mozley, *William Tyndale* (New York, 1937), p. 142; *Letters and Papers of Henry VIII,* V, No. 148 and VI, No. 661; Edward E. Lowinsky, "A Music Book for Anne Boleyn," *Florilegium Historiale: Essays presented to Wallace K. Fergusan,* ed. J. G. Rowe and W. H. Stockdale (Toronto, 1971), p. 188; for the works dedicated to her, see William Marshall, *The forme and maner of subjection for pore people practysed in the cities of Hypres in flaunders* (London, 1535) and Francois Lambert, *The summe of Christianitie,* ed. Tristram Revel (London, 1536); Samuel Clarke, *A Martyrologic Containing A Collection of All the Perscutions* . . . *to the end of Queen Maries Reign* (London, 1652), p. 78.

9. Major W. H. Tapp, *Anne Boleyn and Elizabeth at the Royal Manor of Hanworth* (London, n.d.), p. 3; J. Enoch Powell and Keith Wallis, *The House of Lords in the Middle Ages* (London, 1968), pp. 552-559; George Wyatt, "Extracts From the Life of The Virtuous Christian and Renowned Queen Anne Boleigne written at the close of the Sixteenth Century," *The Life of Cardinal Wolsey by George Cavendish*, ed. George Singer, 2nd ed. (London, 1827), p. 427.

10. Some historians have suggested an earlier date for the wedding. See Herbert Maynard Smith, *Henry VIII and the Reformation* (London, 1962), p. 32; a reading of the dispatches of the Imperial Ambassador to England in the early months of 1533 can leave little doubt that the marriage took place in January of that year. See *Calendar of State Papers Spanish* IV:2:2, 642 and 674; for a discussion of the appeals statute, see G. R. Elton, *Policy and Police* (Cambridge, 1972), p. 179.

11. Henry Ansgar Kelly, pp. 241-261; John Bellamy, *The Tudor Law of Treason* (Buffalo, N.Y., 1979), pp. 40 and 135.

12. Dale Hoak in "Rehabilitating the Duke of Northumberland: Politics and Political Control, 1549-53," *The Mid-Tudor Polity c. 1540-1560*, ed. Robert Tittler and Jennifer Loach (Totowa, N.J., 1980) has challenged W. K. Jordan's view that Edward made the succession decisions. See pp. 48-51; and W. K. Jordan, *Edward VI, The Threshold of Power* (Cambridge, Mass., 1970), p. 516.

13. Mortimer Levine, *Tudor Dynastic Problems, 1460-1571*, (New York, 1973), pp. 71-87.

14. Ibid.; Margaret Clifford, daughter to the Duchess of Suffolk's younger sister, was also included in the succession.

15. Ibid.; for this warning about the marriages of his sisters, see Allan G. Chester, ed., *Selected Sermons of Hugh Latimer* (Charlottesville, Va., 1968), p. 57.

16. Mortimer Levine, *Tudor*, pp. 85-87.

17. Hester W. Chapman, *Lady Jane Grey* (London, 1962), pp. 42 and 144 and *Two Tudor Portraits* (Boston, 1960), pp. 154-164.

18. W. K. Jordan, p. 530; see also D. M. Loades, *Two Tudor Conspiracies* (Cambridge, 1965), p. 6; there were Yorkist male claimants and Henry, Lord Darnley, an eight-year-old descendant of Margaret, Queen of Scotland; for a discussion of a Protestant sermon, see John Stowe, *Two London Chronicles*, ed. C. L. Kingsford, the Camden Miscellany, XII, third series, vol. 18 (London, 1910), pp. 26-27; see also Paula Louise Scalingi, "The Scepter or the Distaff: The Question of Female Sovereignty, 1516-1570," *Historian*, XLI (1978), 59-75.

19. John Proctor, "The Historie of Wyat's Rebellion," *Antiquarian Repertory*, ed. Francis Grose, et al., 4 vols. (London, 1808-1809), III, 69; for a modern analysis, see D. M. Loades, pp. 16-17.

20. D. M. Loades, pp. 13-19 and 115.

21. Roger Ascham, *The Schoolmaster*, ed. Lawrence V. Ryan (Ithaca, 1967), p. 36; *Calendar of State Papers Domestic*, I, 184 and 217; Hester W. Chapman, *Two Tudor*, pp. 195, 216 and 226-230; Richard Davey, *Nine Days'*, pp. 181 and 210 and *The Sisters of Jane Grey* (New York, 1912), pp. 291-292.

22. Mortimer Levine, *Tudor*, p. 90: D. M. Loades, pp. 10 and 138.

23. It was the opinion of the Spanish Ambassador in England that she had made this promise by March, 1559. See *Calendar of State Papers Spanish, Elizabeth*, I, 45.; Hester W. Chapman, *Two Tudor*, pp. 195, 216, and 230.

24. Mortimer Levine, *The Early Elizabethan Succession Question 1558-1568* (Stan-

ford, Calif., 1966), pp. 62-83; *Calendar of State Papers Spanish, Elizabeth,* I, 273; Sir John Harington, *A Tract on the Succession to the Crown* (London, 1880), p. 33.

25. Hester W. Chapman, *Two Tudor,* pp. 226-230; Patrick Collinson, *The Elizabethan Puritan Movement* (Berkeley, Calif., 1967), p. 149.

26. Antonia Fraser, *Mary, Queen of Scots* (New York, 1970), pp. 50-83.

27. *Calendar of State Papers Spanish,* X, 393, *Calendar of State Papers Domestic,* I, 197.

28. John Knox, "The First Blast of the Trumpet Against the Monstrous Regiment of Women," *The English Scholar's Library of Old and Modern Works,* No. 2, ed. Edward Arber (New York, 1967), pp. 3-55; for a discussion of the early Elizabethan propagandists, see Mortimer Levine, *Early,* pp. 30-114.

29. John Knox, pp. 55-61.

30. Christoper Goodman, *How Superior Powers Oght To Be Obeyd of Their Subjects* (Geneva, 1558), pp. 3-53; Anne Boleyn had been a peeress and Lady Ann Berkeley, second wife of Thomas, sixth Lord Berkeley, was granted a special commission by Henry VIII to hear and determine riots and misdemeanors. See Henry Ellis, III, 142. Cecily, Duchess of York, had been a hereditary sheriff of Worchestershire in the fifteenth century; for the Cecil letter see James E. Phillips, "The Background of Spenser's attitude toward Women Rulers," *Huntington Library Quarterly,* V (1941), 12.

31. James Phillips, p. 23; Hastings Robinson, ed., *Original Letters Relative to the English Reformation,* Parker Society, 2 vols. (London, 1842-1845), II, 743-744; John Aylmer, A3-B3, D-D3, and H2-3; for another response by Richard Bertie, see Add. Ms. 48,043, ff. 1-9, British Library.

32. John Aylmer, K-K2; the Rev. Samuel Denne, "A brief Survey of a part of Canterbury Cathedral, as described by Eadmer and Gervase," *Archaeologia,* XI (1794), 388.

33. Claire Cross, *The Royal Supremacy in the Elizabethan Church* (New York, 1969), p. 23; A. G. Dickens, *The English Reformation* (New York, 1964), p. 19.

34. Claire Cross, pp. 24 and 47; for a discussion of the statutes, see J. E. Neale, *The Parliaments of England,* 2 vols. (New York, 1953-1958), I, 65-75; Thomas Lever, a Marian exile, may have assumed a leadership role among the Protestants in convincing the Queen to drop the title of head, see John Strype, *Annals of the Reformation,* 4 vols. (Oxford, 1824), I-i, 194; Norman Jones of Utah State University has argued persuasively that the Catholics were more responsible than the Protestants for the Queen's concessions. See his Ph.D. dissertation, "Faith by Statute: The Politics of Religion in the Parliament of 1559," Cambridge, 1978.

35. Sir Thomas Smith, *De Republica Anglorum* (Menston, England, 1970), pp. 12-13 and 19.

36. John Stowe, *Annales, or a Generall Chronicle of England* (London, 1631-1632), p. 143; see also *Grafton's Chronicle* (London, 1569), p. 40; William Lambarde, *An Alphabetical Description of the Chief Places in England and Wales* (London, 1730), p. 110.

37. William Camden, *Britannia,* ed. Edmund Gibson, 2 vols. (London, 1722), I, 168.

5

Religious Persecution, 1533–1558

To obtain his divorce, Henry VIII abolished Papal authority in England, but declined to make major doctrinal changes, a decision that forced many Protestants to flee into exile or to suffer martyrdom for their heretical beliefs. While the royal supremacy prematurely encouraged some reformers, it also alienated a few Catholics, among them the celebrated martyrs, Sir Thomas More and John Fisher, Bishop of Rochester. Despite these divergent opinions, the great majority of Henry's subjects, who were still able to hear the familiar Latin Mass at their parish churches, routinely accepted the new royal supremacy. After the death of Catherine of Aragon in 1536 and the rapprochement of Henry VIII and her nephew, Charles V, some Catholics even hoped for a resurrection of Papal authority, but the English King declined to renounce his powers over the Church.

It was during the reigns of the first two of his three children that initially reformers and then conservatives won settlements of their choice. In the Act of Uniformity of 1552, the Parliament of Edward VI authorized a Church with services and doctrine which clearly denied the Catholic sacramental system, but after Mary's succession in 1553, still other Parliaments abolished this settlement and restored the Papal supremacy, inaugurating a period of persecution that resulted in the burning of many heretics, including a remarkably large number of women.

In the late medieval period women may have attended religious services in greater numbers than men, a custom that was satirized in a 1525 publication of Wynkyn de Worde, *Here begynneth an interlocuyon with an argument betweyxt man and woman whiche of them could prove to be most excellent*. While the author asked his readers to decide for themselves which sex was the winner of this literary struggle, he seems to have left little doubt as to his own prejudice:

> More men there be in pryson
> In Chaynes bounde for theyr offence
> More women come into sermon
> To lerne godys lawes, with dylygence.[1]

Women also supported various deviant religious causes, but usually without suffering martyrdom. While in 1511 and 1512, for example, approximately one-third of the 74 heretics questioned were female,only about one-tenth of the 60 or so religious radicals actually executed in the reign of Henry VIII were women. The same willingness to conform was evident among conservative Catholic women. Between 1532 and 1540 when Thomas Cromwell was enforcing the Reformation statutes, of 110 people executed for treason, all but 5 were men, for most women reluctantly agreed to obey the newly enacted religious laws.[2]

A brief study will be made in this Chapter of those women who suffered great material or spiritual loss between 1533 and 1558 when three different monarchs imposed a variety of settlements upon the country. An attempt will also be made to determine why increasing numbers of women refused to recant their beliefs, an act that could have saved their lives during the intensified persecution of Mary's reign. By failing to recant as their predecessors had done, these mainly lower-class women challenged the socialization of their culture that had normally led them to submit to symbols of authority. Finally, the question of whether the Protestant view of the family, of marriage, and of childbirth resulted in a height-ened social esteem for Englishwomen will be explored.

One of the few Catholic women to be executed for treason between 1532 and 1540 was a nun, Elizabeth Barton, known as the Maid of Kent. Her story has proved to be an embarrassment to her Church because of her admission that her divine messages warning against the royal divorce were fabrications. Reportedly, she continued to confess her deceit even at her place of execution, conduct characterized as "equivocal" by David Knowles, who has denied her the status of martyr. This judgment seems unnecessarily harsh in view of her story, and, indeed, a recent biographer, Alan Neame, has termed her a "proto-martyr."[3]

Before she gained the notoriety that led to her death, Elizabeth Barton had been a servant to Thomas Cobb, steward of the archiepiscopal estates at Al-dington, Kent. At Easter, 1525, when at the age of fifteen she because ill, she was assured by the Blessed Virgin in a trance that she would be cured in August. After the prophesy was fulfilled, William Warham, Archbishop of Canterbury, had the details of her illness and recovery reviewed by Dr. Edward Bocking, a Benedictine Monk, who was so favorably impressed by her essential honesty and innocence that he became her spiritual adviser.[4]

Shortly thereafter, the Maid was permitted to enter the Benedictine convent of St. Sepulchre near Canterbury where her recurring seizures led her to believe that she had been entrusted with divine messages for society. Gaining audiences with both Thomas, Cardinal Wolsey, whom she rebuked for neglecting the spiritual needs of the Church, and with Henry VIII, whom she predicted would be deposed if he married Anne Boleyn, Barton also claimed the favor and support of many celebrated churchmen, including Archbishop Warham and Bishop Fisher.

Early in the divorce controversy, Henry VIII had apparently tolerated a variety of interpretations of the crucial Levitical verse, but by 1533 when Cranmer had succeeded Warham as Archbishop and when Anne Boleyn had replaced Catherine as his consort, he was less willing to permit the public expression of those opinions. The nun's visions against the second royal marriage and the publicity that they received led Cranmer and the Council to interrogate her. Under extreme pressure, she finally admitted that her revelations were false. After sermons were preached against her, outlining the history of her illness, the seizures, the visions, and her confessions, she and some of her friends, including Bocking, were executed for treason. Trances similar to hers are the symptoms of epilepsy combined with hysteria and are common manifestations in the lives of many worthy people with reputations for "virile sanctity." Unquestionably, her seizures were genuine but sometimes their messages, especially the ones opposing the royal divorce, were invented. As Bocking and her other associates were all hostile to the King's marital schemes, it is likely that their opinions had an effect, "if only a subconscious one" upon her revelations.[5]

In contrast to the Maid of Kent, most of the other Catholic female victims of the Reformation merely suffered financial hardship and social dislocation. Even though their lives were spared, the distress of these professed women, who were expelled from their convents by the government of Henry VIII, should not be minimized or discounted, for most of them only reluctantly returned to secular life. Their troubles officially began in 1536 with the passage of the first Act of Dissolution, which confiscated the possessions of all houses worth less than £200, a category that included 103 nunneries, although because of exemptions only 75 were actually dissolved. This statute made no reference to the moral fitness of the professed, for it was the promise of financial gain that prompted the new Supreme Head of the Church to approve the suppressions. These religious were given the option of release from their vows or transference to one of the wealthier monasteries which continued in existence. Of the 261 nuns affected by the first dissolution, some 36 chose to reject communal living, a remarkably low number, especially noteworthy because 34 of them had lived in 8 small houses where the tone of spiritual life had been particularly low. The suppression of the remaining monasteries was hastened by the Pilgrimage of Grace, a rebellion that spread across several northern counties in late 1536. When it was finally subdued, those houses which had supported the Pilgrimage were forfeited to the crown. At the same time the King's agents had been pressuring other convents to surrender to royal authority. By the passage of the final Act of Dissolution in 1539, little remained of English monasticism, the last survivor of which, Waltham Abbey, was confiscated in 1540.[6]

Most of the professed continuing in houses after the first wave of suppressions in 1536 were granted annual pensions, on the average about five pounds for men and about three pounds for women. These sums are only average figures, for stipends were assessed on the basis of social hierarchy, a scheme that provided some abbesses with as much as forty pounds and some novices with as little as a few shillings. Even those who were awarded three-pound annuities soon found that their net income amounted to much less. Besides the inflation that quickly lowered their real value, the annuities were decreased in other ways. The pensioners had to pay annual eccelesiastical tenths to the government as well as extortionate fees to the disbursement officials of the Court of Augmentations. Often low on funds, the treasury created interminable delays, and in August, 1552 ordered a complete stop on all payments. The uncertainties caused by taxes, inflation, fees, and delays led some in despair to sell their pensions to speculators, who were often royal officials.[7]

Although their five-pound stipend was no more than a subsistance wage by the 1540s, the monks did have opportunities to become schoolmasters, tutors, or clergymen. In the diocese of Lincoln, for example, fifty-two percent of the ex-religious received ecclesiastical preferments. In addition, there is evidence that in anticipation of the dissolution some monks sold the advowsons owned by their houses to friends and relatives, who agreed to appoint them to these livings as they became vacant. While it is true that a few of them had to forego their annuities when they found other means of support, many succeeded in retaining two incomes. Because of their employment possibilities, it is certain that the dissolution was accomplished with less hardship for the monks than for the nuns.[8]

Since most of the women were of gentle birth, they could not be expected to take menial jobs, and they were ill prepared to compete with merchants in the more respectable trading positions. Even the usual financial source available to secular women was forbidden to them for the government did not permit the ex-religious to marry. There is evidence that some purchasers of the monastic estates did provide financial assistance to nuns previously housed there, recognizing by this aid that the dissolution more drastically affected the livelihood of the women than that of the men. A few nuns may have received appointments as governesses but most had to depend upon their meager pensions to give them some small welcome into the households of friends or relatives, an unlikely possibility for the aged and diseased. Even some of the women like Joan Pawtlyner, who were fortunate enough to receive three-pound annuities, were regarded as "very poor" by government officials in a 1555 survey.[9]

Given the general financial distress of the nuns, the conclusion of W.A.J. Archbold that because of their "good social standing," they needed less aid than did the employable monks, is an insensitive if not hostile reaction to their crisis. Their desire to remain in their convents suggests that for many their only security lay in monasticism. Some prioresses and abbesses with large pensions may well have been admitted with warmth into the homes of relatives and friends, but these nuns accounted for no more than 119 of the approximately 1,900 sisters.[10]

Because the dissolution statutes did not forbid them to live communally, a few were able to continue their vocations by pooling their meager resources. A "woman of strong personality and intellect," Elizabeth Throckmorton, for example, the last abbess of Denny, a convent of the Order of Minoresses in Cambridge, returned with two or three nuns to her home in Coughton, Warwickshire, where they observed the order of the rule as closely as they could until her death in 1547. Although this practice was commoner among the women, apparently at least one group of monks also continued to live with their prior at Worsborough.[11]

In 1549 Edward VI signed a statute allowing clerical marriage, an act that seems to have been popular among the clergymen, for when his sister, Mary, succeeded to the throne, she had many of them removed from their positions on the grounds that they had married. The number of deprived priests varied from county to county, amounting to as many as one-fourth in Essex and to as few as one-tenth in Yorkshire. As almost a decade after the final dissolution had elapsed before the enactment of the Edwardian statute, many of the ex-religious may have been rather old to enter matrimony for the first time. Despite their advanced age, some nuns did marry, for a 1555 census indicated that approximately one-fourth of those at Lincoln had married while none at Norwich had done so. During the reign of Mary, the ex-religious who could be identified were forced to separate from their spouses. A former nun, Margaret Basforth of Thornsby, for example, was ordered to depart from her husband, Roger Newstead, and never to speak to him again except in the company of others, but later evidence does indicate that the two resumed their marriage. The changing royal attitudes must have greatly confused and distressed these women and men.[12]

The total annual revenue of the dissolved houses was £136,362 of which only £15,000 belonged to the nunneries. In comparative terms the amount that the women lost was small, so small that it is tempting to treat the suppression of their houses as insignificant. Although the income was tiny, it was all that they had. When it was seized, it did not go to compensate them in any other way, as there was no place for them in the colleges or in the schools refounded by Henry VIII and Edward VI. It is also true that the 1,900 nuns had constituted only a small percentage of Englishwomen, but for those few, at least, the convents had offered leadership training. A nun had been able to aspire to be an abbess or prioress or occasionally to prepare for a career in her house's elementary school. Some women, like those at Syon Monastery had served as spiritual inspirations to their contemporaries. Except during Mary's reign, when there was an attempt to revive monasticism, even these meager opportunities were lost because of the dissolutions. Some single women had formerly been able to retain their self-respect and society's esteem by becoming nuns, but after the Protestant success, they had to learn to live with ridicule or become brides.[13]

While Catholics were expelled from their convents and were executed for denying the royal supremacy, some radicals were also persecuted for rejecting Catholic doctrine. Of the sixty or seventy Protestant martyrs in the reign of Henry VIII, only four or five were women, among them the young aristocrat, Anne Askew. She was the daughter of Sir William Askew or Ayscough of Lincolnshire and the reluctant wife of Thomas Kyme, whose name she discarded after he evicted her from their home because of her religious convictions. That her contemporaries considered her husband's rejection significant is confirmed by John Bale, the sometime Bishop of Ossory, who included in his "simple elucidation" of Askew's two heresy examinations a statement from St. Paul's First

Epistle to the Corinthians that a woman could depart from an unbelieving husband if he would not live with her.[14]

Quick-witted and imbued with spiritual tenacity, Askew's elusive answers, when she was first questioned in 1545, frustrated her inquisitors. Finally resorting to attacks upon her sex to compel her obedience, they quoted St. Paul's First Corinthian Epistle in which women were cautioned to be silent, but the churchmen had not counted on their victim's thorough knowledge of the New Testament. Confidently informing her accusers that St. Paul had meant only to forbid women "to speak in the congregation by way of teaching," she admonished them "to find no fault in poor women, except they had offended the law." Just before she was released from custody, Edmund Bonner, Bishop of London, required that she sign a statement of faith. She complied, but carefully added a few words of her own to the text, an action that so infuriated his lordship that he complained that she "was a woman, and that he was nothing deceived in [her]."[15]

Arrested again in the summer of 1546, Askew and her associates were examined by the King's Council at Greenwich. In a four-hour session, Thomas Wriothesley, the Lord Chancellor, and Bishop Gardiner, among others, attempted to convince her to sign a "bill of the sacrament," a demand that she refused because she could not agree that the Eucharist was the "flesh, blood and bone" of Christ. After a second lengthy session, she was convicted as a heretic at the London Guildhall and condemned to die.[16]

Subsequently, she was transferred to the Tower of London for further questioning because both Sir Richard Riche and Wriothesley hoped that she would implicate in her sacramental heresy some of the ladies at court, especially Katherine, Duchess of Suffolk; Anne, Countess of Hertford (the future Duchess of Somerset); and Lady Joan Denny. Upon her refusal to give information against them, although she did admit that a messenger had brought her some money from Hertford and Denny, the two interrogators according to Bale, "took pains to rack [her] with their own hands, till [she] was nighe dead," but her God had given her the "grace to persevere." All Protestant propaganda aside, torture was an unusual technique in religious interrogations and unprecedented when employed against a gentlewoman already condemned to die. In fact, torture had been almost unknown in England until the ministers of Henry VIII had inaugurated its use. On July 16, 1546, at the age of twenty-five, Askew's crippled body was carried to the place of execution where she was burned.[17]

Less than one year later, Henry VIII was succeeded by his son, Edward, who was guided by a Regency Council largely committed to Protestantism. Near the end of his short reign, the young King was willing to challenge his father's order of the succession to ensure a continuing line of reformed monarchs, but neither he nor his Council had the desire to purge Catholicism from the kingdom in the Smithfield fires. Only two individuals, both Anabaptists, one of them a woman, Joan Bocher alias Joan of Kent, died for their religion during his reign.

The Anabaptists were groups of radical Protestants so called because they rejected infant baptism, but they differed widely in their other beliefs, some denying predestination, others rejecting the trinity, and still others renouncing all private property. While more conservative reformers like the Lutherans and the Zwinglians had disagreed among themselves as to the precise doctrine that should replace the sacramental system of the Roman faith, they had unanimously agreed to condemn the Anabaptists because of their association with social revolution. Although most of the Anabaptists executed in the early Tudor period were foreigners, Bocher has been identified by Michael R. Watts as a former Lollard who had abjured her heresy at Colchester, Essex in 1528 and who had been imprisoned as a heretic for two years at Canterbury in the early 1540s. She seems also to have been personally acquainted with the martyred Anne Askew.[18]

Whatever her nationality, the celebrated martyrologist, John Foxe, stated disdainfully that she had died for opinions he did not think necessary to include in his work. In fact, the reason for her martydom was her denial that Christ was incarnate of the Virgin Mary. The only one among the several Anabaptists arrested in April, 1549 who refused to recant, Bocher reminded her inquisitors that only a short time before, Anne Askew had been burned for "a piece of bread," a sacramental doctrine that the Church of England had recently adopted. They were now, she contended, planning to execute her for "a piece of flesh," a belief that she was confident the Church would similarly accept.[19]

In contrast to Joan of Kent, who was burned in May, 1550, other Protestants during the reign of the young King had been relatively free to implement their designs in England, removing images, replacing the Latin mass with an English prayer service, preaching justification by faith, denying transubstantiation, and promoting clerical marriage, but their worldly paradise ended in July, 1553 when their young Josiah died of acute pulmonary tuberculosis. Despite the efforts of John, Duke of Northumberland, to alter the order of succession, Mary Tudor, a devout Roman Catholic, was crowned as Queen.

By the end of 1554 she was the wife of Prince Philip, the future King of Spain, and was no longer the Supreme Head of the Church, for her Yorkist cousin, Reginald, Cardinal Pole, had returned from exile to preside over the submission of the English Church to Papal authority. To gain precedence in the new Queen's Privy Council, Bishop Gardiner, her Lord Chancellor, only recently released from prison where he had languished during the reign of Edward VI, pressed for revival of the heresy statutes. Apparently, he was convinced that most of the accused would recant, but he misunderstood Protestant commitments. Unlike former heretics, these radicals had served in positions of authority or had been encouraged in their faith by reformers in high echelons of the Church. When interrogated by clergymen whom they viewed as usurpers of offices formerly held by leaders, like Thomas Cranmer, Archbishop of Canterbury, many heretics held firmly to their views. By 1553 Protestantism was no longer identified only with social outcasts and powerless individuals, for it had been, for a short time, the faith of the monarch, himself. Except for Archbishop Cranmer, who recanted only to find himself still destined for the stake where he publicly abjured his recantations, the victims usually refused to deny their reformed beliefs. Often, like Anne Askew, they died for "a piece of bread."[20]

While there were a few more victims than the 275 reported by John Foxe, the martyrologist, only those he identified will be referred to here. Most of the victims were of the lower social orders, mainly laborers and tradespeople, for only 21 churchmen and 9 gentlepeople were burned. Remarkably, 55 women, about one-fifth of the total number, died for their beliefs. Only 2 of these women were burned during 1555, the first year of persecution when about 80 men went to the stake, but in the two years that followed, the number of female martyrs steadily increased, rising to 20 in 1556 and to 28 in 1557, while the number of male victims correspondingly decreased, falling to less than 60 in 1556 and to less than 50 in 1557. In the latter year, 1557, only about 18 more men than women died for their faith, a surprising ratio when contrasted with the much smaller proportion of female victims in the reign of Henry VIII.[21]

In 1558, when the Queen was critically ill, the ferocity of the persecution, which claimed about forty lives, only five of them women, waned somewhat. On November 10, 1558 at Canterbury, just one week before the death of Mary, the last martyrs were burned, among them an aged widow named Katherine Knight alias Tynley and a maid named Alice Snoth. Angered that they were executed so near to the death of the Queen, Foxe charged Nicholas Harpsfield, Archdeacon of Canterbury, and Richard Thornton, Suffragan Bishop of Dover, with particular cruelty in their pursuit of heretics, even arguing that they were more relentless than Edmund Bonner, Bishop of London. While the Marian persecution was more ferocious in Canterbury than in any other country town, it did not meet the standard set in London where the competency and efficiency of the Church courts were responsible for the deaths of 113 heretics.[22]

A. G. Dickens has reported that most of the female victims were poor widows, but only ten of the fifty-five can be so identified, although there were another six women whose marital status is unknown. Even if these six were widows, an unlikely status for them all, the combined total of sixteen does not equal that of the twenty-eight who were married women. Technically, eight of the wives were widows when they died, their husbands predeceasing them as martyrs, but at the time of their interrogation for heresy, they were still married. There were also eleven maiden victims, including at least two that were blind.[23]

Throughout his descriptions Foxe usually dwelt longer upon the stories of the male victims than the female ones. As he turned to the events of 1557, when twenty-eight women were burned, he displayed increasing impatience at having to relate information about so many lower-class women. Finally, while writing about four female and three male victims at Canterbury, his fury could no longer be contained:

What heart will not lament the murdering mischief of these men, who for want of work do so wreak theer time on silly poor women whose weak imbecility the more strength it lacketh by natural imperfection, the more it ought to be helped, or at least pitied; and not oppressed of men that be stronger. . . . blessed be the Lord Omnipotent, who supernaturally hath embued from above such weak creatures with such manly stomach and fortitude, so constantly to withstand the uttermost extremity of these pitiless persecutors.[24]

The reason for the significant increase in female martyrdom cannot be readily explained. Not generally enthusiastic about the persecution of women, the male reformers, themselves, were inconsistent in their support of their steadfast female associates. In his "simple elucidation" of Anne Askew's examination, John Bale, it is true, treated with scorn her accusers' suggestion that St. Paul had forbidden women to speak of the word of God by offering examples of several learned New Testament women, but he was defending the martyrdom of a well-educated gentlewoman who had been so cruelly racked that she had to be carried to the Smithfield fire. While, like Bale, Foxe wrote favorably of Askew's martyrdom, he seemed somewhat impatient with the large number of lower-class victims in 1557. Although he did praise them for their courageous spirit, he also referred to their "weak imbecility" and lashed out at their "pitiless" inquisitors. Even the authorities seemed to tire of the "weaker vessels" whom they apparently could not silence. One "silly creature," according to Foxe, still insisted on referring to the Mass as a "foul idol" when told by James Turberville, Bishop of Exeter, that it was "no woman's matters" to speak of the sacrament.[25]

Without consistent support from the male reformers and even with contradictory statements in the scriptures about the desirability of women to speak out on religious issues, that one-fifth of the Marian martyrs were females remains a surprising fact. It would be erroneous to suggest that the twenty-eight wives simply followed their husbands into heresy. While eight were married to martyrs, some women left their husbands widowers in the faith, and others deserted their conservative spouses to join the movement. One man, in fact, lost two wives to the persecutors while two husbands actually reported their spouses to the authorities.[26] Any attempt to explain the comparatively large number of female victims will remain incomplete, but it would be instructive to consider the impact of the martyrdom of Anne Askew.

Members of minority groups who have been excluded from positions of power and wealth tend to model themselves after achievers of their race, sex, or ethnic group. In the twentieth century increasing numbers of Black Americans have aimed for positions in the fields of entertainment and sports where pioneering Blacks have had highly visible success. While Tudor women were at least numerically equal to men, most were, with the exception of the royal family, prevented from holding political, economic, or religious positions of significance. It is possible that Anne Askew served as a role model for these lower-class Protestant women who might not otherwise have viewed themselves as sufficiently important to die for their faith. A well-educated gentlewoman with quick wit and spiritual tenacity, her torture and death provided an example to the members of her sex of the ideal martyrdom, transcending by the intensity of her heroism all class barriers. More important than the mere fact of her death was the publicity that she received for it. When John Bale chose to publish "a simple elucidation" of her two heresy examinations in which he claimed that she was "canonized in the precious blood of the Lord Jesus Christ," he made a sympathetic version of her story available to a wider audience than that of any other female martyr of England.[27]

Just how many of his contemporaries read Bale's account will never be known, but Bishop Gardiner, one of Askew's inquisitors, complained to Somerset, then Lord Protector of England, that the book was "spread abroad" and "in these parts common." It may well be that an acquaintance of Askew, the Edwardian martyr Joan of Kent, who knew the precise nature of her heresy, had read or at least had heard about Bale's "simple elucidation."[28] Askew's example cannot be dismissed in attempting to find reasons for the relatively high percentage of women victims of Mary's reign, particularly as there is a special psychology to martydom in which believing brothers and sisters take courage from the vindication of the persecuted to prepare themselves for the same spiritual challenge.

Some of the Marian martyrs had belonged to underground congregations which were founded in London and Colchester after the reintroduction of the Latin Mass into the churches. The London congregation usually met in the mornings and in a variety of places with women sometimes acting as hostesses. One of its members, Margaret Mearing, left interesting evidence of Christian forgiveness. Concerned about the need for secrecy, the chief pastor, John Rough, excommunicated her because she had brought strangers into the congregation and seemed unnecessarily inquisitive about its operations. When, shortly thereafter, Rough was imprisoned at Westminster, Mearing gained entry to his cell by the simple ruse of pretending to be his sister and comforted him, thereby placing herself under suspicion and arrest. The two were burned together at Smithfield in December, 1557. In towns other than London and Colchester people met together in groups which cannot be called congregations as they had no regular clergy, but they are noteworthy because they were sustained by the efforts of women. A group at Stoke in Suffolk, for example, emerged as the result of many parishioners, "especially the women" absenting themselves from Catholic services.[29]

Other zealous women were witnesses for their faith in the routine of their everyday lives. In 1556, Paul Bush, a Catholic priest and former Bishop of Bristol, became so incensed by the statements of Margaret Burges, the wife of a Wiltshire clothier, that he printed an exhortation to her. He had met Burges, he said, at dinner at a friend's house in Gloucester where they had begun a rather heated conversation that had been continued after dinner and had finally been terminated only by her departure with her friends. Her "rash temeryte" in denying the doctrine of transubstantiation grossly offended Bush because, as he pointed out, the dispute should have been settled by his quoting the verse from Matthew in which Christ said, "I am the Body." As he had just recently been deprived of his bishopric on the grounds that following the legalization of clerical marriage in the reign of Edward VI, he had chosen to take a wife, since deceased, it is possible that his decision to print the exhortation was an attempt to draw royal attention to his firm commitment to other Catholic sacraments.[30]

Many Protestants died in England for their faith, but some others fled abroad to wait for the succession of a more sympathetic monarch. The Marian exiles were, on the whole, wealthier than the martyrs probably because the poor usually have much more difficulty in emigrating at times of danger. In eight congregations, a total of 788 persons have been identified, 472 of them men, of whom 166 were gentlemen, the largest single social class among the exiles. In her biographical study of the emigrants that was published in 1938, Christina Garrett presented very little information about the women apparently because she was primarily interested in the political impact of the male exiles in Elizabethan England. She listed 100 wives, 25 unescorted women left unnamed, 146 children and adolescents never distinguished by sex, and 45 unidentified servants. Arranged alphabetically, the biographies focused on the 472 men, causing at least one historical distortion, for it is possible to read about the exile of Katherine, Dowager Duchess of Suffolk, only by turning to a statement under the heading of Richard Bertie, who is important largely because he was her second husband. Indeed, he, himself, recognized that his marriage to a noble woman gave him special social status. At the top of a manuscript he wrote in 1558 defending the succession of women as monarchs, he identified himself as "husband to ye lady Catherine Duchess of Suff."[31]

With her father's death in 1526 the wardship of Katherine, the daughter and sole heiress of Lord William Willoughby de Eresby and Mary de Salinas, one of Catherine of Aragon's Spanish ladies, had been granted to Charles Brandon, Duke of Suffolk, with the expectation that she would become the wife of his only son, the Earl of Lincoln. Seven years later, the fourteen-year-old girl married her guardian, who was then over forty, only a few weeks after the death of his third wife, Mary, the French Queen. The Duchess subsequently gave birth to two sons, the elder becoming the heir to Suffolk after the death of Lincoln in 1534. Although the family tradition that Suffolk became a Protestant during the last years of his life may be incorrect, there is no doubt that after his death in 1545, his Duchess did become a convert. Both Riche and Wriothesley had hoped to implicate her in the heresy of Anne Askew.[32]

After the succession of Edward VI, the Duchess retired to Grimsthorpe Castle in Lincolnshire where she abolished holy days and removed images from chapels. Tragedy struck her family in 1551 when both her sons died on the same day of the sweating sickness, causing the Dukedom of Suffolk to revert to the husband of her stepchild, Frances Grey, Countess of Dorset, the elder daughter of Brandon and the French Queen. Hugh Latimer, a famous reformed preacher and later a Marian martyr, was the guest of the Dowager Duchess in 1552 and 1553 at which time he may well have married his hostess to Richard Bertie, the son of a stone mason and one of her gentlemen ushers. Because when noble ladies married beneath their social class they had the right to retain their former surnames and titles, she continued to be addressed as Lady Suffolk after her second marriage.[33]

With the reenactment of the heresy laws, she decided to go into exile. In June, 1554 her husband traveled to the continent and by the end of that year she had joined him. Somewhat unsympathetic to the refugees whose biographies she published, Garrett wrote that it is impossible to believe that her ladyship was in desperate straits when she left. It took her five weeks to travel from London to Gravesend, accompanied by a household of thirteen, including a major-domo, a gentlewoman with six servants, a joiner, a brewer, a kitchen-maid, a laundress, a Greek rider of horses, and a fool. Undoubtedly, the Queen had no desire to prevent the departure of the Duchess, whose Spanish mother had earlier risked her life to comfort Catherine of Aragon after her divorce from Henry VIII. Ultimately, Lady Suffolk returned to England to continue her support of the Protestant faith, a devotion that led one of the most celebrated Puritan leaders, John Field, to dedicate a religious work to her in 1580.[34]

In her volume on the exiles, Garrett made occasional references to women who probably belonged to the category labeled "unescorted women." It is disappointing that the author did not publish a list of their names, for they were as willing as the male exiles to suffer hardships for their faith. One of the few "unescorted" women identified by Garrett was Alice Agar, first referred to in the biography of her son, Thomas. A widow, Agar arrived in Geneva in advance of her son and later married another Protestant exile there, an act that caused her to be named also in her new spouse's biography. Had it not been for her male relatives, no record of her commitment to her faith would have appeared in Garrett's book.[35]

Another unescorted woman, Anne Locke, was mentioned in the biography of James Yonge of Frankfurt, only because she had delivered a message to him from John Knox. A devoted Protestant, Anne, who was subsequently joined by her husband, Henry, a mercer of London, had left England at the persistent urging of Knox. It was probably because her husband was able to complete some business transactions on the continent that he was not also listed by Garrett as a religious exile. Anne was a friend of the Duchess of Suffolk, to whom she dedicated her English translation of the French Sermons of John Calvin in 1560. As she later married Edward Dering, a reformed minister, and was prominent in the Puritan movement, the story of her exile should have been included in Garrett's book. Indeed, Patrick Collinson has thought that her life was noteworthy enough to be the subject of a scholarly article.[36]

In the first half of the sixteenth century, about sixty Protestant women were executed for their faith while countless others died in prison, were persecuted, or forced into exile. Generally, it has been assumed that the Reformation brought to England enlightened concepts and ideas that led to a measurable rise in the esteem of women as individuals. For that reason, it would be instructive to investigate early Protestant attitudes toward family life, childbirth, and marriage to gain a better understanding for what it was that these Englishwomen were willing to make such tremendous sacrifices and to ascertain more fully whether reformed society was a more comfortable place for them to live.[37]

In his impressive study of domestic life in early modern England, Lawrence Stone argued that the "open lineage family" gave way in the middle of the sixteenth century to the "restricted patriarchal family," the dominant form until the middle of the seventeenth century. He identified the patriarchal family as one in which the loyalty of its members to their lineage and patron declined as their passive obedience to the father or the head of the household increased. Within that framework a new emphasis was placed upon the relationship of the spouses to each other and to their children, the components of the nuclear family. Stone gave to Protestantism, with its sanctification of the father's vocation as the religious adviser of his wife and children, the primary cultural role in this change.[38] While there is no doubt that Protestants did advocate this transition in domestic function and emphasis, it is also evident that these theories were adapted from the ideas of the Christian humanists.

Historically, Catholicism has been associated with the ideal of celibacy while early Protestantism has been linked more closely with the ideal of marriage, but these categories are too arbitrary. The fifteenth-century Italian humanists, especially Leon Battista Alberti in his work *The Family,* had lauded good marital relations and a "mutually sustaining" companionship between spouses. Adopting this approach, many Tudor humanists, Erasmus, Sir Thomas More, Sir Thomas Elyot, Richard Hyrde, and Juan Luis Vives had promoted unions in which partners exchanged ideas, in which they had compatible relationships and in which they gave emotional support to each other. Marriage was not just for procreation and the avoidance of sin but was also for the comfort and companionship of life. Erasmus even doubted that God looked with more favor upon the virgin state than upon married life.[39]

In addition, many other Protestant concepts evolved from humanism. The first Protestant translator of the scriptures into English, William Tyndale, was greatly influenced by Erasmian thought. It was, after all, the Dutch scholar's challenge to make the Bible available in the vernacular tongues that Tyndale had accepted when he had committed himself to his translation project. If some of the attitudes about marriage and domestic life of Cranmer and Tyndale are compared to those of Erasmus and More rather than to those of medieval Catholic philosophers, Protestantism seems less novel and less innovative in its social aspects. As Supreme Head of the Church even Henry VIII reinforced the family as the center of religious instruction and learning in his first Royal Injunctions issued in 1536.[40]

Christian humanism was only one small source of Protestant philosophy, for despite some similarities in their familial attitudes, they still had fierce differences about religious doctrine and human nature. While Sir Thomas More had a public debate with William Tyndale over several issues, Erasmus disassociated himself from most Protestants, including the celebrated reformer, Martin Luther. Justification by faith instead of good works, the denial of many other of the Catholic doctrines so essential to the sacramental system, such as transubstantiation, and a destructive hostility to images, to holy days, and to the veneration of the saints caused innumerable rifts between Protestants and Christian humanists. While many of the early humanists had ridiculed a good part of the medieval trappings of Catholicism, they often viewed the cures of Protestantism as worse than the disease itself, for a reform not a schism in Christendom had been their goal. It will be instructive to review some of the changes effected in the Edwardian Church to determine the extent of humanist influence in the early Reformation.

The hope of Protestants that Henry VIII's assumption of the royal supremacy was the first step in a program to reform the Church doctrinally had not been fulfilled, but in 1547 when his son, Edward, became King, the schismatic Church was transformed into a Protestant one. This change was accomplished in several Parliamentary statutes, among them the two Acts of Uniformity which authorized the use of two standard prayerbooks. James McConica has described the Book of Common Prayer of 1549 as Erasmian because it was in great part merely a English version of the Sarum Use, the Latin service most widely used in Henrician England. While the words of this first prayerbook were vague enough to make some Catholics believe that their sacramental system would survive intact, the words of its successor, the second Book of Common Prayer, left no doubt of doctrinal deviation. In 1552 the Church settlement became more Protestant than it was ever again to be in Tudor England.[41]

Despite their rejection of Catholic doctrine, the reformers maintained in both of these prayerbooks a special and somewhat degrading service for new mothers. Believing that childbirth was an act that rendered women unclean, the Catholic Church had, following Judaic tradition, authorized a purifying ceremony that the reformers decided to continue with minor changes. While the first prayerbook had simply changed the title of the medieval service to "The Order of the Purification of Weomen," the more Protestant prayerbook of 1552 changed it to "The Thankes Geving of Women after Childe Birth commonly called the Churching of Women." Speaking for many reformers, Hugh Latimer justified retaining this service so that the new mother could give God special thanks for a safe delivery. It was, he also said, the public recognition that she was capable again of performing "acts as other women" and having "company with her Husband. . . . For Women . . . be as well in the favor of God before they be purified as after." Even as he was defending it as merely a thanksgiving service, Latimer, continued to refer to the women as "purified" and suggested that there were acts which they ought not to perform before the churching.[42]

Undoubtedly, upon hearing the traditional Catholic service that utilized the 121st Psalm, most parishioners, still fearing that women who died without churching would be denied Christian burial, failed to note any distinction in meaning between the Protestant service and that of the translated Sarum Use. The retention of this ceremony, despite the government's repeal of Candlemas Day, seems to indicate that the early Protestant attitude toward childbirth was not a marked improvement to that of Catholicism.[43]

Because he was a popular Edwardian preacher, Latimer's ideas about childbirth and marriage are of significance to any study of Tudor Protestantism. It was he who had warned the boy King of the manifold dangers of permitting his sisters to inherit the throne, a warning that may have been an important factor in the subsequent decision to alter the succession. In another of his sermons, Latimer approved the Genesis curse condemning women to bring forth children in pain and sorrow. Apparently, to excuse his insensitivity to the dangers of childbirth, he also asserted that even though women suffered greatly at the time of delivery, they later "remembered not the pain" because of the "soul brought forth into the world." Since clergymen were still fulminating against the use of anesthetics in Victorian England because God had intended for women to endure pain during their deliveries, this remarkably outrageous attitude held sway for centuries.[44]

Although the Catholic churching service remained largely the same, except that it was said in English, more extensive changes were made in the marriage ceremony as authorized by the two Edwardian prayerbooks. The reformers believed that God had instituted marriage for three purposes. While two of them, for procreation and for avoidance of lust and fornication, had long been recognized by the Roman Church, the third reason, for mutual comfort, was added by the Protestants whose goal, following and elaborating upon humanist guidelines, was to promote newer, closer relationships between spouses. For the first time the wedding vows, themselves, were said before a priest in the body of the Church and not just at its porch. After this exchange, the priest gave a marriage sermon printed in the prayerbooks in which St. Paul was liberally quoted. Men were ordered to love and cherish their brides, and women were required to be respectful, submissive, and reverent to their spouses. While Church courts continued to enforce private marriage vows, fines and other penalties were used to discourage those clandestine unions.[45]

Mutual comfort of spouses meant more than just personal affection for each other. Adopting part of the Erasmian philosophy on family education and fellowship, Protestants generally agreed that lower-class individuals should be given elementary religious instruction. It was thought that husbands and wives should be taught to read the scriptures together in translation and to instill religious precepts in their children. Henry VIII had originally adopted this policy when in 1538 he had authorized the setting up in parish churches of English Bibles for all to read. In 1543, apparently after widespread disputes over Biblical interpretations, the King had signed into law a statute that had forbidden Bible reading by women and the following lower-class men: artificers, prentices, journeymen, serving-men of the rank of yeomen and under, husbandmen, and laborers. Noblemen, gentlemen, and merchants could read it in their families while noblewomen and gentlewomen could study it privately. This attempt to limit lower-class knowledge of the scriptures was later swept away by Protestants who reaffirmed that portion, at least, of the Erasmian educational program, although they also believed that the "unlearned and the laity" should not be given the scriptures without official interpretations to guide them.[46]

It was in their attitudes toward the training of the aristocratic and propertied people that the educational and family ideas of the Christian humanists most obviously differed from those of the Protestants. Following the optimism of Quintilian about human nature, Erasmus and More believed that a classical education could teach people to behave morally and ethically within traditional Christian guidelines. The most felicitous marital relationship, they argued, was one in which the partners had a mutual understanding and enjoyment of classical literature, both pagan and Christian. The ideal of these humanists was a family headed by a Christian male governor, well grounded in the classics, whose learning would enable him to reform the ills of society: crime, poverty, warfare, a poor school system, and a corrupt Church, and whose wife, similarly educated, would be able to provide learned companionship for him at home and to assist him in offering moral training to their children.

By contrast, Protestants imbued with the pessimism of St. Augustine, emphasized that human nature was essentially corrupt and rejected the belief that education could transform individuals into more moral creatures. Most viewed education as a tool in teaching people about the divine ordinances written in the scriptures and other holy works. Through Biblical instruction, it was thought, people whose salvation or damnation had been divinely predetermined, could best be taught how to honor, glorify, and obey God. Generally, the Protestant ideal was a family headed by a pious male parishioner, whose first concern was Church reform, and whose Christian wife, by virtue of her religious training, would support his piety and assist him in instilling Godly precepts in their children.[47]

Except for a few moral works, the reformers disapproved of the reading of pagan literature because for them generally morality without reference to Godliness was an irrelevant topic. In his catechism, Alexander Nowell, the Elizabethan Dean of St. Paul's, later stated this idea quite succinctly: "For this age of childhode ought no lesse yea also much more to be trayned with good lessons to godliness, than with good artes to humanitie." Tyndale earlier had spoken for many Protestants in *The Obedience of a Christian Man* when he admonished his readers first to "Seek Christ in their mates." Most reformers also discouraged the household instruction of children in Latin vocabulary, as Sir Thomas Elyot had suggested in the *Governour,* for fear that knowledge of this language would lead to clandestine Catholic devotions. While some Protestant boys, especially those who attended grammar school, would continue to be required to study Latin, it became increasingly less likely that the homebound girls would be given that opportunity. Although there were a few Protestant humanists, like William Cecil and Sir Nicholas Bacon, who valued the classical education of their wives, most of their reformed contemporaries did not appreciate that viewpoint. Indeed, after an outburst of excellence in Greek and Latin studies among young women between the years 1540 and 1550, this training for them began to disappear.[48]

The reformers' effort to enhance the powers of husbands over their wives, as evidenced in the marriage service of the Edwardian prayerbooks, was part of a general attack on clerical privilege and status. It had long been the custom in England, among both Catholics and Protestants, to tell scurrilous jokes about the human failings and weaknesses of priests, stories which were generally accepted as true because on the whole the clergymen were an uneducated group of lower-class men. Many had become priests in the same way that guild apprentices became masters, through apprenticeships in which the trade was learned. It was by this attack on the elite position of the poorly educated, often illiterate parish priest, that the early Reformation was largely popularized.[49]

Partly because the vows of celibacy, though often ignored, helped to set the parish priest apart in a separate caste, Protestants consistently favored clerical marriage. To defend their position, they turned to the Bible for their arguments. First, they quoted from the Book of Genesis, where it is written that woman was created to be a helpmeet unto man, to prove that marriage, itself, was a divine ordinance, and secondly, they quoted New Testament verses with comments about married bishops, priests, and deacons to prove that it was also instituted for churchmen. Recognizing that only a few men had the gift of chastity, the reformers repeatedly referred to the epistle of St. Paul in which he had offered marriage as a remedy for the sins of lust and fornication, and they frequently warned that a priest who failed in his holy vows gave a perilous example of sexual immorality to his parishioners.[50]

While their promotion of clerical marriage stripped the clergy of the special position allotted to them as celibate servants to Christ, who had himself lived and died a virgin, Protestants also attacked the priests' ability to perform the miracle of the Mass and denied to them the power of the private confessional through which many husbands feared priests, often ridiculed for their sexual incontinence, gained emotional control over women. A joke about this control protected Thomas Lawney, a Kentish minister, who was known to favor clerical marriage, from the wrath of the conservative third Duke of Norfolk in 1539. When this nobleman asked him whether priests may have wives, Lawney replied: "I cannot well tell whether priests may have wives or no: but well I wot, and am sure of it . . . that wives will have priests." The Duke left "merrily, laughing at Lawney's sudden and apt answer."[51]

In *Utopia,* Sir Thomas More's cure for priestly authority over women was to institute clerical marriage and to establish husbands as the confessors of their wives. While he reaffirmed his personal support for priestly celibacy, most of the Protestants adopted his fictional innovations as part of a general attack on clerical elitism. These concepts are clearly evident in the writing of the early reformers. William Tyndale wrote that a woman had to accept orders from her husband as though they were from God, and Thomas Becon, a chaplain of Archbishop Cranmer, wrote that one of the husband's duties was to teach his wife spiritual truth. She should, Becon went on to quote liberally from St. Paul, remain silent in the congregation, seeking religious guidance and instruction only from her husband at home. Theoretically, the spiritual powers of Protestant men over their wives and children, which were executed through the medium of family prayers and scripture readings, increased dramatically when the elitism of the priesthood was abolished.[52]

While promoting matrimony as the natural human condition, even for clergymen, the reformers were quite willing to recognize that celibacy was still a special religious gift for some men but not for women. The preordained fate of women was as wives and mothers, family roles which were regularly emphasized in the writing of Protestants, who indiscriminately interchanged the words, wife and woman, a semantic indifference indicating that for reformers the identity of a woman was subsumed in her role as a wife. The failure to grant women identities independent of their family roles may have been a result of their acceptance of the medieval assumption that women did not have as much control over their baser emotions as did men. Husbands were warned to maintain a constant vigilance over their wives, who might use their feminine wiles like Eve or Jezebel of old to usurp mastery of the family, thereby creating a monstrous regiment on the most fundamental social level.[53]

One Protestant effort that could have been of immeasurable assistance to women and men trapped in destructive marriages did not succeed. It was their hope to make remarriage possible in some divorce cases, but to do so they had to change the canon law of England, by which there were only two ways to dissolve a union, *a mensa et thoro,* a separation for adultery, heresy, apostasy, or cruelty, with no remarriage possible, or *a vinculo,* a separation with remarriage possible, because the union, illegally contracted, was declared null and void. A major disadvantage to *a vinculo* was that in England it resulted in the union's offspring being declared illegitimate.[54]

A committee, first authorized by Henry VIII, to make recommendations for reform of the canon law completed a report in 1551 called *Reformatio Legum Ecclesiasticarum* that, although it reflected the belief of many Protestants, failed to achieve Parliamentary sanction in Tudor England. It had recommended divorce with remarriage possible for adultery, dissertion, and male impotence, but because of its rejection, the only dissolution that canon law approved, which was not synonymous with annulment, was the *a mensa et thoro* separation.[55]

Like many other Protestants, Hugh Latimer had argued for graver penalties for adultery than mere divorce. In a sermon before Edward VI in 1550 he had proposed capital punishment for convicted adulterers, a cure that he believed would eradicate the widespread lechery in England. Adopting the attitude of Erasmus, reformers also argued for equal application to men and women of the regulations concerning sexual immorality, but instead, even the *a mensa et thoro* separations, which were often followed by illegal marriages, came to be applied by a double standard. Ordinarily, a woman could not obtain a separation for simple adultery, as a man could, but had to prove aggravated circumstances, such as the introduction of her husband's mistress into the household. Once legally separated, a wife found that she was "almost wholly destitute of civil rights," for the divorce had not restored her to the status of a single woman. She was still her husband's mate, with no power before the law to enforce contracts into which she entered. Finally, even when she was the innocent party in the suit, her spouse automatically obtained custody of their children. This discrimination against women was greater in England than in any other Protestant country.[56]

It was in the Edwardian period that an aristocrat first turned to Parliament for help in a marital case because of the inflexible divorce laws. William Parr, Marquess of Northampton, the brother of Queen Katherine, had married Anne Bourchier, daughter to Henry, second Earl of Essex, in 1541. By 1547 he had sufficient doubt as to the paternity of her children to obtain an *a mensa et thoro* divorce and to have the offspring declared illegitimate by Parliamentary statute. Confused about his marital status, or so he claimed, the Marquess took a second wife while a Church commission was still deliberating about whether or not he could remarry during the lifetime of his first wife. Outraged by his action, the King's Council, following the advice of religious experts, ordered him to separate from his second spouse, Elizabeth Brooke, daughter to George, ninth Lord Cobham. In 1552 Northampton finally sought and won Parliamentary approval of the second union, a decision that was without precedent in England, for even Henry VIII had established the validity or the invalidity of his marriages by Church commissions. Although this decision was later overturned, Northampton set the precedent for frequent legislative action in divorce cases of the aristocracy in the Stuart period. Lower-class people, without access to Parliament, were left with the simple expedient of remarrying illegally, hoping that their new unions would not be challenged in Church courts.[57]

While a final contrast of women in Catholic and Protestant cultures will be made in Chapters 8 and 9, it is impossible to argue here, given the comments of the early Protestant leaders and the statutes enacted in Edwardian England, that women gained measurable esteem through reformed influence in government and society. It is true that Catholics, both conservative and humanist, had regarded the female sex as inferior, but this outlook was one shared by the Protestants, who adopted many of the familial views of Erasmus and More. In fact, whenever the attitudes of the reformers deviated from those of the Christian humanists, the theoretical esteem and opportunity of women suffered from the changed emphasis. However limited had been the educational plan of Erasmus and More, for example, it was still less restrictive for women than that of most Protestants.

With the destruction of the monasteries, virtually the only social and economic future left for women was as wives, for society remained scornful of single women. While Protestants continued to view celibacy as a special religious gift for men, they failed to provide a vocation for young women in which virginity was esteemed. Furthermore, as brides, women had to participate in a Church ceremony in which they were told that reverence for their husbands had been divinely decreed. Though this state-imposed indoctrination, the Church blessed men's spiritual control of their spouses. The priesthood of believers, that celebrated Protestant concept, was to be exercised by a community of husbands and fathers on behalf of their female dependents.[58] Whether or not these familial ideas were successfully implemented, Protestantism, like Christian humanism, in theory at least, offered a more diminished role for women in relationship to their husbands than had medieval Catholicism.

NOTES

1. G. R. Owst, *Preaching in Medieval England* (Reprint, 1965), p. 173; *Here begynneth an interlocucyon with an argument betwyxt man and woman whiche of them could prove to be most excellent* (London, 1525).

2. Clair Cross, " 'Great reasoners in scripture:' the Activities of Women Lollards, 1380-1580," *Medieval Women: Studies in Church History,* ed. Derek Baker (Oxford, 1978), pp. 359-380; A. G. Dickens, *The English Reformation* (New York, 1964), p. 30; for information about those who died for Protestantism in the reign of Henry VIII, see John Foxe, *Acts and Monuments,* ed. the Rev. George Townsend, 8 vols. (Reprint, 1965), I, IV, and V; Geoffrey Elton, *Policy and Police* (Cambridge, 1972), p. 390.

3. Dom David Knowles, *The Religious Orders in England,* 3 vols. (Cambridge, 1959), III, 191; Alan Neame, *The Holy Maid of Kent* (London, 1971), p. 351.

4. Dom David Knowles, III, 182-466.

5. Thomas Cranmer, *Miscellaneous Writings and Letters,* ed. John E. Cox (Cambridge, 1846), pp. 64-66; John E. Paul, *Catherine of Aragon and her Friends* (New York, 1966), p. 172; L. E. Whatmore, "The Sermon Against the Holy Maid of Kent," *English Historical Review,* LVIII (1943), 463-475; Alan Neame, pp. 77 and 172; Dom David Knowles, III, 184-191; *Calendar of the Letters and Papers of Henry VIII,* VI, No. 1589; E. J. Devereux, "Elizabeth Barton and Tudor Censorship," *Bulletin of the John Rylands Library,* XLIX (1966), 91-107.

6. G.W.O. Woodward, *The Dissolution of the Monasteries* (New York, 1966), pp. 2 and 73-74; Dom David Knowles, III, 157, 298-319, and 470; occasionally the funds of nunneries were transferred to monasteries. See Abbot F. A. Gasquet, *Henry VIII and the English Monasteries* (London, 1906), p. 27; Peter Heath, ed., *Bishop Geoffrey Blythe's Visitations,* Staffordshire Record Society, fourth series, vol. 7 (Stafford, 1973), p. xxxv; A. G. Dickens, pp. 122-128 and 143; Walter C. Richardson, *History of the Court of Augmentations, 1536-1554* (Baton, Rouge, La., 1961), p. 178; G.A.J. Hodgett, ed., *The State of the Ex-Religious and former Chantry Priests in the Diocese of Lincoln, 1547-1574,* Lincoln Record Society, vol. 53 (Hereford, 1959), pp. xi-xx; Richard Watson Dixon, *The History of the Church of England,* 2nd rev. ed., 6 vols. (London, 1884-1902), II, 548.

7. Dom David Knowles, III, 406-466; nuns were receiving £2 6s 8d in the reign of Elizabeth. See A. G. Dickens, p. 146; apparently the nuns in Essex received more generous pensions. See J. E. Oxley, *The Reformation in Essex* (Manchester, 1965), p. 238.

8. A. G. Dickens, p. 146: G.A.J. Hodgett, pp. xi-xvi; Geoffrey Baskerville, "The Depossessed Religious in Surrey," *Surrey Archaeological Collections,* XLVII (1941), 13.

9. A.F.C. Bourdillon, *The Order of Minoresses in England* (Manchester, 1926), p. 90; G. Baskerville, "The Married Clergy and Pensioned Religious in the Norwich Diocese, 1555," *English Historical Review,* XLVIII (1933), 211 and 221.

10. A. G. Dickens, p. 145; F. A. Gasquet, pp. 91 and 183; W.A.J. Archbold, *The Somerset Religious Houses,* Cambridge Historical Essays, No. 6 (Cambridge, 1892), 103-104; Arthur Collins, *Historical Collections of the Noble Family of Windsor* (London,

1754), pp. 45-53; Gerald H. Ryan and L. J. Redstone, *Temperley of Hintlesham* (London, 1931), p. 33.

11. Joyce Youings, *The Dissolution of the Monasteries* (New York, 1971), p. 13; A.F.C. Bourdillon, pp. 80-90; Dom David Knowles, III, 412; A. G. Dickens, p. 147; G.W.O. Woodward, p. 152; F. A. Gasquet, p. 452; J. E. Oxley, p. 239.

12. G. Baskerville, *English Historical Review,* p. 205; Dom David Knowles, III, 21; G. Baskerville, "The Dispossessed Religious after the Suppression of the Monasteries," *Essays in History Presented to Reginald Lane Poole,* ed. H.W.C. Davis (Oxford, 1927), p. 460; A. G. Dickens, pp. 145 and 245.

13. A. G. Dickens, p. 52; there were a few schoolmistresses in Tudor England. See Norman Wood, *The Reformation and English Education* (London, 1931), p. 77; positions as governesses seem to have been more prestigious and higher paying. In 1638 Hannah Woolley considered her transfer from the job of schoolmistress to that of governess as a promotion. With her small knowledge of Italian and her ability in arithmetic and writing, she was considered better educated than most of her female contemporaries. See Ada Wallas, *Before the Bluestockings* (London, 1929), pp. 17-18; Eileen Power, p. 98.

14. John Foxe, V, 537-550; John Bale, *Select Works,* ed. the Rev. Henry Christmas (Cambridge, 1849), pp. 180 and 199; for details about her family, see Derek Wilson, *A Tudor Tapestry* (Pittsburgh, 1972), pp. 155-160.

15. John Bale, pp. 155, 158 and 177-178.

16. Ibid., pp. 201 and 224.

17. Ibid.; John Foxe, V, 545; see *Letters and Papers of Henry VIII,* XXI-i, No. 1546 and No. 1181; the other ladies at court were Anne, Countess of Sussex and Anne, Lady Fitzwilliam; John Bellamy, *The Tudor Law of Treason* (Buffalo, N.Y., 1979), pp. 110-120.

18. There were also "half-way" Anabaptists who repudiated predestination but did not object to infant baptism. See M. M. Knappen, *Tudor Puritanism* (Chicago, 1939), p. 149; Champlin Burrage, *The Early English Dissenters* (New York, 1967), p. 41; Michael R. Watts, *The Dissenters* (Oxford, 1978), p. 9; Daniel Neal, *The History of the Puritans,* 2 vols. (New York, 1848), I, 49.

19. John Foxe, V, 704; her religious views were similar to those of Melchio Hoffman of Munster. See Champlin Burrage, p. 41 and A. G. Dickens, p. 237; John Strype, *Ecclesiastical Memorials,* 3 vols. (Oxford, 1822), II-i, 335.

20. D. M. Loades, "The Enforcement of Reaction, 1553-1558," *Journal of Ecclesiastical History,* XVI (1965), 56-66; John Foxe, VI, 590; *Calendar of State Papers Spanish,* XIII, 138; Sir John Harington, *A Tract on the Succession to the Crown* (London, 1880), pp. 78 and 100-101.

21. A. G. Dickens, p. 266; see Carol Levin, "Women In the Book of Martyrs as Models of Behavior in Tudor England," *International Journal of Women's Studies,* IV (1981), 196-207.

22. John Foxe, VIII, 253, 321, and 504; Gina Alexander. "Bonner and the Marian Persecution," *History,* LX (1975), 374.

23. A. G. Dickens, p. 266.

24. John Foxe, VIII, 325.

25. John Bale, p. 155; John Foxe, VIII, 325 and 498.

26. John Foxe, VIII, 326, 401, and 467.

27. John Bale, p. 246; there were, of course, stories of martyrs from the early Church. *The Golden Legend* was first translated and published by Caxton in 1483. Its last printing

was in 1527. See Helen C. White, *Tudor Books of Saints and Martyrs* (Madison, Wisc., 1963), pp. 41 and 67.

28. John Foxe, VI, 30 and 39; John Strype, *Ecclesiastical Memorials*, II-i, 335.

29. A. G. Dickens, pp. 273-275; John Foxe, VIII, 450-451.

30. Paul Bush, *A brief exhortation . . . to one Margarete Burges wyfe to Jhon Burges, clotheare of Kyngeswode in the countie of Wiltshire* (London, 1556).

31. Christina Garrett, *The Marian Exiles* (Reprint, 1966), pp. 32 and 87; Add. Ms. 48,043, f. 1, British Library.

32. Peregrine Bertie, *Memoirs of Peregrine Bertie, Eleventh Lord Willoughby de Eresby* (London, 1838), pp. 12-27; in 1546 John Hooper included the Duke of Suffolk in a list of those who supported the gospel in England, but who had only recently died. See Hastings Robinson, ed., *Original Letters Relative to the English Reformation*, Parker Society, 2 vols. (London, 1842-1845), I, 33-38; for modern biographies of the Duchess, see Evelyn Read, *Catherine, Duchess of Suffolk* (London, 1962) and Lady Cecilie Goff, *A Woman of the Tudor Age* (London, 1930).

33. Frances Grey was, of course, the mother of Lady Jane Grey.

34. Christina Garrett, p. 11; Theodore de Beze, *The other parte of Christian questions and answeares,* trans. John Field (London, 1580), dedicatory letter.

35. Christina Garrett, pp. 69 and 292; another unescorted woman was Mistress Wilkinson. See Ruth Hughey, "Cultural Interests of Women in England from 1524 to 1640 Indicated in the Writing of Women," Ph.D. dissertation, Cornell University, 1932, p. 185.

36. Christina Garrett, p. 347; Patrick Collinson, "The Role of Women in the English Reformation. Illustrated by the Life and Friendships of Anne Locke," *Studies in Church History,* II (1965), 258-272; Lewis Lupton, *A History of the Geneva Bible,* 10 vols. (London, 1977), IV, 12-23; Jasper Ridley, *John Knox* (New York, 1968), pp. 247-248; after her third marriage to Richard Prowse, an Exeter draper, she published her translation of a French work by John Tafflin, *Of the Markes of the children of God* (London, 1590).

37. Richard T. Vann, "Toward a New Life Style: Women in Pre-Industrial Capitalism," *Becoming Visible: Women in European History,* ed. Renate Bridenthal and Claudia Koonz (Boston, 1977), p. 199; Natalie Davis, *Society and Culture in Modern France,* (Stanford, Calif., 1975), pp. 88-89.

38. Lawrence Stone, *The Family, Sex and Marriage in England, 1500-1800* (New York, 1977), pp. 7, 123-128, 141, and 653.

39. A. G. Dickens, *The Age of Humanism and Reformation* (Englewood Cliffs, N.J., 1972), p. 19; Kenneth Charlton, *Education in Renaissance England* (London, 1965), pp. 31 and 205; Erasmus, *A ryght frutefull epystle in Laude and prayse of matrymony,* trans. R. Tavernour (London, c. 1530).

40. Sir Thomas Elyot, *Defence of Good Women* (London, 1545); Juan Luis Vives, *Office and Dueties of a Husband* (London, 1553); E. E. Reynolds, *Margaret Roper* (London, 1960), p. 38.

41. Henry Gee and W. J. Hardy, *Documents Illustrative of Early Church History* (Reprint, 1966), p. 269; James McConica, *English Humanists and Reformation Politics* (Oxford, 1965), pp. 235-239.

42. This ritual was based on ancient Jewish tradition; Ernest Rhys, ed., *The First and Second Prayerbooks of Edward VI* (London, 1910); Allan G. Chester, ed., *Selected Sermons of Hugh Latimer* (Charlottesville, Va., 1968), p. 169.

43. Kenneth Charlton, p. 205; the Rev. John Henry Blunt, *The Annotated Book of*

Common Prayer (New York, 1876), p. 524; unmarried mothers could not be churched until after penance was done; Puritans objected to the ceremony because it resembled the Jewish service of purification. See Horton Davies, *Worship and Theology in England* (Princeton, 1970), p. 267; see also Francis Proctor and William Howard, *A New History of the Book of Common Prayer* (New York, 1901), pp. 638-640; T. F. Thistleton-Dyer, *British Popular Customs* (London, 1876), p. 54.

44. Matilda Gage, *Women, Church and State* (Reprint, 1972), p. 434; Hugh Latimer, p. 153.

45. John Cordy Jeaffreson, *Brides and Bridals,* 2 vols. (London, 1873), I, 262-266.

46. J. W. Adamson, "The Extent of Literacy in England in the 15th and 16th Centuries: Notes & Conjectures," *The Library,* fourth series (1929), 172; John Bruce, ed., *The Works of Roger Hutchinson,* Parker Society (Cambridge, 1842), p. 293.

47. For a revised opinion of the Protestants as social reformers in the reign of Edward VI, see G. R. Elton, "Reform and the 'Commonwealth Men' of Edward VI's Reign," *The English Commonwealth, 1547-1640, Essays in Politics and Society, Presented to Joel Hurstfield,* ed. Peter Clark, et al. (Leicester, 1979), pp. 23-38; see also Douglas Bush, *The Renaissance and English Humanism* (Toronto, 1939), p. 83.

48. William Tyndale, *Doctrinal Treatises and Introduction to Different Portions of the Holy Scriptures,* ed. Henry Walter (Cambridge, 1848), p. 199; Marjorie Keniston McIntosh, "Sir Anthony Coke: Tudor Humanist, Educator, and Religious Reformer," *Proceedings of the American Philosophical Society,* CXIX (1975), 239-240; Alexander Nowell, *A Catechisme, or first Instruction and Learning of Christian Religion,* trans. John Norton (London, 1571); see also Thomas Becon, *The Catechism,* ed. John Ayre, Parker Society (Cambridge, 1844), p. 50; Richard Mulcaster, *Positions (1581)* (New York, 1971), pp. 30, 238, and 259; for a government statement agaist the reading of pagan literature in grammar schools, see *Acts of the Privy Council of England,* XIII, 389.

49. F. W. Brooks, "The Social Position of the Parson In the Sixteenth Century," *Journal of the British Archaeological Association,* X, third series (1945-1947), 23-37.

50. Henry C. Lea, *The History of Sacerdotal Celibacy in the Christian Church* (Reprint, 1957), pp. 405-426; John Foxe, V, 579; William Tyndale, pp. 254 and 314; W. E. Campbell, *Erasmus, Tyndale and More* (London, 1949), pp. 142-143; Charles George and Katherine George, *The Protestant Mind of the English Reformation, 1570-1640* (Princeton, 1961), pp. 265-266.

51. Thomas Becon, pp. 334-340; John Strype, *Memorials of the Most Reverend Father in God Thomas Cranmer, Sometime Lord Archbishop of Canterbury,* 2 vols. (Oxford, 1822), I, 49.

52. William Tyndale, pp. 171 and 200; Charles George and Katherine George, p. 259.

53. Hugh Latimer, pp. 61 and 153.

54. Chilton Powell, *English Domestic Relations, 1487-1653* (Reprint, 1972), pp. 8-9.

55. Sir Lewis Dibdin and Sir Charles E. Chadwyck-Healey, *English Church Law and Divorce* (London, 1912), pp. 46-70; some early Protestants, for example, William Tyndale, were opposed to divorce.

56. Hugh Latimer, pp. 57, 64, and 144-145; Lulu McDowell Richardson, *The Forerunners of Feminism in French Literature of the Renaissance from Christine of Pisa to Marie de Gournay,* (Baltimore, 1929), pp. 47-54; George Elliott Howard, *A History of Matrimonial Institutions,* 3 vols. (Chicago, 1904), II, 77-87; Chilton Powell, pp. 65-75;

A Berrell, "Women Under the English Law," *Edinburgh Review*, XLXXXIV (1896), 330-340; C. S. Kenny, *The History of the Law of England as to the Effects of Marriage on Property and on the Wife's Legal Capacity* (London, 1879), p. 148.

57. *Letters and Papers of Henry VIII*, XVIII-i, No. 67; John Strype, *Ecclesiastical Memorials*, III-i, 843; John Foxe, VI, 537 and 542; *Acts of the Privy Council of England*, II, 164, *Calendar of State Papers Spanish*, XII, 175; Howell A. Lloyd, "The Essex Inheritance," *Welsh History Review*, VII (1974), 23; *Calendar of State Papers Spanish, Elizabeth*, I, 591.

58. Rosemary Ruether, ed., *Religion and Sexism* (New York, 1974), p. 297; Protestants did not support the spiritual authority of the husband, however, if he remained Catholic when his wife converted to reformed views. For more discussion, see Chapter 8.

6

The Reformation
Generation

The Christian humanists had failed to popularize their theories on female education in the 1530s partly because of the disgrace of the women who can be identified as learned. The divorce of Catherine of Aragon, which was soon followed by the execution of Sir Thomas More and the persecution of his family, brought public disrepute to the women humanists of the first generation. It became unfashionable at court, or indeed elsewhere, to praise the accomplishments of Margaret Roper and her sisters, of Margaret Clement, or even of the Princess Mary, whose royal title was transferred to her half-sister, Elizabeth.

For an insight into the unwillingness of the aristocracy to extend classical instruction to their daughters, it will be helpful to review the training of the royal maids of honor. The competition for an appointment to serve Henry VIII's consorts was keen because the maids were in a position to develop valuable social contacts and to contract important marriage alliances, as, for example, the celebrated one of Queen Katherine Howard, who had been an attendant of Henry VIII's fourth wife, Anne of Cleves. In 1540 when Katherine succeeded Anne as the King's fifth wife, nearly sixteen years had elapsed since the publication of Richard Hyrde's dedicatory letter to the *Pater Noster,* the first work in English advocating a humanist education for women. There is no reason to believe that during that time any maid of honor was a classicist, a conclusion that is based not only on the overwhelming contemporary silence about their language skills or the apparent ignorance of a few of them like Katherine Howard, but also on the availability of specific evidence about the instruction of two young women whose relatives struggled valiantly to obtain court appointments for them.

Honor Grenville, wife first of Sir John Basset by whom she had seven children, and second of Arthur, Viscount Lisle, an illegitimate son of Edward IV, attempted to obtain places for her Basset daughters, Anne and Catherine, in the households of Anne Boleyn and her successor, Jane Seymour. To prepare them for these appointments, Lady Lisle had her girls taught to read and to write French and English, to play the lute and the virginals, to choose and to wear stylish clothes properly, and to sew, an education that despite its limitations was far superior to the instruction previously given to Jane Basset, Lady Lisle's stepchild, who at the age of thirty was unable to sign her name. After distributing gifts to important courtiers and giving some quails to Queen Jane in 1537, the Viscountess was able to win a place at court for only one daughter.[1] Because of her determination, it is possible to conclude that she would have offered her children any linguistic training, including Latin, had she thought it an advantage in fulfilling her social aspirations for them.

Two men at court who continued to support the ideas of the humanists for female education were Sir Thomas Elyot and the King, himself. In 1540 Elyot dedicated his publication, the *Defence of Good Women,* whose heroine was a learned woman, to Anne of Cleves, thus associating himself publicly with Thomas Cromwell, the chief architect of Henry VIII's fourth marriage. Set in the third century A.D. the *Defence* was a dialogue between two Romans about the female sex. The first disputant, Caninus, derogated women with a quote from Aristotle that they were a work of nature "unperfect," never contented, always complaining and rebuking others, and the second disputant, Candidus, defended their cause with a review of the inconsistencies in Aristotelian thought and a reminder of the story of Penelope, the long-suffering and constant mate of Ulysses. To settle the argument, Caninus agreed to a meeting with Zenobia, widow of Odenatus, King of Palmyria, who was reputed to be a perfect woman.[2]

The two men learned from Zenobia that she had not married until she was twenty years old because she had devoted her teenage years to the study of moral philosophy. It was this advanced education, along with her expertise in the Greek, Latin, and Egyptian languages, that had led the King of Palmyria to seek her for his consort. As his wife she had revered him after God and as his widow she had governed wisely on behalf of their children whose education she had carefully supervised. Even though she had led her troops in battle against the Romans when they invaded her country, her conquerors had treated her with honor because of their appreciation for her exceptional qualities. Overwhelmed by the history of this outstanding Queen, Caninus withdrew his earlier contention that women were by nature "unperfect."

Although Pearl Hogrefe dismissed this treatise as an overly complimentary view of women rulers, it actually reflected its author's philosophy quite well.[3] Its primary purpose was to support the views of More and other humanists that wives ought to be educated to provide their husbands with learned companionship and their children with moral training. Because Elyot defined the perfect woman by her family relationships, the successful heroine of the *Defence* had necessarily to be an individual like Queen Zenobia, who was both an obedient consort and an exceptional regent, rather than a woman like Queen Isabella, who ruled Castile in her own right.

Ultimately, it was not the humanist publications but the King's decision to welcome Princess Mary back to court and to offer her half-brother and half-sister classical instruction that prompted a few noble families to adopt this training for their girls. Determined to perpetuate his dynasty, if necessary even with his daughters, Henry VIII provided them with a rigorous education similar to that of his sons. By his death because of the fashion he had helped to popularize, there were enough women at court reading Latin, if not Greek, for Nicholas Udall, the former schoolmaster of Eton, to praise them for their industry.[4]

In this Chapter the instruction of the royal children and the influence of their stepmother, Queen Katherine Parr, on their academic accomplishments will first be examined. Next, the reasons that the four noble families of Grey, Seymour, Howard, and Fitzalan, all of whom had a child named in honor of Prince Edward's mother, Queen Jane Seymour, decided to offer classical training to their daughters will be reviewed. A study of the female classicists who were not members of the secular nobility will also be made with the intent of discovering why their parents chose to offer them classical instruction. These women included one daughter of a bishop, four of a Protestant gentleman, the wife of a bourgeoisie, and the grandchildren of the More circle. Finally, some conclusions will be made about the content and quality of their training.

Sympathetic biographers have exaggerated the roles of the King's first and last wives in the instruction of the royal children. Although Catherine of Aragon did have considerable input into Mary's training, Henry was clearly concerned with every detail of her upbringing and was also responsible for the splendid education of his next two children, the Duke of Richmond and the Princess Elizabeth. While the King sought advice from More and other scholars about tutors for his natural son, he provided the opportunity for his younger daughter, who was declared illegitimate in 1536 the year of Richmond's death, to learn Italian, French, Latin, and Greek from various instructors, among them William Grindal, a pupil of Roger Ascham, the author of *The Schoolmaster*.

The fourth surviving royal child, Edward, had Protestant tutors whom most modern scholars, including Pearl Hogrefe, have maintained were appointed by Katherine Parr, a conjecture that is based on the false assumption that she was both a committed Protestant and an experienced classical scholar at the time of her marriage to Henry. Widowed for the second time only six or seven months before she became his consort in 1543, Katherine's most immediate religious loyalties had been linked to conservative religious politics, for her second husband, John Neville, Lord Latimer, had been involved in the Pilgrimage of Grace. More importantly, the statement of her faith, that was published in 1547 under the title of *The Lamentacion of a synner,* cannot be described as a Protestant treatise. Called a "classic of Tudor devotional literature" by James McConica the *Lamentacion* has statements that are entirely compatible with the beliefs expressed in the fifteenth-century tract, *De Imitatio Christi,* a work celebrating the tenets of the Dutch mysticism that had such a profound effect upon the thought of Erasmus. Probably authored by Thomas à Kempis, the *De Imitatio* became one of the most popular religious treatises in Tudor England after its first appearance in translation in 1504. Echoing some of its sentiments, Katherine confessed that her faith was based on meditation, prayer, and a personal experience with Christ and denied that salvation was merited. Piety, faith, humility, and a zealous reading of the scriptures, she thought, would help to restore the unity of Christendom, a goal that Erasmus would have approved.[5]

Although she may be described as Erasmian in her personal faith, it is doubtful that when they were children either she or her younger sister, Anne, wife of William Herbert, the future Earl of Pembroke, had been educated as humanists. While it is true that they both displayed an interest in classical Latin at the Henrician court, there is no evidence that they developed advanced skills in that language. When in 1545, Roger Ascham, whose stylistic techniques included Ciceronian imitations, sent a copy of the *De Officiis* to Lady Herbert, he advised her in a Latin letter, as though she were a new classical scholar, to study it with diligence. In the following year, nine-year-old Prince Edward, who had been writing Latin letters since he was seven, praised Queen Katherine's progress in Latin composition, implying by his statement that his skills were more advanced than were hers. To dismiss his remark as "innocent" as did Pearl Hogrefe is to misread his character and the rigor of his instruction even in the nursery. Indeed, as most of the Queen's exquisite handwriting and all of her printed works are in English, it is evident that she never devoted much effort to Latin composition and none at all to classical translations.[6]

Katherine's correspondence with Cambridge University in 1545 offers some insights into her attitude about ancient literature. In her reply to suppliant letters from the University administrators, she scolded them for writing to her in Latin and not "in our vulgar tonge, aptyst for my intelligence." Then admitting that she had become a "cheryscher of the lernyd state," as a person of her vocation ought to be, she also warned them against the study of pagan works, particularly of Greece, because these ancient values might corrupt the purity of the Christian faith.[7]

While she was neither a Protestant nor a classicist in 1543, she was also not the patroness of the instructors of her stepchildren. There is absolutely no evidence to support the claim that it was she who ordered the reorganization of the Prince's household school just before his seventh birthday. It is more likely that the young boy's father and his advisers had already decided to adopt the advice in Elyot's *Governour* to remove a pupil of seven years of age from the nursery and entrust him to tutors for advanced study of Latin and for beginning lessons in Greek. In 1544 Sir John Cheke, the first Regius Professor of Greek at Cambridge University and the King's physician, was appointed the Prince's Greek tutor. Since Katherine deplored the study of pagan literature, she would not have favored, much less sought, Cheke's appointment, but, in any event, the King, who had long possessed the *Institutio principis Christiani,* a handbook by Erasmus for the instruction of royal heirs, would surely not have permitted a new wife, however learned, to assume responsibility for the education of his only male child.[8]

While she did influence the choice of instructors for Elizabeth, her involvement was largely a negative one. In 1548 with the death of William Grindal, Elizabeth asked Katherine, who was then Queen Dowager, to replace her deceased tutor with Ascham who was, himself, a former pupil of Cheke. Perhaps because he usually assigned pagan authors to his students, Katherine only reluctantly agreed to Elizabeth's request for his appointment, a hesitation that would have been deplored by Margaret Roper, who had futilely sought Ascham for her children.[9]

Despite these reservations, it is obvious that by encouraging Edward to write Latin letters to her and by supervising the religious training of his sisters, Katherine had a positive influence on their education. Forming a link between the second generation of women humanists as represented by Elizabeth, who was young enough to be her child, and the first generation as represented by Mary, who was only four years her junior, there is evidence that the Queen encouraged them both to read Christian works. In 1544 Elizabeth rendered into English a treatise written by Margaret of Navarre from a copy that belonged to Katherine, a translation that, along with the young girl's rendition of the fourteenth Psalm, was published in 1548 by John Bale, the sometime Bishop of Ossory, under the title of *A Godly Medytacyon of the christen Sowle.* A few years earlier, in 1545, Queen Katherine had authorized her own first publication, *The Prayers styring the Mynd unto heavenlye medytacions,* a collection of her favorite prayers written by others, that was issued nine times by 1559 and was reprinted with the *King's Psalms* in 1568. As the Princess rendered this volume into Latin, French, and Italian for her stepmother, it can reasonably be concluded that the Queen had also suggested this project, particularly as Elizabeth's later extant efforts, are primarily of secular authors.[10]

The Queen also encouraged her elder stepdaughter to translate religious works. When Katherine decided to promote the publication of an English version of Erasmus' Latin Paraphrases on the New Testament, she chose Mary as one of the translators, although because of illness, the Princess was unable to complete her assignment. The finished English Paraphrases were so well received that both Edward and Elizabeth issued injunctions requiring parish churches to purchase copies of them.[11]

Katherine must be judged a successful consort even though she had been Queen for less than four years at Henry VIII's death in 1547. When given high office she rose to the challenge admirably for nothing she had previously done had carried the promise of her accomplishments as his wife. While she and her sister turned to a study of Latin to encourage the scholarship of the royal children, Katherine, herself, was responsible for the publication of three books. Since she was one of only eight Englishwomen to have published at all between 1486 and 1548 and one of only three, including Marjery Kempe and Anne Askew, to have a statement of her faith appear in print, her scholarly attainments were, indeed, remarkable.

Even though Catherine's younger stepdaughter, Elizabeth, was educated after the public disgrace of most of the Christian humanists, their pedagogy had a significant influence on her training, since her tutors, among them Ascham, based their instructional methods and techniques on those of Sir Thomas More. As he was both the instructor of Elizabeth and the author of *The Schoolmaster*, published posthumously in 1570, Ascham's work serves as an excellent introduction to the humanism of the second generation. In his celebrated treatise that was written after a dinner conversation in the chamber of William Cecil about the flogging of students at Eton, Ascham strongly championed gentle methods of instruction and denounced the increasingly popular custom of finishing the education of young men by sending them off on continental tours which included many vice-ridden places like Italy.[12]

While he was a "propagandist" for the improvement of vernacular literature by imitation of the classics, he remained convinced that Latin was the language most satisfactory for scholarly expression. In *The Schoolmaster* he ridiculed those who worshipped Chaucerian English or Petrarchan Italian as their "gods in verses," claiming that he personally "would needs be counted like unto [More]," whose classic, the *Utopia*, had been written in Latin. When Ascham published in English, he excused his use of the vernacular as a need to reach the widest possible audience, but ironically it is for the simplicity and vigor of his native prose and not for his classical erudition that he owes his place in literature.[13]

Partly because of her long, successful reign, Elizabeth, who was his pupil for about two years, is the best known woman humanist of the sixteenth century. Ascham wrote in 1550 that her mind had no "womanly weakness," and that she was more intelligent and more industrious than the young men he had taught at the university. In the mornings, he revealed, she read the Greek of Isocrates and Sophocles and in the afternoons the Latin of Cicero and Livy as well as patristic authors and the New Testament.[14]

While she gained an appreciation for the moral guidance of ancient philosophers as a result of her work with Grindal and Ascham, she also developed an enthusiasm for the ideals of the vernacular literature that circulated at her father's court. Surrey, Wyatt, and other Henrician courtiers brought the Italian culture into fashion by their interpretations of the Petrarchan love sonnet in their poetry that honored an unobtainable love rather than an erudite wife. There is no doubt that the vernacular tongue that Elizabeth most esteemed was Italian, a language in which she had instruction as a child and in which her earliest letter, dated in 1544, was written. Her continuing efforts in that language as well as in French were so successful that by 1550 when she was seventeen Ascham was able to boast that she knew both as well as English.[15]

As an adult she maintained her expertise in Italian by reading regularly with Baptista Castiglione, who is identifiable as her instructor largely because of his imprisonment three times in the Tower of London in the reign of Queen Mary. In 1557 when the unsympathetic Venetian Ambassador reported the third arrest of Castiglione, he gave an assessment of Elizabeth's linguistic abilities that confirmed the earlier one of Ascham. The diplomat admitted to his superiors that as a linguist Elizabeth excelled her sister, for besides Latin, he said, she had "no slight knowledge of Greek," and took so much pleasure in speaking Italian that she "will never speak any other language with Italians." At her accession the next year, Elizabeth expressed great disappointment at the Venetian decision to end their embassy to England and welcomed the reversal of that policy in February, 1603 just a few weeks before her death with the words, "high time." She later confessed to the new diplomat: "But I do not know if I have spoken Italian well, still I think so for I learnt it as a child, and I believe have not forgotten it." Until 1584 when she ordered their expulsion, she had preferred to use this language with the Spanish Ambassadors, who could just as easily have communicated with her in French or even in the Latin that one of these diplomats informed his King she spoke with "eloquence."[16]

French was the only other vernacular tongue in which contemporary scholars, including Ascham, claimed that she was fluent. Her version of Margaret of Navarre's work that appeared in 1548, had, according to its editor, John Bale, caused learned men on the continent to rejoyce at her faith and her expertise in languages "specyally in noble youth & femynyte." Although French and Italian are the sole foreign vernacular languages in which she had remarkable skills, she did boast to a visiting ambassador in 1598 that at her succession she had known six tongues better than her own. While this is a highly exaggerated claim, it is possible that she developed some small skill in Spanish during the reign of her sister and that she may have learned to read a little German.[17]

Although many Protestant divines lauded Elizabeth's scholarship, it was often from surprise that as a woman she had any linguistic skills at all. These patronizing assessments and the flattery of others who hoped to win her friendship have made it difficult to evaluate her abilities. On the basis of their analysis of a few extant translations, T. W. Baldwin and other scholars have denied that she was fluent in Latin, implying that all of the contemporary praise was mere flattery. These modern appraisals are not convincing because they fail to take into account that her efforts were largely either the unpolished work of a student or that of a ruler pursuing a pleasurable diversion in the few leisure moments available to her. In 1561 when Sir Anthony Cooke presented her with his Latin version of a Greek work as a New Year's gift, he may have touched upon the primary difficulty in evaluating her extant translations when he remarked that if she would only devote more time to her studies, she would be able to translate the original of the piece he was sending to her better than anyone else. While her skills surely would never have been rated the finest in England, it is likely that they did deteriorate markedly during her reign when she had to neglect her scholarship because of the press of royal business. Indeed, after she had responded in impromptu Latin to a Polish ambassador in 1597, she remarked that she had been required to resurrect her old, almost forgotten, Latin vocabulary. There is, furthermore, no means by which modern scholars may determine her expertise in conversation, generally the medium by which even unfriendly ambassadors judged her to be an elegant linguist. None of her contemporaries who commented on her fluency ever suggested that she had inferior linguistic abilities. Only modern scholars evaluating her out of context have come to that conclusion.[18]

With the death of her father in 1547, Elizabeth moved to the Chelsea home of her stepmother who was soon secretly planning a fourth marriage. Just a few months after she was widowed, the Queen Dowager wed Thomas Seymour in what has customarily been characterized as a love match because of her remark in a letter to her new husband of her frustrated attempt to become his wife four years earlier in 1543. The long-held assumption that, as Lady Latimer, Katherine had first sought marriage with Thomas for romantic reasons needs to be reassessed.[19] It is well to remember that no courtier had a closer family tie to the future boy King of England in 1543 than had Thomas, her intended groom, except for his older brother, Edward, the future Duke of Somerset, who was already married, and the somewhat aged Henry VIII, whose sixth wife she became.

The issue of whether Katherine had a lingering passion for Thomas that was confirmed by marriage in 1547 must also be explored in the context of their relationships with other members of the royal family. When they married, she was Queen Dowager with custody of Elizabeth, who was then second in line to the throne, and he was the young King's uncle with plans to obtain custody of Jane Grey, whose place in the succession came immediately after that of Elizabeth. Surely it was political and social ambition that led Katherine to marry Thomas and to assist him in the competition with his elder brother, the Lord Protector, for supremacy in the kingdom, a struggle that sometimes took the form of bitter rivalries with her sister-in-law, Anne Stanhope, the wife of Somerset, over the possession of royal jewelry and social precedence at court. Ennobled as Lord Seymour of Sudeley, Katherine's new husband bribed the young King with pin money, schemed to marry him to Jane Grey who came to reside in the Seymour household, and played flirtatious and intimate games to win emotional ascendancy over Elizabeth.[20]

Because Seymour remained determined to pursue his dynastic goals after the death of the Queen Dowager in childbirth, he contemplated marriage with Elizabeth and sought continued custody of Jane Grey, his proposed bride for the King. When his schemes and other conspiracies against the Protectorate were revealed in 1549, his brother, Somerset, finally agreed to his arrest and execution. Under the leadership of the Duke, the King's Council also tried to prove that Elizabeth had encouraged Seymour in his marital designs, a charge that if substantiated could have caused her to be dropped from the succession, but despite her arrest and the interrogation of her servants, the government could find no evidence to warrant legal action against her.

While Elizabeth's status was endangered by the suspicion that she was involved in Seymour's conspiracy for power, Jane Grey's immediate political position was salvaged by her parents' alliance with John Dudley, the future Duke of Northumberland, who was able to engineer the defeat of the Lord Protector. It was undoubtedly because Jane had an opportunity to become Queen by succession as well as by marriage to Edward VI that her parents had provided her with instruction in Latin, Greek, French, Italian, and Hebrew, a linguistic training similar to that provided for the royal children. John Foxe, the martyrologist, later claimed that her learning had been superior to that of Prince Edward. She married Guildford Dudley, a son of Northumberland, and ruled as Queen of England for nine days in 1553 before she was imprisoned and ultimately executed by her cousin, Mary, the new monarch. All that has survived of Jane's erudition, besides the testimony of Ascham and other contemporaries, are her letters and prayers, some of which were published by Foxe, in 1563.[21]

Roger Ascham did not believe that Katherine Grey, the middle child, was as remarkable a scholar as her elder sister. In 1550 when he extolled the academic achievements of several young English women, Jane was the only one of her family to earn praise for her learning. About one year later in a personal letter to Jane, Ascham complimented her for reading Plato and expressed the hope that her sister would develop a similar love of ancient literature. Because shortly before her death in 1554, Jane asked Katherine to read a Greek book she was forwarding to her, it is likely that her younger sister had at least some elementary instruction in that language as well as in Latin. By contrast, Mary, the third Grey daughter, who was only nine years old in 1554 when her father, the Duke of Suffolk, was executed, probably had only vernacular skills, a linguistic training that is evident by the lack of classical works in her personal library.[22]

Among the descendants of Henry VII, the first Tudor monarch, four women in Edwardian England had a humanist education: his granddaughters, Mary and Elizabeth, and his great-granddaughters, Jane and Katherine Grey. There were learned women in at least three other noble households. Besides the desire that their dependents achieve enough educational distinction to compare favorably with the fashion set at court, the heads of these families, Edward Seymour, Duke of Somerset, Thomas Howard, third Duke of Norfolk, along with his heir, Henry, Earl of Surrey, and Henry Fitzalan, twelfth Earl of Arundel, hoped to match their offspring with royalty. It is noteworthy that, like Lord Suffolk, these noblemen all had daughters called Jane who were named in honor of Henry VIII's third Queen and who were reputed to be the most outstanding scholars in their families.

The Duke of Somerset, who ruled England on behalf of his young nephew, was the father of three sons and six daughters. Traditionally, his assertive wife has been blamed for exacerbating the conflict between her husband and her brother-in-law, Lord Seymour, but her role does not seem so outrageous when it is analyzed in the context of their dispute that actually focused on questions about possible royal marriages for her children. The major cause of the controversy may have been Somerset's desire to marry his heir, Edward, Earl of Hertford, to Jane Grey, the ward of Lord Seymour, whose goals by contrast were to make her the consort of Edward VI and to replace his elder brother, Somerset, as Lord Protector of the young King. Besides the rumor that Somerset wanted Jane Grey, who was third in line to the throne, as wife for his heir, it was widely believed that he planned to wed his well-educated daughter, also named Jane, to the King, himself. Although when he lost the Protectorship, he flatly denied that he had schemed for this dynastic union, Somerset's failure in

1547 to implement the marriage treaty between Edward and his five-year-old cousin, the Queen of Scotland, surely prompted him and his Duchess to consider more seriously the possibility of another royal alliance for the Seymour family. Indeed, in 1548 Jane and her sister, Margaret, thanked Edward graciously in a Latin letter for his "literary gift."[23]

Unfortunately, there is little extant information about the education of Anne, Margaret, and Jane, Somerset's three learned girls, except that they had a superb command of Latin, are reputed to have learned Greek, and studied French with their tutor, Nicholas Denisot. In 1550 after their Latin distichs commemorating the death of Margaret of Navarre had been published, Ascham praised their fine ability, comparing their skills favorably to Jane Grey and to Elizabeth, and even the celebrated French author, Pierre de Ronsard, complimented their abilities in a poem. They were the first women to have an original Latin work appear in print in the sixteenth century.[24]

In 1559 among several women that he praised for their humanist education, William Barker, the author of *The Nobility of Women,* singled out Jane as the most learned Seymour daughter. Like Jane Grey, her Uncle Seymour's proposed bride for the King, Jane Seymour also gained an unusual amount of attention from prominent Protestant divines, among them Martin Bucer and Paul Fagius, with whom she had corresponded by 1550 when she was only nine years old. In his book, *The Governance of Virtue,* that he dedicated to Jane, Thomas Becon, Archbishop Cranmer's chaplain, complimented her parents for instructing her in "good literature," an approval that may offer a clue to her education. In some of his earlier writings on the instruction of children, Becon had admonished parents to forbid their daughters to read books about Robin Hood and had recommended that schoolmasters teach the verses of David rather than the literature of Virgil, Ovid, and Horace. Since Becon praised their reading material, it is extremely unlikely that Jane and her sisters read many pagan classics, especially as their mother, who was a renowned patroness of Protestant authors, surely approved the works that were assigned to them for translation.[25]

Besides Somerset and Suffolk, two other noblemen had female dependents who were indisputably classical scholars. Although their families came to represent the best of Catholic recusancy in Elizabethan England, it is difficult to categorize them by religion for their immediate concern was not the purity of their faith but the survival and social enhancement of their lineage through intermarriage with the royal family. The result was just the opposite of their goals: the Arundel and Norfolk families allied together socially and politically to find disgrace, imprisonment, political exile, and death in Tudor England.

While contemporaries made frequent references to their attempts to obtain royal alliances for their sons and grandsons, the evidence that Norfolk and Arundel schemed for similar unions for their female dependents is based mainly on supposition. Given the political ambitions of the two noblemen, it is likely that these girls were educated as humanists to help further their family's position at court through advantageous marriages. In the case of Norfolk, in particular, it is reasonable to conclude that he considered the feasibility of obtaining royal alliances for his granddaughters since two of his nieces had been consorts of Henry VIII and his daughter had wed that monarch's natural child, the Duke of Richmond.

It was the three girls and two boys of Norfolk's heir, Surrey, by his wife, Frances de Vere, daughter of the fifteenth Earl of Oxford, who were given Greek and Latin instruction. In 1544 after the Duke had sought Roger Ascham's assistance in procuring a tutor for his grandchildren, he appointed Hadrianus Junius, an eminent Dutch scholar, to that post. Apparently, Jane, the eldest grandchild, who was born in 1537, benefited most from the two years of this tutor's instruction, as the next oldest child, Thomas, the future fourth Duke remained an indifferent scholar. Upon Surrey's return from France in 1546, his children wrote a still-extant letter to him in Latin that nine-year-old Jane probably composed [26]

Surely there was a direct connection between the political ambitions of Norfolk and his decision to extend classical training to his granddaughters, for at least since the birth of Prince Edward in 1537, the Duke had been competing with the Seymours, the boy's maternal relatives, for power at court. After Surrey's elder son, Thomas, was born in 1538, for example, Norfolk promoted the appointment of his new grandson to the household of the infant Prince. It is likely that he also considered the possibility of betrothing his well-educated granddaughter, who was a namesake of Queen Jane Seymour, to the young Edward. [27]

After Surrey's execution and Norfolk's imprisonment in the Tower of London, the children were placed in the custody of their father's sister, Lady Richmond, a cultured woman and a dedicated Protestant. For the next few years they lived in her London townhouse and at Reigate Castle in Norfolk with their tutor, John Foxe, who was so impressed by Jane's skill in Greek and Latin that he compared her scholarship favorably to the most learned men of her day. Later, the author, William Barker, wrote of Jane, who had married Charles Neville, sixth Earl of Westmoreland, that "few men maye compare with her."[28]

With their grandfather Norfolk's release from prison in 1553, the children were returned to his care and given Catholic instruction while Foxe, who had previously taught them Protestant doctrine, became a Marian exile. This mixed Christian training prevented some of the Howard offspring from developing deep religious ties, for dynastic ambitions remained a strong concern of at least two of them, Thomas, fourth Duke of Norfolk from 1554, and his youngest sister, Margaret, the wife of Henry, Lord Scrope of Bolton. When Mary, Queen of Scots, fled into England in 1568, she was placed in the custody of Lord Scrope, Governor of Carlisle and Warden of the West Marches. It may well have been Lady Scrope who passed on to her husband's royal prisoner, her brother Norfolk's message, offering to become Mary's husband and to support her as Elizabeth's heir to the English throne. After Mary's removal to Tutbury in 1569, the Northern Rising, which was led by the Earl of Westmoreland, husband to Norfolk's sister, Jane, broke out in support of the Duke's royal marriage but was crushed with the assistance of Lord Scrope, despite his own marital ties to the Howard family. [29]

One well-educated sister of the fourth Duke of Norfolk, Katherine, was not involved in the dynastic intrigues of the family although she was ultimately affected by them. The wife of Henry, eleventh Lord Berkeley, Katherine, like her husband, was an avid deer hunter. By the early 1570s, the English Queen and her close associates viewed the Berkeleys with hostility partly because of Norfolk's plotting with the Scots Queen, but also because of Lady Berkeley's refusal to agree to the betrothal of her two daughters to two sons of Sir Henry Sidney, a brother-in-law of Elizabeth's favorite, Robert Dudley, Earl of Leicester. In retaliation the Queen not only visited Berkeley Castle in its owners' absence and slaughtered twenty-seven stags in one day, but she also encouraged lawsuits by relatives of Leicester against the Berkeleys, a process that tied up their lands and what was left of their fortune in litigation for years. When at one point, Lady Berkeley attempted to pacify the Queen, she is said to have exclaimed: "Noe, noe, my lady Berkeley, wee know you will never love us for the death of your brother."[30]

Fortunately, when John Smyth, a member of her household, chose to write a history of the Berkeley family, he made several personal comments about his mistress. Describing Lady Berkeley as a haughty woman, who was overly proud of her lineage, Smyth also repeatedly referred to her eloquent speech and to her great learning. She was, he said, "skillful in French" and "perfect in Italian," but he also revealed that in her old age she had purchased a copy of Cicero to brush up on her Latin grammar. Smyth's wonderful revelations of the solace her classical studies gave Lady Berkeley only serve to highlight the glaring lack of information about the education of other prominent Tudor women.[31]

It was only by chance that Lady Berkeley's brother, Norfolk, was unmarried in 1569 and thus free to join the conspiracy with the Scottish Queen, for he had by then survived three wives, the last one dying in 1567. His first spouse had been Mary Fitzalan, the younger daughter of the Earl of Arundel, one of the most eminent peers in the kingdom. While his interest in scholarship was genuine, Arundel may have educated his two girls as classicists because he wished to stay abreast of or even go beyond the fashion in education established at court. After the death of Thomas Cranmer in 1556, for example, the Earl combined the Archbishop's books with his own collection of English and classical works to create a library that became the "showplace" of England.[32]

While there is no direct evidence that his goal in educating his daughters was to make them attractive as consorts for the young King, there is ample information about his schemes to obtain other royal alliances for his family. In the reign of Mary, the Spanish had believed that he was planning to have his heir and only son, Henry, Lord Maltravers, marry Princess Elizabeth, and even Edward Courtney, Earl of Devon, had confessed that his own willingness to marry the Queen's sister as part of the Wyatt conspiracy of 1554 had been based on the information that if he did not, Maltravers would. Later, after the death of his heir, the twice-widowed Arundel, himself, began to court Elizabeth.[33]

Born about 1541 the Earl's daughter, Mary, the first wife of Norfolk, died in

1557, after giving birth to both her father's and her husband's male heir, a son named Philip, later the Earl of Arundel but never the Duke of Norfolk as he was not permitted by the crown to inherit his father's title. Little is known of Mary's short life except that she was a classicist, for there are extant four Latin manuscripts with pieces from Greek and Latin authors, two of which she completed before her marriage and two afterwards. It has sometimes been claimed that the two manuscripts which are signed "per Mariam Arundell" were done by her stepmother, Mary, daughter of Sir John Arundel and widow of Robert Ratcliffe, Earl of Sussex, who married the Earl of Arundel in 1545, but as they are written in the same exquisite Italian hand as the two which were signed by Mary as the wife of Norfolk, they are doubtless of her composition. By the Tudor period the Fitzalan children were using their family's title as their surname.[34]

At the age of about twelve Mary's elder sister, Jane, married Lord Lumley, a classmate of her brother, Maltravers, at Queen's College, Cambridge. Generally recognized as the more brilliant of the two girls, Jane has been identified as the first person to render into English a work of one of the Greek dramatists: *Iphigenia at Aulis* by Euripides. Denying that her Greek skills were very advanced, some modern scholars have suggested that the piece was a mere translation of Erasmus' Latin version that had earlier appeared in a volume with the original play. There is no doubt that her work was a classroom exercise, but to denounce it because of its reliance on Latin aids without also pointing out that many Tudor translations depended on such assistance is demeaning to the originality of the piece. Despite the real limitations of her work, she deserves credit for a pioneering effort that one modern scholar has suggested was "extraordinary and rare for one of her years and her period." As all of her extant manuscripts, like those of her sister, are translations of ancient works, it can be conjectured that her father, who acquired books only in his native English and in classical languages for his library, chose not to have his two daughters tutored in French or Italian. After Lady Lumley's death without issue in 1578, her husband not only had engraved on her sepulchre that she was an obedient daughter and a loving wife but also that she was without equal in her knowledge of Greek and Latin.[35]

When Arundel died in 1580, almost two years after Lady Lumley, he left more than 1,000 volumes, including some manuscripts and books of his daughters, to her widower, who combined them with his own collection to create the largest private library in England. At Lumley's death in 1609, the royal family gained possession of the library that was ultimately transferred to the British Museum.[36] While it is fortunate that through the Arundel-Lumley collection the manuscripts of these women have been preserved, the rarity of their survival highlights the problem in finding evidence of Tudor women who were trained as humanists. Often the disgrace, the exile, or the execution of the parents of classical scholars, as for example, the Howards, the Seymours, and the Greys, has led to the destruction of most of their work.

Besides the secular nobility and the members of the More circle, there were very few, perhaps only three other households in which girls were educated as classicists. In all three cases the most important factor in the educational decisions affecting these women may have been the deep Protestant commitment of their parents. One of these families was headed by John Hooper, a Bishop of the Church of England. Politically, the bishops were lords, who normally had the right to serve in the upper house of Parliament, a position that they were unable to enforce socially since the continuing animosity toward priestly marriage prevented them from finding wives among the nobility. In the last years of the reign of Henry VIII, while John Hooper was residing as a religious refugee in the Low Countries, he had, despite his priestly status, married Anne de Taerclas, an esteemed Latin scholar. With Edward's succession and the legalization of clerical marriage, the Hoopers returned to England where he served as chaplain to the Duke of Somerset until he was invested as Bishop of Gloucester after a short imprisonment had first convinced him of the wisdom of donning the mandatory episcopal vestments that he scorned as Popish garments.[37]

Their daughter, Rachel, who was born before 1548, was taught English, German, French, and Latin, and of these languages, her father was particularly proud of her progress in Latin. Because of his execution as a Marian heretic and his wife's forced flight to the continent when Rachel was still quite young, there is little extant information about her. It is possible that she was provided this advanced education because her mother wanted her daughter to have linguistic training similar to her own, but since the Hoopers, as Protestants, also believed that marriage was the proper female vocation, it was probably their hope to teach Rachel to be a respectful and obedient Christian wife through the reading of religious texts.

Hooper was the only Edwardian bishop to have a female child instructed in Latin, a uniqueness that was based in part on his decision to marry prior to the legalization of clerical unions in England. Rachel Hooper was the sole legitimate daughter of a clergyman who was old enough to be considered for inclusion among the second generation of women humanists. Even in the next generation no other bishop's daughter had classical training, the result, no doubt, of the decision of Tudor bishops to de-emphasize the use of Latin in their households as part of their Protestant commitment to creating a favorable reception in the kingdom for official vernacular versions of the scriptures and Church services. In the second and third generations, as in the first, the implementation of humanist education for English women remained largely a lay movement.[38]

Outside the More circle, Anthony Cooke was the only member of the gentry class known to have provided his female issue with instruction in the ancient languages of Latin, Greek, and Hebrew, as well as in Italian and probably French. While it is possible that the remarkable intelligence of his five girls was the most important factor in his decision to offer them this advanced linguistic training, the religious zeal that later led him to become a Marian exile must also be considered. The elder two daughters, Mildred, born in 1526, and Anne, born in 1528, began their education when most of the major Christian works were accessible in languages other than English. While their father was surely determined to challenge their intellect, he must also have decided that the best way for them to learn religious doctrine was through a study of ancient Christian writings. Although he may also have assigned them some profane philosophy to read, Sir Anthony, like Katherine Parr, seems to have feared that a familiarity with pagan ethics, especially those of ancient Greece, would lead to a corruption of Christian values. In his introduction to a St. Cyprian translation that can be dated about 1541, this fear is evident in his denial that princes would benefit from a knowledge of Platonic philosophy.[39]

Although none of Mildred's manuscripts was published, her contemporaries were well aware of her expertise in translating Greek authors such as the Church Fathers, Basil, Cyril, and Chrysostom. Even her tutor, Giles Lawrence, an eminent Greek Professor of Christ's Church, Oxford, remarked that Mildred "Egalled if not overmatched" all other Greek experts. As an adult she may also have read Greek with Charles Utenhove, an esteemed Flemish poet. When in 1550 she presented a Greek translation to the Duchess of Somerset, Ascham compared her skills favorably to those of Jane Grey, a compliment that he spoiled somewhat by claiming that it was difficult for him to decide whether Mildred was to be most envied for her learning, for her noble father, or for her prudent husband. In 1545 when she became the wife of William Cecil, the widower of Mary Cheke whose brother was the tutor of Prince Edward, Mildred entered into a marriage that approached the ideal predicted by the Christian humanists. A scholar who continued to read classical authors and the Latin Bible throughout his life, William's devotion to his wife and to his offspring has often been noted by his biographers.[40]

The most published scholar among the sisters was Anne, whose vernacular and Latin translations were printed in her lifetime. In 1550 her English version of the Italian sermons of the ex-friar Bernardino Ochino, then a religious refugee at Canterbury, were published and in 1570 an enlarged version of the sermons appeared. Anne wrote in the preface of her translation that she had learned the language over the "Godly exhortacyons" of her mother, Anne Fitzwilliams, who had probably feared that her daughter would read Petrarchan love sonnets rather than religious works. She also noted, "If oughte be erred in this translation, remember it is a womans, yea a Gentylwomans, who comenly are wonted to lyve Idilly, a maidens ye never gaddid farder than her fathers house to learn the language." Despite this disclaimer, her work was truly remarkable. In 1550, the year it first appeared in print, John Coke, a minor official of Edward's government, boasted that England had divers learned gentlewomen, but he listed only three: Margaret Roper, Margaret Gigs, and Anne Cooke.[41]

After her marriage to Nicholas Bacon, Anne translated into English from the Latin, John Jewel, Bishop of Salisbury's work, *Apologia pro Ecclesiae Anglicanae,* a treatise written to defend English Protestantism on historical grounds. In 1564 her version was printed at the behest of Matthew Parker, Archbishop of Canterbury, who explained in its introduction that he had acted without her knowledge "to prevent such excuses as her modesty would have made in stay of publishing it." Her excellent translation of Jewel's work that the Society for Promoting Christian Knowledge still circulates, has prompted C. S. Lewis to remark, "If quality without bulk were enough, Lady Bacon might be put forward as the best of all sixteenth-century translators." This was extraordinary praise for a woman living in a century replete with far-more celebrated scholars.[42]

One of the most interesting Cooke women because of her long life and her high social ambitions was the third daughter, Elizabeth. After the death of her first husband, Sir Thomas Hoby, in 1566, she married Lord John Russell, who to her great disappointment predeceased his father, the second Earl of Bedford in 1584, thereby depriving her of the title of countess. Some evidence of her classical scholarship survives in Latin and Greek verses engraved on the tombstones of her husbands and other family members and in notes penned to her nephew, Sir Robert Cecil. Besides Anne, she was the only Cooke sister to see her own work in print, for in 1605, when she was well over seventy, her translation of a Latin book of John Poynet was printed under the title, *A Way of Reconciliation of a Good and Learned Man*.[43]

Partly because their husbands were far less important in Elizabethan England than the spouses of their three elder sisters, very little evidence has survived about the scholarship of the other two Cooke women. The most important record of the linguistic skill of Catherine, who married Henry Killigrew, is a Latin poem she composed to ask for Cecil's assistance for her husband. In the appeal, which was published posthumously in 1591, she requested Mildred's intercession with her husband, William, the Queen's secretary, to obtain the reversal of the government's decision to send Killigrew on an undesirable diplomatic mission. There is almost no extant information about the other daughter, Margaret, who died in 1558 shortly after her wedding to Sir Ralph Rowlett.[44]

Among the bourgeoisie, only one woman, Catherine Thysmans alias Tishem, is known to have been a classical scholar. A Flemish woman who may have had English ancestors, she married Wouter de Gruytere of Antwerp in 1558 and because of Spanish persecution fled with him to Norwich in 1565. While she has been praised for her knowledge of English, French, Italian, Latin, and Greek, there is no extant evidence of the quality of her training, although she did read Galen and helped prepare her son, Janus Gruter, for an esteemed academic career.[45]

While Queen Mary's linguistic skills have been examined by modern scholars, few have noted that she had at least as many, if not more, learned women at her court as did her sister, Elizabeth. Of the Edwardian scholars, at least two of the Cookes, Anne and Margaret, two of the Seymours, Jane and Margaret, and one of the Greys, Katherine, attended her regularly. In addition to having her sister, Elizabeth, occasionally present, Queen Mary welcomed visits by Arundel's daughters, the Duchess of Norfolk and Lady Lumley. Her accession also made it possible for Mary Basset, a member of the politically disgraced More circle, to associate with the court.

Before her death in 1544 Margaret Roper had provided a humanist education for her three daughters, of whom only one, Mary, tutored by Dr. John Morwen, became a celebrated Greek and Latin scholar. With the demise of her first husband, Stephen Clarke, Mary Roper wed James Basset, a son of Sir John Basset and Honora Grenville, Viscountess Lisle. Throughout her adulthood Mary translated ancient works, as her grandfather had advocated. During the reign of Edward VI, she bound together in one volume her translations from Greek into Latin of the first book and into English of the first five books of Eusebius' *Ecclesiastical History* for presentation to the King's sister, Mary. After the succession of the Princess, William Rastell printed Sir Thomas More's *English Works* that included Lady Basset's version of the second part of her grandfather's *History of the Passion,* originally written in Latin. Rastell noted that the excellence of her translation had caused many learned people to protest that it had deserved publication in a separate volume. She was the only woman to have her work appear in print during this reign.[46]

Besides Margaret Roper, the other outstanding woman of More's circle had been Margaret Gigs, the wife of John Clement and the mother of five daughters to whom she taught Latin and Greek. Apparently, at least three of the young women did not return from exile with their parents at the succession of Queen Mary: one, Winifred, who was the wife of William Rastell, the printer of More's *English Works,* died at Louvain in 1553 and another two, Margaret and Dorothy, joined nunneries there, the former professed at St. Ursula's by 1557 and the latter at St. Clare's by 1555. Two daughters did return to England: Bridget, the wife of Robert Redman and the godchild of Mary Clarke Basset, and Helen, the wife of Thomas Pridieux of Devonshire.[47]

With some refinements, the few parents who had their daughters taught to read ancient literature did so for the reasons that the Christian humanists had advanced: to train them as suitable companions for their husbands and as Godly mothers for their children. The four noble families of Grey, Seymour, Howard, and Fitzalan surely gave their girls the classical training that was then fashionable at court with the hope of making them attractive as potential consorts to Prince Edward after whose mother the most learned of their daughters had been named. Marriage into the royal family was not an unreasonable goal since Henry VIII had wed four Englishwomen, among them a Seymour and a Howard, and since his natural son, Richmond, had married a Howard. The purpose of the instruction of the girls of the More circle was to teach them to perform their marital roles in a pious and virtuous manner within their own social milieu although as Catholics the prospect of becoming a nun remained for them a viable alternative. While it is true that Bishop Hooper, a Protestant, and Sir Anthony Cooke, an Erasmian in faith until his conversion to Protestantism sometime in the 1540's, were eager for their daughters to learn the reformed brand of Christianity, an important part of their girls' early training had to focus on their future roles as wives and mothers since the alternative of joining a religious order was not available to them.

It is interesting to note that it was largely the male relatives of the second generation of women humanists who hired their instructors and who made most of the decisions affecting the content of their academic training. While both Margaret Roper and Margaret Clement of the More circle directed their daughters' education, there is no reason to believe that the other mothers performed a similar supervisory role. Indeed, the slim evidence of their involvement is a somewhat negative one, for, as has been noted, Lady Cooke protested her daughters' instruction in Italian and even Katherine Parr, upon gaining custody of the orphaned Elizabeth, only acquiesced, after her first objections, in Ascham's appointment as her stepchild's tutor. The Duchess of Richmond was the sole woman, outside the More circle, with an unquestionably positive role in providing a humanist education for some of her young relatives. When she obtained the wardship of her Howard nieces after the death of their father and the imprisonment of their grandfather, she chose to continue their classical instruction under the direction of John Foxe. It is possible to speculate that because Lady Hooper was a Latin scholar and Lady Somerset was a patroness of Protestant authors that they, too, had some influence on the academic training of their daughters. Clearly, Henry VIII until his death, the Duke of Norfolk until his imprisonment, the Duke of Suffolk until his death, the Earl of Arundel, and Sir Anthony Cooke were primarily responsible for the education of their female dependents.

Although the paucity of evidence makes it extraordinarily difficult to generalize about the academic content of the instruction of the second generation of women humanists, it is still possible to organize them into three rough groupings: Christian humanism, Protestant humanism, and a combination of Christian and court humanism with Protestant overtones. While it can be concluded that the Roper and Clement daughters had the education promoted by Sir Thomas More and other Christian humanists, little specific information exists about their training except that they were tutored in Greek and Latin. Of the learned women of this generation who did not belong to the martyr's intimate group, only Arundel's daughters approached More's ideal in education. Although there is abundant evidence that Jane and Mary Fitzalan read a wide variety of both Latin and Greek pagan authors, as More and Erasmus had advocated, there is no record that they had had any vernacular instruction other than in their native tongue.

While the Fitzalan women remained within the conservative Catholic tradition, the other women scholars outside the More circle were trained by reformed tutors. Largely because of the pervasive role of Protestantism on the education of the families in the second academic category: the Greys, Seymours, Hoopers, Cookes, and Thysmans alias Tishem, only Jane and Katherine Grey, who were successors to the throne, read a wide variety of Greek pagan literature. It is an interesting contrast that Jane Grey studied Plato because her parents were educating her as a queen regnant as well as a queen consort while the Cooke sisters did not read that author because their father denied that even princes needed to understand Platonic philosophy. Not very much detail has survived about the instruction of the Seymour girls, but because of Becon's approval of their training, it can be reasonably concluded that their parents, like Sir Anthony Cooke, did not have them read many profane works.

The Howards and the Princess Elizabeth were as deeply affected by the Italian Renaissance and by Christian humanism as by the Protestant Reformation. Unfortunately, little information has survived about the instruction of the Howard women but as Surrey the poet was their father and as John Foxe the future martyrologist became their tutor, their education was a blend of pagan and Christian ethics through a study of vernacular and classical languages. Reared in a tradition similar to that of her Howard cousins, although her continued study of Greek indicates she was more greatly influenced by Christian humanism than they, the Princess Elizabeth was strongly attracted to secular literature. Consequently, as an adult when she could choose her academic exercises she favored the translation of pagan authors to those of the Church Fathers and, like Lady Berkeley, preferred Italian to all other vernacular languages. Of the second generation of women humanists outside the More circle, she, alone, remained single by choice, personifying in her public life as Queen the divine virgins of pagan mythology and the unobtainable love of Petrarchan sonnetry.

By adopting the educational program of More and Erasmus for his children, Henry VIII had made classical training fashionable among the nobility who were ambitious for royal alliances. The significance of the Tudor example in promoting this limited acceptance of classical instruction can best be tested by looking ahead to its rejection in the reign of Elizabeth. As she had no children of her own to be educated, the nobility lost the incentive to instruct their female offspring in ancient languages. The only aristocrats who could aspire to marry into the royal family were gentlemen who came to recognize, however reluctantly, that their Queen would never wed. Because the personal qualities of Elizabeth began to be looked upon as exceptional, if not eccentric—her marital status, her education, her regnancy, even her longevity—fewer noble parents would choose to educate their daughters as classicists.

NOTES

1. Mary A. E. Green, *Letters of Royal and Illustrious Ladies of Great Britain*, 3 vols. (London, 1846), II, 76, 137, 295, and 311 and III, 153; for a new edition of these letters, see Muriel St. Clare Byrne, *The Lisle Letters*, 6 vols. (Chicago, 1981); for a list of the maidens in 1540, see *Letters and Papers of Henry VIII*, XIV-i, No. 572; Jane Dormer, daughter of William Dormer and Mary Sidney, was a frequent playmate of Prince Edward. Although she was well educated, she was not a classicist. See Henry Clifford, *The Life of Jane Dormer, duchess of Feria*, trans. Canon E. E. Estcourt, ed. Joseph Stevenson (London, 1887), p. 59.

2. Sir Thomas Elyot, *Defence of Good Women* (London, 1545); see also Lyn Yates, "The Uses of Women to a Sixteenth Century Bestseller," *Historical Studies*, XVIII (1979), 422-434.

3. Pearl Hogrefe, *Sir Thomas More's Circle* (Urbana, Ill., 1959), p. 204.

4. Nicholas Udall, *The first tome or volume of the Paraphrase of Erasmus upon the newe teste* (London, 1549), preface to St. Luke.

5. Her first husband was Edward, Lord Borough; *Letters and Papers*, XVIII-i, No.

894; for evidence of her assistance to conservative Catholics, see *Correspondence of Matthew Parker,* Parker Society, (London, 1853), p. 19 and "Sir Nicholas Throckmorton," *Dictionary of National Biography*; James K. McConica, *English Humanists and Reformation Politics* (Oxford, 1967), p. 251; Thomas à Kempis, *The Imitation of Christ,* trans. Ronald Knox and Michael Oakley (New York, 1960); William P. Haugaard, "Katherine Parr: The Religious Convictions of a Renaissance Queen," *Renaissance Quarterly,* XXII (1969), 331.

6. John Allen Giles, *The Whole Works of Roger Ascham,* 3 vols. (London, 1865), I-i, 89 and 111-112; Roger Ascham, *The Schoolmaster,* ed. Lawrence Ryan (Ithaca, N.Y., 1967), p. xxxv; see Pearl Hogrefe, *Women of Action in Tudor England* (Ames, Ia., 1977), p. 183.

7. Pearl Hogrefe, *Women of Action,* p. 183; Anthony Martienssen, *Queen Katherine Parr* (New York, 1973), pp. 21-28; C. Fenno Hoffman, "Catherine Parr as a Woman of Letters," *Huntington Library Quarterly,* XXIII (1960), 349-367; John Strype, *Ecclesiastical Memorials,* 3 vols. (Oxford, 1822), II-ii, 337.

8. John Strype, *The Life of the learned Sir John Cheke, Kt.* (Oxford, 1821), pp. 21-26; John Strype, *Memorials,* III-i, 514; James K. McConica, p. 215; Samuel Clarke, a Puritan minister born in 1599, wrote that John Cheke was appointed by Henry VIII. See *A Martyrologie containing a Collection of all the Persecutions . . . to the end of Queen Maries Reign* (London, 1652), p. 180; Erasmus, *Education of a Christian Prince,* trans. Lester K. Born (New York, 1963), p. 28; and John Palsgrave, *The Comedy of Acolastus,* ed. P. L. Carver, Early English Text Society, old series, vol. 202 (London, 1937), pp. xlii-lx.

9. Lawrence V. Ryan, *Roger Ascham* (Stanford, Calif., 1963), pp. 102-103.

10. This psalm was taken from the Vulgate where it is numbered thirteen; see also David Scott Kastan, "An Early English Metrical Psalm: Elizabeth's or John Bale's?" *Notes & Queries,* N.S. 21 (1974), 404-405; Cyril James Davenport, *English Embroidered Books* (London, 1899), pp. 32-55; *Letters and Papers,* IV-i, No. 370; Leicester Bradner, *The Poems of Queen Elizabeth I* (Providence, R.I., 1964), p. 79 and Ruth Hughey, "Cultural Interests of Women in England from 1524 to 1640 Indicated in the Writings of Women," Ph.D. dissertation, Cornell University, 1932, p. 22; later, Elizabeth did translate Boethius, who was probably a Christian.

11. Nicholas Udall, preface to St. Luke; Henry Gee and W. J. Hardy, *Documents Illustrative of Early Church History* (Reprint, 1966), p. 421.

12. Roger Ascham, *The Schoolmaster,* p. 5.

13. Ibid., pp. 146-147; Patricia Thomson, "Wyatt and Surrey," *English Poetry and Prose, 1540-1674,* ed. Christopher Ricks (London, 1970), p. 35.

14. Roger Ascham, *The Schoolmaster,* p. xvii.

15. Ibid.

16. *Calendar of State Papers Venetian,* VI-ii, 457 and 1058 and IX, 529 and 533; John Allen Giles, I, lxiii; *Calendar of State Papers Spanish, Elizabeth,* I, 303, II, 491 and 579, and III, 25.

17. Mary A. E. Green, III, 176; G. B. Harrison, trans. *De Maisse* (London, 1931), p. 109; *The Memoirs of Sir James Melville,* ed. A. Frances Steuart (London, 1929), p. 97; Elizabeth, *The godly Medytacyon of the christen Sowle,* ed. John Bale (Wesel, 1548), preface.

18. *Calendar of State Papers Venetian,* VI-ii, 1057; Leicester Bradner, p. xv; George P. Rice, *The Public Speaking of Queen Elizabeth* (New York, 1951), p. 103; T. W.

Baldwin, *William Shakspere's Small Latine and Lesse Greeke,* 2 vols. (Urbana, Ill., 1944), I, 284; Elkin Calhoun Wilson, *England's Eliza* (Reprint, 1966), p. 444.

19. Anthony Martienssen, pp. 224-227.

20. *Calendar of State Papers Domestic,* I, 13; I am doing research on the myths about Katherine.

21. Richard Davey, *The Nine Days' Queen* (London, 1909), pp. 14 and 172; John Foxe, *The Acts and Monuments of,* ed. George Townsend, 8 vols. (Reprint, 1965), VI, 384 and 415-425; Hastings Robinson, ed., *Original Letters Relative to the English Reformation,* Parker Society, 2 vols. (London, 1842-1845), I, 4-11.

22. Richard Davey, *The Sisters of Jane Grey* (New York, 1912), p. 291; John Allen Giles, I, lxx.

23. Samuel Haynes, *A Collection of State Papers Relating to Affairs in the Reigns of King Henry VIII, King Edward VI, Queen Mary, and Queen Elizabeth . . . left by William Cecil, Lord Burghley,* 2 vols. (London, 1740-1759), I, 69 and 80-81; *Calendar of State Papers Spanish,* IX, 19-20; Richard Harold St. Maur, *Annals of the Seymours* (London, 1902), p. 395; John Smyth, *The Berkeley Manuscripts,* ed. Sir John Maclean, 2 vols. (Gloucester, 1833), II, 430; Leonard Howard, *A Collection of Letters and State Papers . . .* (London, 1765), p. 276; for a sympathetic statement about the Duchess, see J. G. Nichols, "Female Biographies of English History," *Gentleman's Magazine,* CLXXVII (May, 1845), 371-381.

24. Mary A. E. Green, III, 245; Georgiana Hill, *Women in English Life from Medieval to Modern Times,* 2 vols. (London, 1896), I, 135; for the poem by Ronsard see Amy Aubrey Locke, *The Seymour Family* (London, 1911), p. 75, note 1; John Allen Giles, I, lxx; Kathleen Lambley, *The Teaching and Cultivation of the French Language in England during Tudor and Stuart Times* (Manchester, 1920), pp. 83-84; Richard St. Maur, p. 394; Pearl Hogrefe, *Tudor Women: Commoners and Queens* (Ames, Ia., 1975), p. 106.

25. William Seymour, *Ordeal by Ambition* (London, 1972), pp. 277, 344, and 353; Mary A. E. Green, III, 199; William Barker, *The Nobility of Women,* ed. Richard Warwick Bond (London, 1904), p. 154; Hastings Robinson, I, 2; Thomas Becon, *The Early Works,* ed. John Ayre (Cambridge, 1840), pp. 396-399; John Strype, *Memorials,* II-ii, 8; Lily B. Campbell, *Divine Poetry and Drama in Sixteenth Century England* (Berkeley, Calif., 1959), pp. 32-33; J. E. Jackson, "Wulfhall and the Seymours," *Wiltshire Archaeological and Natural History Magazine,* XV (1875), 200.

26. Neville Williams, *Thomas Howard, Fourth Duke of Norfolk* (New York, 1964), pp. 3-12; James McConica, p. 211; for Junius, see Jan Van Dorsten, *The Radical Arts,* 2nd ed. (Leiden, 1973), pp. 131-134.

27. F. R. Grace, "The Life and Career of Thomas Howard, Third Duke of Norfolk," M.A. thesis, Nottingham, 1961, p. 212; Sir John MacLean, *The Life of Sir Thomas Seymour, Knight* (London, 1869), pp.3-5.

28. Neville Williams, pp. 12 and 24; John Foxe, I, 24; William Barker, p. 154; apparently Foxe tutored only three children: Jane, Thomas, and Henry. See James Mozley, *John Foxe and his Book* (Reprint, 1970), pp. 28-37.

29. Antonia Fraser, *Mary, Queen of Scots* (New York, 1969), p. 417; for the Rising, see Chapter 10.

30. John Smyth, II, 290, 336, and 369.

31. Ibid., II, 382-384; another contemporary described her brother, Henry Howard, Earl of Northampton, as proud because his ancestors had married with royalty. See Godfrey

Goodman, *The Court of King James the First,* ed. John B. Brewer (London, 1839), p. 50; it was Northampton who wrote a treatise on philosophy for her. See G. F. Nott, *The Works of Henry Howard, Earl of Surrey and of Thomas Wyatt the Elder,* 2 vols. (London, 1815-1816), I, 429-430.

32. The fourth Duke married secondly Margaret, widow of Henry Dudley and daughter of Thomas, Lord Audley, and thirdly, Elizabeth Leybourne, widow of Thomas, Lord Dacre; *The Lumley Library: The Catalogue of 1609,* ed. Sears Jayne and Francis R. Johnson (London, 1956), pp. 1-11.

33. Patrick Tytler, *England Under the Reigns of Edward VI and Mary,* 2 vols. (London, 1839), II, 405; Lord Maltravers married Anne Wentworth in 1555; *Calendar of State Papers Spanish,* XII, 267 and 231 and XIII, 438.

34. John Nichols, *Literary Remains of King Edward the Sixth,* 2 vols. (London, 1857), I, lxiv; Mark A. Tierney, *History and Antiquities of the Castle and Town of Arundel,* 2 vols. (London, 1834), I, 347-348; Mary A. E. Green, II, 346; J. G. Nichols, "Life of the Last Fitz-Alan, Earl of Arundel," *Gentleman's Magazine,* CIII (1833), 499-500; Edith Milner, *Records of the Lumleys* (London, 1904), p. 88; see also Chapter 9.

35. Edith Milner, p. 89; J. G. Nichols, "Life of the Last Fitz-Alan," p. 491; Lady Jane Lumley, *The Iphigenia at Aulis of Euripides,* ed. Harold H. Child, (London, 1909), pp. v-vii; Frank D. Crane, "Euripides, Erasmus, and Lady Lumley," *Classical Journal,* XXXIX (1944), 223-228; Henry B. Lathrop, *Translations from the Classics into English from Caxton to Chapman, 1477-1620* (Reprint, 1967), p. 31; David H. Green, "Lady Lumley and Greek Tragedy," *Classical Journal,* XXXVI (1941), 547; for a comment about Elizabethan translations, see G. K. Hunter, *John Lyly: The Humanist as Courtier* (Cambridge, Mass., 1962), p. 39; for material about her funeral, see Add. Ms. 35,324, f. 118, British Library.

36. Lady Jane Lumley, pp. i-vii; *The Lumley Library,* pp. 1-11.

37. Hastings Robinson, I, 74 and 114; Ruth Hughey, "Cultural," pp. 142-198; John Strype, *Memorials,* II-ii, 4.

38. See contemporary views on the study of Latin in Bishop John Woolton, *A Treatise of the immortalitie of the soule* (London, 1576), dedicatory letter and Richard Mulcaster, *Positions* (New York, 1971), pp. 30, 238, and 259; see also Richard Greaves, *Society and Religion in Elizabethan England* (Minneapolis, 1981), p. 331.

39. Marjorie Keniston McIntosh, "Sir Anthony Cooke: Tudor Humanist, Educator, and Religious Reformer," *Proceedings of the American Philosophical Society,* CLXX (1975), 235-250; Sir Geoffrey Fenton, *Monophylo, A philosophicall discourse of love* (London, 1572), letter of dedication.

40. For some dedications to Mildred, see Thomas Wilcox, *A short yet sound commentarie: written on that Woorthie worke called: The proverbes of Solomon* (London, 1589) and Thomas Marsh, trans., *A medicinable morall that is the two bookes of Horace his Satyres* (London, 1566), letter of dedication; Thomas Dannett, ed., *The Historie of France* (London, 1595), letter of dedication; and John Sharrock, trans., *Elizabeth Queene* (London, 1585), letter of dedication. See also, John Allen Giles, I, lxx; for information about Charles Utenhove and Cecil's patronage, see Jan Van Dorsten, *The Radical Arts* pp. 16, note 2 and 126; and "Literary Patronage in Elizabethan England," *Patronage in the Renaissance,* ed. Guy F. Lytle and Stephen Orgel (Princeton, 1982), pp. 191-206; Bernard Beckingsale, *Burghley, Tudor Statesman, 1520-1598* (New York, 1967), pp. 16 and 249-250; James McConica, p. 259; Conyers Read, *Mr. Secretary Cecil and Queen Elizabeth* (New York, 1955), pp. 105.

41. Ruth Hughey, "Lady Ann Bacon's Translations," *Review of English Studies*, X (1934), 211; M. A. Scott, introduction; E. E. Reynolds, *Margaret Roper* (London, 1960), p. 40.

42. Ruth Hughey, "Lady Ann," p. 211; M. A. Scott, p. 250; C. S. Lewis, *English Literature in the Sixteenth Century Excluding Drama* (Oxford, 1954), p. 307; Marjorie Keniston McIntosh, p. 240; Robert Tittler, *Nicholas Bacon* (Athens, Ohio, 1976), p. 51; *Calendar of State Papers Spanish*, I, 18.

43. Ruth Hughey, "Cultural," p. 112; Charlotte Kohler, "The Elizabethan Women of Letters," Ph.D. dissertation, University of Virginia, 1936, p. 154; Lady Russell's translation of Poynet's work was via the French edition brought out by Sir Anthony Cooke, on which Poynet's name did not appear. Apparently, she and the rest of the family thought Sir Anthony had written it. See Majorie Keniston McIntosh, p. 244, note 74.

44. Bernard Beckingsale, *Burghley*, p. 105; John Strype, *Memorials*, III-ii, 22; Sir John Harington, *Ludovico Ariostos' Orlando Furioso*, ed. Robert McNulty (Oxford, 1972), p. 434; In addition to the Cookes, one other gentlewoman may have been a classicist. Because Elizabeth Fane's *Twenty-one Psalms and 102 Proverbs*, printed in 1550, is no longer extant, it cannot be determined if it contained her translations. Her contemporaries remained silent about her language skills. John Foxe, VII, 234 and 246 and VIII, 584; John Strype, *Memorials*, III-i, 226 and 434 ff.; Ruth Hughey, "Cultural," p. 29; Robert Crowley, *Pleasure and payne, heaven and hell* (London, 1551), letter of dedication; John Gough Nichols, *Narratives of the Days of the Reformation*, Camden Society, vol. 77 (London, 1859), p. 346.

45. George Ballard, *Memoirs of British Ladies* (London, 1752), p.144; Leonard W. Forstor, *Janus Gruter's English Years* (Leiden, 1967), pp. 20-21.

46. Mary Basset, who died in 1572 with no daughters, had two sisters, Elizabeth, who died with no issue before 1557, and Margaret, who died after 1577 with no daughters; *Calendar of State Papers Venetian*, VI-i, 207; there is some question about whether it was Basset or her mother who translated Eusebius. See Pearl Hogrefe, *Tudor Women*, p. 106; Mary Basset, *St. Thomas More's History of the Passion*, ed. P. H. Hallett (London, 1941), pp. x-xiv.

47. A. W. Reed, *Early Tudor Drama* (Reprint, 1969), p. 87; Mary Basset, pp. x-xiv; Dr. John Clement said in his wife's epitaph that she had taught their children Latin and Greek. See Catherine Durrant, *A Link between Flemish Mystics and English Martyrs* (London, 1925), p. 420; William F. Peryn, *Spirituall exercyses and goostly meditacions* (London, 1557), letter of dedication to Dorothy; Sir Henry Ellis, "Account of the Convent of English Nuns formerly settled at Louvain in South Brabant," *Archaeologia*, XXXVI (1855), 74-77; Dom Adam Hamilton, *The Chronicle of the English Augustinian Canonesses Regular of the Lateran at St. Monica's in Louvain*, 2 vols. (London, 1904), I, 18-25; Elizabeth S. Bier, "Education of English Women Under the Stuarts," M.A. thesis, University of California at Berkeley, 1926, pp. 47-50.

7

The Mid-Elizabethan Generation

The cross-fertilization of humanist ideas and reformed beliefs resulted in an outpouring of literary excellence in the reign of Queen Elizabeth. Most of this literature was written by Protestants who adopted freely from the poetry and philosophy of the Henrician court and the Christian humanists. Their acceptance of the challenge of Sir Thomas More's *Utopia* to employ their classical training in the service of the commonwealth is evident in the many works that they wrote to instruct the governing class in public and private morality. With the pastoral literature of Virgil to inspire them, some Elizabethans followed the lead of Sir Philip Sidney in using poetry, in its broadest sense of fiction, rather than philosophy or history as the medium to express these views.[1]

It was not only the native and the classical cultures that influenced this literature but the near contemporary societies of Italy and France. Often expressing their ideas in the poetic form that was disdained by Plato, the Elizabethans ironically chose to employ themes that were sometimes blends of the Platonic images of God as infinite beauty, truth, and goodness with Christian concepts of the afterlife. An important precursor of their ideas was the Neoplatonism of the Florentine Marsilio Ficino, who believed that earthly love was a step on the ladder to "ecstatic reunion with the Godhead." The author of two tracts that were published in 1474, Ficino postulated that the lover's emotion in which a deep feeling for the loved one was reconciled with divine adoration and self-love needed reciprocity to reach the highest stage of spiritual perfection. Essential to his philosophy was the notion that ideal love originated in beauty, a quality that was less evident in men than in women. Because their beauty gave them a significant earthly role in the ultimate reunion with God, women were widely reputed to be instructors of men in the cult of love. The verses of Petrarch, whose work was a major inspiration for the Tudor love sonnet, had foreshadowed this mystical tone. His celebrated love for the beautiful Laura after it had been purified by the sorrow of her death became the ideal earthy love and was transformed into the love of God.[2] These Elizabethans not only admired the romantic literature of Italy, but they also respected the poetry of French authors such as Robert

Garnier, who wrote drama in the Senecan style, and Clément Marot, who translated King David's Psalms.

Although they adopted Neoplatonist concepts in their celebration of women's superiority in love, English poets did not change the climate at court or in the country that fostered the social and economic subservience of women. Ian Maclean has argued that marriage, an institution favored by both the Christian humanists and the reformers, remained the greatest hindrance to the application of Neoplatonist ideas to society. After marriage, men dominated public life while women were left at home to direct households. Even at court where the romantic literature was circulated first in manuscript, there were regular places only for those women who were personally selected to attend the Queen and none for the wives of her courtiers.[3]

The monarch honored by these poets was somewhat out of touch with the genius of their generation. Although her name has been given to this literary outburst, Elizabeth was not an intimate part of the motion that gave it its direction and prominence. She was an offstage presence inspiring but not creating the celebrated literature of her reign. A student of Ascham and a second-generation humanist, the Queen turned to ancient philosophy for moral guidance and seems to have discouraged the reading of her secular verses despite their praise and publication by authors such as Richard Puttenham. It was her classical translations that she admired enough to bestow as gifts, including, for example, one of Cicero and one of Seneca to John Harington.[4]

Although Elizabeth viewed native poetry in a less serious vein than did the humanists of the third generation, who composed their works for moral inspiration as well as for entertainment, her remoteness to their literary world can be overstated. While she did not customarily favor poets, she regularly financed aristocrats such as Robert, Earl of Leicester and Henry Carey, Lord Hunsdon, who supported a wide variety of artists and scholars. More importantly, no monarch better understood how to use contemporary literature to buttress her position in the kingdom. By appearing at official court functions or on progresses where the ideal union of love and beauty was depicted in poetry and drama, she became the embodiment of the spiritual perfection that the poets were celebrating. She was quite willing to be praised as the Gloriana of Spenser's *The Faerie Queene,* to be lauded as Astraea, the virgin of Virgil's *Fourth Eclogue,* or to be worshipped as Diana, the virgin goddess of the hunt. This "idealization of Elizabeth expressed the imaginative life of her age, which made of her a complete symbol for the good and beautiful in sovereignty and womanhood."[5]

Ironically, it is only to the 1580s when the Queen was about fifty years old that these tributes linking her to the classical cult of love and its eternal beauty can be traced. By the standards of her day, she was an old woman when these poetic ideals began to be associated with her, a circumstance that must have served to highlight the difference in age and outlook between her and her young courtiers. As early as 1575, Sir Philip Sidney referred to the forty-two-year-old Queen as "somewhat advanced in years." Protesting their passionate devotion to her only as part of the courtly and poetic conventions of the day, it is possible that neither he nor the other young courtiers felt any personal affection for her.[6]

Although the literary accomplishments of Philip Sidney and Edmund Spenser, two of the most famous Elizabethan poets, are well known, the efforts of Sidney's sister, Mary, Countess of Pembroke, the most important private poetess and patroness of Elizabethan literature, have until recently been largely ignored. In this Chapter her accomplishments will be highlighted by comparing and contrasting them to the efforts of her more renowned brother in whose memory she wrote and published. Because the underlying theme of this book is to trace the degree to which English society adopted the classical training advocated for women by Sir Thomas More, the quality of her education will also be examined. To further place her talents in perspective, it will be necessary to review the classical scholarship of other Tudor women to determine whether it is possible to identify them as third generation humanists.

Lady Pembroke's literary contribution was inspired by the premature death of her brother, the "shepherd poet." Born in 1554 to Sir Henry Sidney and his wife, Mary, daughter to the Duke of Northumberland, Philip's social status had been greatly enhanced as he reached adulthood because he was also the heir of his childless maternal uncles, Robert, Earl of Leicester, and Ambrose, Earl of Warwick. After receiving a humanist education and serving on minor diplomatic missions, he won appointment as Governor-General of the garrison town of Flushing.

In 1586 he died from wounds at the Battle of Zutphen after a chivalric gesture that caused him to be memorialized by his contemporaries. Having noted that a ally lacked leg armor, he discarded his own only to be mortally wounded in the thigh. To give heightened interest to the story of his injury and death, it was reported that as he lay suffering on the battlefield, he disdained the offer of water, directing the refreshment to a poor, dying soldier nearby with the immortal words, "Thy necessity is yet greater than mine." Deeply mourned by the court and the country, it was less for his remarkable poetic talents than for the chivalric style of his death that he was long remembered by his contemporaries although the posthumous printing of his manuscripts soon added important literary evidence to his legendary greatness. It was "a consciously created ideal."[7]

His chivalric death has caused him to be associated with the ideal courtier of Baldessar Castiglione's *The Book of the Courtier,* printed in Italian in 1528 and published in English translation in 1561 by Sir Thomas Hoby, first husband of the learned Elizabeth Cooke. One of the most popular of the courtly and etiquette books in Elizabethan England, the work was set at the court of Guidobaldo, Duke of Urbino, in whose service Castiglione had been employed. Because of the Duke's ill health, his wife, Elisabetta, had presided over the daily after-dinner entertainment in which their guests elected to participate in dialogues to define the ideal courtier. They described their hero as a nobly born soldier-scholar-poet who combined his proficiency in arms with a taste for letters and music and who had gentle speech and manners which were unaffected yet sophisticated enough for courtly conversation.[8]

The ideal lady as well as the perfect courtier was defined. Like her male counterpart, the lady was expected to be of noble birth, to avoid affectation in her speech and manners, and to have learning in letters and music. While the courtier was also asked to provide his prince with military service, the lady had no occupation except that of a useful ornament in the entertaining of guests with her beauty and her erudite conversation.[9]

Although Philip has often been described as the embodiment of the ideal courtier, his sister, Mary, born in 1561 the year that Hoby's English translation was first published, has been associated with the presiding Duchess rather than with the court lady. This was the highest of compliments, for Castiglione had greatly admired Elisabetta, crediting her presence at the palace for the chain of camaraderie that existed among the courtiers and the ladies.[10] It was because she attended Queen Elizabeth as maid of honor for only a short time during her adolescence that Mary Sidney did not gain recognition as the ideal court lady although even when she was fourteen, her intelligence had been remarkable enough to be noted by an anonymous writer. In a tribute written in 1575 to honour the beauty and grace of the royal maids, this poet singled out Mary for her "wit":

> Tho yonge in years yet olde
>   in wit, a gest dew to your race.
> If you holde on as you begin
>   Who ist youle not deface?[11]

At the age of sixteen, she married William Herbert, second Earl of Pembroke, the forty-three-year-old widowed nephew of Katherine Parr,and retired to Wilton, his principal seat in Wiltshire, to begin the patronage of scholars that has led her admirers to describe her as Castiglione's Duchess.

Since she became a famous poetess and patroness of literature, her level of education and her literary efforts need to be reviewed for the purpose of determining the role of women in Elizabethan literary circles. Later writers, including her biographer, Frances Young, have sometimes assumed even in the absence of contemporary records that besides her proficiency in French and Italian, Lady Pembroke was also skilled in Latin. While it is certain that her elder brother, Philip, attended Shrewsbury School, there is less firm evidence about the early instruction of her and the other Sidney children, although the younger boys may have been enrolled in some local school. Indeed, there can be found among the Sidney family accounts of the 1570s records of the purchases of Latin books and a satchel to carry them for use at school by Robert, who was two years younger than Mary. The expenditures noted specifically for the girls included fees for an Italian tutor and for items such as pins, lute strings, a French book, and articles of clothing. The family was preparing their sons for admission into a university and the girls for entrance into polite society and for marriage. In 1575 when Mary became a maid of honor to Queen Elizabeth, her brother Robert was enrolled at Oxford University.[12]

Because the aristocracy generally had not adopted the humanist instructional program for women, her parents had little incentive to provide her with an education that differed from the usual vernacular training for girls of her rank and position. Even in the 1530s when there had been several households with women humanists only the Cookes outside the More circle had been of the gentry class. While it is likely that Sir Anthony Cooke had chosen to instruct his daughters in classical languages to direct them "toward the specific purpose of coming to the true understanding of God's word," later reformers disdained teaching girls Latin. Many were convinced that women were emotionally immature and would be easily seduced into religious heresy by the Papists or even by the Devil if they became conversant in Latin. As early as 1565, for instance, a woman was accused of witchcraft for saying prayers in that language.[13]

Because of this social and religious climate, it seems unlikely that Mary Sidney ever developed any great fluency in Latin, but for a final determination of her linguistic abilities, it will be instructive to review the extant evidence dating from her years as mistress of Wilton. Since at least three authors wrote Latin dedications to her, it is possible to argue that they believed she was a classical scholar or they would have composed their epistles in English. To dispute this conjecture, it is only necessary to note that her cousin, Lucy Harington, the wife of Edward Russell, third Earl of Bedford, was honored by a dedication and some epigrams which were written in Latin despite her ignorance of ancient languages.[14]

It would also be reasonable to assume that the Psalms Lady Pembroke began to versify sometime after 1586 were translations taken if not from the original Hebrew then surely from a Latin version. Almost certainly according to G. F. Waller, her model was the French Psalter that Théodore de Béze had completed in 1562 at Geneva using as his foundation the 50 Psalms composed between 1532 and 1543 by Clément Marot. She had turned to this task in the hope of accomplishing the goal of her deceased brother, whose model had also been the Béze-Marot Psalter, to demonstrate the attractiveness of English for expressing divine poetry. From Philip's death until perhaps 1611 the Countess versified 107 Psalms, repeatedly revising her own as well as some of the 43 her brother had completed. Not only does her work have more literary merit than that of her brother but his verses were also greatly improved by her changes.[15]

Unconcerned with the literal accuracy of her efforts, her versions more properly called "imitations" than translations are remarkable for their technical experimentation. Among her verses are 164 distinct stanzaic and 94 distinct metrical patterns, which she arranged in many unique combinations, carefully avoiding the exact repetition of any one combination in all but four instances. Because there is extant a series of her Psalms revisions, it is possible to use them as a means of tracing her growth from 1586 when she tentatively began to revise and rearrange the verses of her brother to the 1600s when she had achieved success as a mature poet. To provide a perspective for her literary talent, her rendition of Psalm 134 is placed here with that of the King James version of the Bible:

PSALM 134 ECCE NUNC

You that Jehovas servants are,
Whose carefull watch, whose watchfull care,
Within his house are spent;
Say thus with one assent:
Jehovas name be praised.
Then let your handes be raised
To holiest place,
Where holiest grace
Doth ay
Remaine:
And say
Againe,
Jehovas name be praised.
Say last unto the company,
Who tarryeng make
Their leave to take:
All blessings you accompany,
From him in plenty showered,
Whom Sion holds embowered,
Who heav'n and earth of nought hath raised.

KING JAMES: PSALMS 134 A SONG OF DEGREES

BEHOLD, bless ye the Lord, all ye servants of the Lord, which by night stand
in the house of the Lord.
2 Lift up your hands in the sanctuary, and bless the Lord.
3 The Lord that made heaven and earth bless thee out of Zion.[16]

Circulating only in various manuscript copies during her lifetime, her verses won enthusiastic praise from some of the most important literary figures, including John Donne, Fulke Greville, Samuel Daniel, Benjamin Jonson, John Davies of Hereford, and Joseph Hall. In 1599 she presented a copy of them to the Queen, signing her dedicatory letter as the sister of that "Incomparable Sidney," and in 1600 her cousin, Sir John Harington, who questioned her independent authorship of them, sent three of them to their mutual cousin, Lady Bedford. While Sir John was almost exactly the same age as Lady Pembroke, it is unlikely that the two ever shared a close, personal friendship, for he had been too young to frequent court when she was a maid of honor and he had probably not visited her at Wilton. That they remained remote acquaintances is evidenced by his speculation that Gervase Babington, Bishop of Worcester, sometime chaplain to her husband, had assisted her in translating the Psalms directly from Hebrew, "for it was more than a woman's skill to express the sence so right as she hath done in her vearses, and more than the English or Latin translations could give her."[17]

While his admiration for her "imitations" caused him to suggest incorrectly that she had taken them from the Hebrew, Harington also left the impression that she could possibly have read them in Latin translation. The entire statement, which is difficult to interpret, was a highly speculative one, important primarily because of its expression of disbelief that she, or any other woman, could "express the sence so right" in her verses. Although it is conceivable that Lady Pembroke had turned to a study of Latin after her retirement from court in 1577, there is no extant record of such scholarship. With her remarkable "wit" and her extraordinary skills in vernacular tongues, she could easily have learned the most popularly used classical phrases and quotations of her day, but the literary and cultural climate at court and later at Wilton was not such as to prompt her to become a trained Latin scholar. Even Bishop Babington, credited by Harington with a close scholarly relationship to Lady Pembroke, did not allude to her classical skills or indeed to the Psalms project in the sermons he dedicated to her and to her husband.[18]

Despite their contemporary praise, modern scholars have until recently ignored her Psalms. Except for a few which were included in a publication of Harington's manuscripts in 1804, her "imitations" did not appear in print with Philip's until 1823. From then until 1963, when a new collection of her verses was issued in a volume with her brother's, only his Psalms, often without her improvements, had been republished, except for a stray one or two of hers that have been printed with an incorrect attribution to him. For too long forgotten or ignored, her Psalms, including the one-fourth that have not yet been printed deserve greater recognition and better exposure through their publication in a separate volume of their own.[19]

As Philip was seven years her senior and had been away at school or on continental tours since her toddler days, it is likely that their close personal attachment and literary association dates from her marriage in 1577 when she was able to invite him to Wilton. It was on such a visit in 1580 during a temporary retirement from court caused by his mounting personal debts that Philip wrote in her honor his famous pastoral romance, "The Countess of Pembrokes Arcadia," for the purpose of teaching the values of virtuous behavior and the art of governing well in a genre that delighted as well as instructed. Although the "Arcadia," an early work of original prose fiction in English, was "crammed with chivalric episodes," it approved of passionate love that led to marriage rather than the adulterous passion often detailed and explored in medieval stories.[20]

At his death in 1586 he left an incomplete revision of the manuscript which was published in 1590 by his friend Fulke Greville under its original title, *The Countess of Pembrokes Arcadia*. Outraged by its inferior quality, the Countess printed her own copy of her brother's revision in 1593 to which she added the last three books of the first "Arcadia" in an awkward attempt to complete the work. Her publication has been the subject of some dispute because of the suggestion in its prefatory letter that she had made changes in the manuscript. While some critics have argued that her reverence for her brother served to prevent her from altering any of his text, others have more reasonably concluded that she made a few of the minor corrections to be found there. Despite some retouching, most of the romance was undoubtedly Philip's work.[21]

It was probably the unauthorized printing in 1590 of the *Arcadia* and the three pirated versions in 1591 of *Astrophel and Stella*, the "first and most energetic" of the Petrarchan sonnet sequences in English, which prompted Lady Pembroke to supervise the publication of some of her and her brother's manuscripts. In 1598 she had the sonnet sequence that was reputed to be a celebration of his love for Penelope, Lady Rich, included in an authorized edition of his works. While this was not a genre that lent itself easily to female authorship, Philip's success in glorifying the lover's feelings and emotions, may have led Lady Pembroke to translate the *Trionfi della Morte*, Petrarch's poem describing the vision in which he met a group of ladies who had witnessed the death of his beloved Laura. In her translation that remained in manuscript until 1912, she reproduced the difficult *terza rima* of the original in an impressive display of her mastery of that technique. Frances Young has praised Lady Pembroke's "ingenuity of phrasing" and "adroit transpositions" in the "finest English version" of this important poem.[22]

A few years before the completion of this Italian translation, she had chosen to turn into English two French works whose publication together in one volume in 1592 symbolized the blending of the classical and Protestant heritage of the Elizabethan Renaissance. The first, entitled *A Discourse of Life and Death*, was an English version of Philippe Du Plessis de Mornay's treatise of 1575 that had emphasized the misery of human condition. Remarkable for its "clear and vigorous prose style," her intent was probably to make available in English the literature of an author whose works Philip, himself, had earlier thought worthy of translation.[23]

A Discourse appeared with her version of a Senecan play by Robert Garnier, "the most eminent French tragedian of the sixteenth century." Entitling her translation *The Tragedie of Antonie*, she displayed considerable skill in turning his Alexandrine verse into English blank verse, a medium just then gaining popularity in dramatic circles. She may have published it in response to Philip's lament in *The Defense of Poesie* that there were almost no tragedies in English that could reach "the height of Seneca's style."[24]

Besides the three vernacular translations and the Psalms project, the Countess of Pembroke wrote two original poems: "The Dolefull Lay of Chlorinda," published in 1595, and "A Dialogue between two Shepherds, Thenot and Piers, in praise of Astraea," printed in 1602. Both of these pieces were also related to the ideas and work of her brother. The "Chlorinda" was actually written two years after Philip's death to mourn England's "dead shepherd":

> Great losse to all that ever him did see,
> Great losse to all but greatest losse to me.

It appeared in Spenser's publication, *Colin Clouts Come Home Again*, and as its style is similar to that of "Astrophel," a poem by Spenser that precedes it in the same volume, there is some question as to whether it was actually his work. In introducing her as the author, Spenser described her as a gentle shepherdess who "in shape and spright" closely resembled her brother. Her other poem, "The Dialogue," which was included in a collection of pieces published by Francis Davison, was written about 1599 to be presented before the Queen on a visit to Wilton which probably never took place. In the work characterized by G. F. Waller as "merely a charming minor piece," two shepherds compete with each other in singing the praises of Astraea, who clearly represents the Queen. Their dialogue is interesting because it reflected two inspirations of the literary Renaissance, the shepherd Thenot praising Astraea with Neoplatonic themes while Piers relied upon Protestant allusions. Years earlier, in 1578, Lady Pembroke's brother had written "The Lady of May," a pastoral drama that had been performed for Elizabeth on one of her country progresses.[25]

Although they praised her as a remarkable poet, because of the scope and extent of her aid to literary figures, her contemporaries knew her better as the "maintainer of Arte," as "Muse's chief comfort," and as "Nourisher of the Learned." While it was customary for noble women to support the efforts of the scholarly and of the Godly, none before, except for members of the royal family, such as Margaret, Countess of Richmond, had done so on such an extensive scale. With a special literary mission to fulfill, Lady Pembroke preferred to promote authors who had previously been favored by her brother or who were willing to follow his poetic leadership as interpreted by her.[26]

The work of one scholar, Samuel Daniel, her children's tutor at Wilton in the late 1580s, best exemplifies some of the qualities which she admired. The 1591 pirated editions of Philip's *Astrophel and Stella* had contained many of Daniel's love sonnets to "Delia," which he dedicated to the Countess in an authorized volume of 1592, explaining that he would not have published his work except for its earlier appearance without his approval. Daniel not only continued the tradition of Sidney's sonnetry, as did many other poets, but he also wrote drama in the Garnier-Senecan style. His original play, *The Tragedy of Cleopatra*, which was dedicated to Lady Pembroke, was composed as a companion piece to her *Antonie*.[27]

While the association of Daniel with Lady Pembroke is well documented, the literary relationship of Edmund Spenser to the Wilton scholars is unclear. It was not until late 1579 when he joined the household of Leicester that Spenser first met Philip Sidney. As he remained with Leicester for only about eight or nine months before departing in July, 1580 for Ireland where he spent most of the remainder of his life, there was probably little literary reciprocity between Spenser and the Wilton scholars. Because at first he had failed to include the Countess among those to whom *The Faerie Queen's* prefatory sonnets were addressed, although one in her honor was later added, Spenser may not, in fact, have sought her patronage until after he had decided to publish this work in 1590. The next year he dedicated to her *The Ruines of Time,* admitting that he was "bounded by manie singular favours to her," and in 1595 published her "Chlorinda" in his *Colin Clouts Come Home Again,* praising her as England's Urania.[28]

Spenser and Daniel, among others, were professional rather than private poets because they wrote for political and financial advancement, but the Queen to whom this growing group of lay writers increasingly looked for aid never compensated them to their satisfaction. After Richard Robinson dedicated a work to her in 1595, for example, he received nothing more than a royal thank you for his efforts. Since there was not yet a copyright law to protect them from plagiarism, these authors needed to attract private if not public patrons to ensure their professional survival. Lady Pembroke was only one of many women whose assistance was successfully sought, although not without some complaints from disgruntled recipients like Thomas Nashe, who in a 1593 work that he had dedicated to a woman, actually admitted his hatred for "these female braggarts that contend to have all the Muses beg at their doors."[29]

Despite their importance as patrons it was difficult for the women to gain acceptance as writers. When the Countess of Pembroke, as a private poet, had decided to have her translations printed, she had done so to honor her brother rather than to win personal acclaim or financial reward. None of the other Elizabethan noblewomen had any secular writings published although a few of them, including the Queen, were the authors of minor pieces that appeared in collections printed by individuals such as Richard Puttenham.[30]

Only three women, all of whose work was published prior to that of the Countess of Pembroke, attempted to win financial rewards for their writing in Elizabeth's reign. This number does not include the six or seven women, like Anne Wheathill in 1584, who may also have been primarily interested in earning money when they had works on religious topics printed. Of the secular authors, one, Isabella Whitney, was the first of her sex to publish a collection of English poetry; another, Margaret Tyler, was the first woman to have an English translation of a Spanish romance printed; and the third, Jane Anger, was the first Englishwoman to write a defense of her sex. There is no reason to believe that the Countess was in any way associated with these three authors, but it will be instructive to review briefly their work as a means of further clarifying her contributions to the literary Renaissance.[31]

The first of these women to publish was Isabella Whitney about whom there is some specific family information partly because her brother Geoffrey was also an author. It is known that he was born in 1548 in Cheshire and that in 1586 he published *A Choice of Emblems,* a book that he dedicated to his patron, the Earl of Leicester. Although Isabella's own age is uncertain, the first evidence of her writing, *The Copy of a Letter lately written in meeter by a yonge Gentelwoman to her unconstant Lover,* published in 1567, identified her, of course, as a young woman.[32]

Her more important work, *A sweet Nosegay or pleasant Posye,* a collection of 110 secular verses, some of which were taken from Virgil and Ovid, and

some of which were of her own composition, was printed four years later in
1573. Knowledgeable in Italian as well as in English, Whitney was widely read
in classical translations, a pastime for which she apologized in her introductory
letter. Anticipating charges that she should have spent her idle moments in
scripture reading, she explained that without a divine at hand to aid her in Biblical
interpretations, she had been forced to read secular works. Her contemporaries
may have found her argument reasonable, for eleven years later in 1584 when
Anne Wheathill published a collection of prayers, she carefully apologized for
completing the project without learned council. Whitney also informed her readers
that her academic studies had been made possible only by the forced leisure of
a serious illness and reassured them with the following verse:

> Had I a Husband, or a House,
> And all that longes thereto
> My self could frame about to course
>   as other women do.
> But til some houshold cares mee tye,
> My boke and Pen I will apply.

The obvious conclusion of her verse is that as soon as a recovery of her health
made it possible for her to return to domestic service, she would have little or
no time to read classical translations.

While Whitney was unique among the women writers because she had two
different works printed, Margaret Tyler was the most successful of the three
because her translation of a Spanish work by Diego Ortunez de Calahorra, entitled
The mirror of princely deeds and knighthood, was issued in two more editions
after its first appearance in 1578. In its dedication to Lord Thomas Howard, the
future Duke of Suffolk, whose parents she had formerly served, Tyler explained
that she had published the translation for financial rewards. She had hoped, she
continued, that her readers would be delighted with her work even though they
might consider its subject matter too "manlike" for a female to translate.

Tyler also answered in advance the anticipated charge that only bold females
wrote of princely deeds. From the first premise of her argument that it was the
custom of men to dedicate books to women that had been written on many topics
including war, law, government, and religion, she moved easily to the second
premise that it was proper and usual for women to read the works composed in
their honor. Her concluding premise that "it is all one for a woman to pen a
storie, as for a man to address his storie to a woman . . ." may have shocked
her readers as much as her decision to publish her "storie," for in 1578 it had
not yet become routine for gentlemen to have their manuscripts printed. Shortly
before the appearance of Tyler's publication, for example, Thomas Whythorne,
a noted musician, wrote that he had suffered "many combats" with his conscience
before he decided to place his music in the "common gaze" of the world by
publishing it.[33]

While Tyler felt compelled to justify translating a work on chivalry, and Whitney had paused to apologize for studying pagan authors, the third writer, Jane Anger, had a far less humble approach. In her work *Iane Anger her Protection for Women,* she responded to a book attacking her sex entitled *Boke his Surfyt in love,* which is no longer extant. During the century after the first printing press was established at Westminster, numerous abusive and complimentary tracts had been published on women, a topic that had proved to be so lucrative to its authors that on occasion a few men had written books both for and against women. Anger apparently joined them as the first woman to defend her sex in English prose.

Even though there were two Jane Angers known to be living in Tudor England, the possibility that the writer was a man using a female pseudonym must be considered. As no woman since Whitney in 1573 had published an original secular work, Anger's book with its bold title, announcing her authorship and with its two prefatory letters pointedly saluting women cast doubts on the honesty of its author. Even the numerous works that were named in honor of Lady Pembroke did not begin to appear in print until the year after the issuance of the *Protection.* Whoever Anger was, she was not of noble or of royal status, and as a routine matter, could have expected some censure for her audacity in publishing any secular work, even one more conservative than a defense of her sex. Undaunted by the certainty of criticism, she included in her prefatory letter an aggressive explanation rather than a humble excuse: "for my presumption I crave pardon, because it was ANGER that did write it. . . ."[34]

If the author was a woman who meant seriously to defend her sex, she failed to accomplish her goal. Intent on exploring the vulnerability of women, Anger blamed them for numerous faults: silliness, credulity, bashfulness, garrulity, and weakness of wit, but also accepted the Neoplatonist philosophy which reveres them as the purer and more beautiful sex. With remarkable versatility, she utilized their alleged greater virtue to defend their inferior status, for without the male headship, she warned, the superior moral nature of women would cause them to fall victim to the heinous sins of pride and self-righteousness. While her female contemporaries often admitted to the weaknesses which Anger exposed in the *Protection,* her analysis still seems strangely out of place in a book devoted to their defense. Indeed, although her work was far more aggressive than that of Tyler, Anger's promotion of the status quo for the sexes was far less radical than the claim of the Spanish translator that women had a right to join a profession.

Obviously, the light verse of Whitney, the prose of Anger, and the translation of Tyler were not accomplished within the guidelines of any philosophical framework. They are used here merely as standards by which the uniqueness of Lady Pembroke's talents may be placed into perspective. Since there were other aristocratic women who were admired for their vernacular scholarship, it is possible that some of them were writing verses as remarkable as many of the minor male Elizabethan poets who are still read. If there were women of this generation besides Lady Pembroke who composed with a serious literary purpose, their work has not survived or has simply gone unrecognized.

Because it was sprinkled with Latin phrases, the text of Anger's work is also important to a discussion of classical training. While her frequent use of Latin does not confirm that Anger, who will be accepted here as a woman in the absence of any other information about her, had the skills of Lady Bacon or even of the Queen, it does prove that she could at least read this language. *The Protection* remains the only evidence that she belongs to a group of Latin scholars that included Magdalen Pridieux, grandchild to Margaret Gigs Clement of the More circle; Anne Cecil, daughter to the learned Mildred Cooke; Lady Arbella Stuart, first cousin to King James VI of Scotland; Elizabeth Grymeston, a Catholic writer; and Jane (Mary) Wiseman, an Augustinian Canoness. Before relating the work of these six women to that of Lady Pembroke, it will be necessary first to investigate the quality of their education and secondly to discover why they were the only Englishwomen of this generation known to have had Latin instruction.

For the purpose of placing the education of Magdalen Pridieux and Anne Cecil in perspective, it will be helpful to make some general statements about the instruction of the other daughters of the second generation of women humanists to ascertain if possible why they were not also given classical training as Sir Thomas More had advocated. Very little evidence has survived about More's great-granddaughters through the female line partly because his martyrdom forced their parents into political disgrace or exile except during the reign of Queen Mary. It was perhaps only among the women of the Clement family that the first generation's educational theories were passed on successively from the first through the second to the third generation. Of Margaret Gigs Clement's five daughters, all of whom were trained as classicists, only Helen Clement, the wife of Thomas Pridieux of Devonshire, had a daughter she could instruct in the Latin language. The child, Magdalen Pridieux, was also educated as a student boarder and not as a novice by her mother's sister, Margaret Clement, the learned prioress of St. Ursula's at Louvain.[35]

Only scattered information can be found about the education of the daughters of the second-generation women humanists who were Protestant. While no record can be found of the grandchildren of Bishop Hooper, whose wife fled into exile, some sparse information is still extant about the children of the Cooke sisters, one of whom was Anne Cecil, about the offspring of Catherine Thysman alias Tishem, who returned to the Low Countries in 1577, and about the noble issue of the Greys, the Fitzalans, the Howards, and the Seymours. Although in the second generation there had been at least sixteen girls among these six families with fluency in Latin, these learned women, in their turn, were the mothers of only sixteen surviving daughters, a number that was no larger because two of the Cookes, two of the Seymours, both Greys, both Fitzalans, one of the Howards, Thysman alias Tishem, and Queen Elizabeth either had only male children or no offspring at all. If the suggestion already made here is accurate that Mildred Cooke was the sole member of the second generation, outside the More circle, to provide her female issue with Latin instruction, it is a shocking comment on the unwillingness of Tudor women to pass on their cultural accomplishments to their daughters.[36]

Mildred and her husband, William Cecil, the future Lord Burghley, had two girls, Anne born in 1556, who studied Latin grammar, and Elizabeth, born in 1564, who probably did not have any such training. Even with tutoring by William Lewin, a distinguished Cambridge scholar, Anne never achieved any great fluency in this language, although her expertise is almost impossible to evaluate as a few Latin phrases in a letter she wrote to her father are the only extant record of her scholarship. After her death in 1588, just one year before that of her mother, Lord Burghley clearly distinguished between her pious abilities and the classical skills of her mother in the Latin inscriptions that he had engraved on their tombs.[37]

At least some of the credit for introducing Anne to Latin scholarship must be given to Lady Cecil who regularly turned to a Latin book of devotions for her meditations and who proved to be a valued friend of advanced education by her aid to university scholars. There is fortunately a contemporary reference to her interest in her daughter's training. In late 1569 when Anne was for a short time betrothed to Philip Sidney, her intended father-in-law, Sir Henry Sidney, informed Lady Cecil that he was sending to them a tutor whom he knew she was desirous of having to teach Anne the French language. It can be speculated that under the supervision of her mother in 1569, the girl turned from her classical studies which were probably begun in the nursery, to vernacular instruction.[38]

It is likely that her husband supported and encouraged Lady Cecil in providing this advanced education for Anne. Despite his celebrated New Year's poem in 1568, exhorting his daughter to spend her idle moments at a spinning wheel, an admonition that would have won the approval of Juan Luis Vives, William's own continuing devotion to ancient literature probably prompted him to approve of having his elder daughter, if not his younger one, instructed in Latin.[39]

No information is available about the instruction of Anne's younger sister, Elizabeth. Because they were more than seven years apart in age, they surely did not share the same tutors, for in the early 1570s when decisions about Elizabeth's education were being implemented, her sister was already the wife of Edward de Vere, seventeenth Earl of Oxford, a former ward of their father. It is possible that after William's ennoblement in 1572 as Baron Burghley, he decided not to extend the same rigorous education to Elizabeth as he had to her older sister, since classical training for women of the lay nobility had previously been adopted only by families with immediate aspirations to marry their offspring into the royal family. The older daughter had received her Latin instruction well before her father's ennoblement.

It was in 1571 just after her fourteenth birthday that Anne Cecil married the twenty-one-year-old Oxford, whose subsequent treatment of her was considered callous in an age when noble spouses were not often solicitous of each other's tender feelings. By 1576 he had denied paternity of their daughter who was clearly his child and by 1581 had received royal punishment for fathering the offspring of a maid of honor. At the time of Anne's wedding, her father, not yet raised to the nobility, had disclaimed any credit for the alliance, protesting that his approval had been granted only after she and Oxford had solicited his consent. While it is probably true that his awareness of the volatile temper of the Earl had led William to seek other husbands for Anne, including Philip Sidney, it cannot be doubted that he was pleased that she was to have such an esteemed noble husband. It is unbelievable that as a girl of thirteen Anne, still characterized at the age of twenty-two as the "sweet little Countess" by the Earl of Warwick, had the strength of character to woo and win Oxford, the darling of the royal court, and then to force her father to submit to the alliance.[40]

While indisputably William hoped to arrange advantageous marriages for his children, Anne's alliance was also consistent with his humanist concepts. Both she and Oxford had received the training that made it possible for them to converse together about ancient literature, although in their case this knowledge did not lead to the close intimate relationship anticipated by the Christian humanists. Since their marriage proved to be equally incompatible with the family's reformed beliefs, as Oxford was for a while a Catholic sympathizer, it was only on the dynastic level that this union succeeded in its early promise. Anne's father lived to see her child, Elizabeth de Vere, the eldest of her three daughters by Oxford, become the wife of William Stanley, sixth Earl of Derby, a claimant to the English throne through his descent from the second daughter of Henry VIII's sister, the Queen of France.

Little information is extant about the early education of the daughters of Lady Cecil's two sisters, Elizabeth and Catherine. Married to Henry Killigrew in 1565, Catherine, who was younger than both Mildred and Elizabeth, had four girls before she died in childbirth in 1583 at about the age of fifty. While there is no surviving record of her children's instruction, a nineteenth-century scholar speculated that her second daughter, Elizabeth, whose third and last husband was Sir Thomas Lower of Cornwall, was brought up with a fondness for classical languages because the inscription on her tombstone, erected in 1638, credited her with "virtue, piety, and learning . . . nothing short . . . of any of her ancestors."[41]

Catherine's older sister, Elizabeth, after she was widowed by the death of her first husband, Sir Thomas Hoby, married Lord John Russell, son of Francis, second Earl of Bedford. It was one of the tragedies of her life that he died in 1584 only one year before the demise of his father whom he would have succeeded as earl. Not only was she deprived of the status of countess but their surviving children, Elizabeth and Anne Russell, could not inherit the family's title. For the remainder of her life, Lady Russell sought social eminence for her daughters. After winning appointments as royal maids of honor for both of them, she schemed to find gentlemen eligible by rank and wealth to become their husbands.[42]

The highlight of her private life was the marriage of her younger daughter, Anne, to Lord Henry Herbert, the heir of Edward Somerset, fourth Earl of

Worcester. The wedding in June of 1600, graced by the presence of the Queen, proved to be the season's social event, but like her brother-in-law, Lord Burghley, Lady Russell had betrayed the tenets of her religion for family connections. Ignoring the admonition of William Tyndal to search for religious compatibility in marriage partners, she approved of the Herbert alliance despite the Catholic sympathies of the young man's family. Her new son-in-law, the future Marquess of Worcester, reared most of his thirteen children, her grandchildren, as Roman Catholics, including at least one daughter who was professed as a nun at Brussels.[43]

Lady Russell had enough energy and vitality at the age of seventy to prepare and publish in 1605 her English version of a Latin work that she dedicated to Lady Herbert. Only one of three translations to be published by a woman in the first forty years of the seventeenth century, the prefatory letter of the book, *A Way of Reconciliation of a Good and Learned Man,* had a reference to her daughter's sincere religious education. Presenting it to her as a New Year's gift, Lady Russell may have hoped that a study of this work would help Lady Herbert retain her Protestantism among her new Catholic relatives.

The reference in this epistle to Lady Herbert's religious training is her mother's only extant comment about the instruction of either daughter. Since they were born to her in the 1570s when she was well over forty years old, her plans for their education were implemented at a time when it had become manifestly clear that fashionable young people no longer translated classical literature. As her major family ambition was the arranging of socially prominent marriages for her children, Lady Russell probably did not seriously consider training them as classicists. In the late 1590s when she began unsuccessfully to seek an alliance for the elder daughter, who died tragically in 1600, she listed her child's best assets as her "virtue, birth, and place" but neglected to refer to her scholarship. By way of contrast, the Christian humanists had considered both classical and religious education as essential criteria in the selection of spouses.[44]

Only three of the second generation noblewomen with classical training had female issue. Almost nothing is known about the education of the two girls of Anne Seymour, Countess of Warwick, by her second husband, Sir Edward Unton, or of the four girls of Jane Howard, the eldest child of Surrey the poet and the wife of the Earl of Westmoreland. The extant information about Frances and Mary Berkeley, the two daughters of Jane's sister, Katherine, Lady Berkeley, indicates that their language training did not include any ancient tongue. Not only did John Smyth, the historian of Lady Berkeley's family, recall clearly that their mother had been particularly anxious for them to learn Italian, but their tutor, Henry Grantham, also dedicated to them an Italian grammar book that he had been forced to translate for their use from its original Latin into English.[45]

That Lady Berkeley and almost all of the other women humanists of the second generation adopted for their girls the vernacular training that was then most popular among their aristocratic friends indicates the strength that peer pressure often has on decisions about education. When even classical scholars neglected to offer Latin instruction to their daughters, there was little chance that ancient literature would remain an important part of the reading material of Tudor women. This trend had become obvious at court by the 1570s, for it was only the second-generation women who spent their idle moments there in the reading of Latin works. Of the identifiable third-generation women Latinists, the only two ever to be present at court were Lady Oxford, who was there frequently with her mother, and Lady Arbella Stuart, who was invited for a few visits before her status as claimant to the throne led to her rustication.

While Lady Oxford was given an advanced education because of her learned mother's influence, the motive for Arbella's training was entirely different. Like the Greys, Howards, Fitzalans, and Seymours of the second generation, her relatives were eager to reap the rewards of royal power. Even her birth can be interpreted as a further step on the social and dynastic ladder ascended by her determined grandmother, Elizabeth Hardwick. Married four times, Elizabeth increased her wealth and position with every husband, moving from the status of a mere gentlewoman in her youth to that of countess in her last union with George Talbot, sixth Earl of Shrewsbury. The father of her children for whom she harbored grand dynastic ambitions was her second husband, Sir William Cavendish. In 1574 Lady Shrewsbury made arrangements with Lady Margaret Douglas, Countess of Lennox, the daughter of Henry VIII's elder sister, the Queen of Scotland, for the marriage of her son, Charles, fifth Earl of Lennox, to Elizabeth Cavendish. By this marriage Lady Shrewsbury's daughter became the sister-in-law of Mary, Queen of Scots, then a prisoner in England in the custody ironically of Lady Shrewsbury's husband. The imprisoned Queen and Lennox's deceased elder brother, Lord Henry Darnley, were the parents of James VI, King of Scotland. While the clandestine marriage of Lennox led to the incarceration of his mother, it also resulted in the 1575 birth of his daughter, Arbella, who was to become the chief alternative to James for the English throne.[46]

Arbella received an education appropriate to a daughter of the English royal family. By the time she was thirteen, her skill in French and Italian was so extraordinary that even Sir John Harington admired her fluency. In 1603 the Venetian Ambassador reported to his superiors that she knew Latin, French, and Spanish and that she spoke Italian extremely well. There is no contemporary evidence that she knew any ancient language besides Latin.[47]

Like all the other women claimants in Elizabethan England, Arbella had a tragic life. By 1600 she had become increasingly impatient with the supervision of her grandmother Shrewsbury and by the refusal of the crown to honor her as she believed her high birth deserved. Had she studied more carefully the experiences of her female relatives with royal blood, Arbella might have been less eager to demand her rights of inheritance. Most of the others had suffered imprisonment: Mary, Queen of Scots, had been executed after nineteen years in custody; Katherine Grey had been kept under close supervision until her death because of her clandestine marriage to the Earl of Hertford; her sister, Mary Grey, had been freed from custody only after the demise of the husband she had secretly wed; and even the Countess of Lennox, Arbella's paternal grandmother, had suffered occasional periods of incarceration. Notwithstanding these examples, in 1602 Arbella schemed to marry William Seymour who, because he was a grandson of the Earl of Hertford and Katherine Grey, was himself a royal claimant. By her incautious behavior she became completely alienated from her grandmother Shrewsbury and was placed in the protective custody of the crown for the remainder of Elizabeth's reign.[48]

In the last decade of the sixteenth century Arbella's status had been the source of much political speculation because of the Queen's refusal to name a successor. Listing Arbella in line to the throne after her cousin, James of Scotland, one contemporary writer reported that because of her English birth there were many who believed that she was the better candidate. Indeed, Catholic nobles with Spanish sympathies favored her because of their opposition to the succession of the monarch of a country that had been so recently allied with France. Before his death in 1601 even the Earl of Essex, a staunch supporter of James, had begun to consider how best to use her presence in England to his political advantage. There were many rumors of her marriage to a wide range of candidates: Rainutio Farnese, son of the Duke of Parma, Henry Percy, ninth Earl of Northumberland, and even King James of Scotland, all of whom had claims, some of them rather distant, to the English throne.[49]

Despite this speculation and the ungrounded fears of some of the Scottish King's supporters that Sir Robert Cecil, the Queen's leading minister after the death of his father in 1598, would marry Arbella to become King himself or would support the candidacy of the sixth Earl of Derby who was the husband of Cecil's niece, Elizabeth de Vere, James succeeded remarkably smoothly to the English throne. The ease of the Stuart succession is a tribute to the political skill of Cecil and his associates and to the "innate capacity for caution and opportunism" of the Scottish King. Even with the growth of tension between England and Scotland in the 1590s that was brought on largely by the uncertainty of the English succession and by the competition of Cecil and Essex, the two monarchs had maintained a personal correspondence that was sometimes cordial. In 1593, for example, Elizabeth said in a letter to him: "You knowe, my deare brother, that sins you first brethed, I regarded alwais to conserve hit as my womb hit had bene you bare." Later, her godson, Sir John Harington, wrote that she was often heard to say, "they were fooles that did not knowe that the lyne of Scotland must needes be next heires."[50]

In this generation Lady Arbella was the only daughter born to an English nobleman to be given a classical education largely because of the inability of the Tudor family to have female issue who could continue the association of the court with humanist training for women. It had been King Henry VIII's support for the classical instruction of his children that had prompted four of his ambitious noble kinsmen to adopt the same educational standards in their households. In their quest for marriage alliances with the Tudor dynasty, and for some special status that would at the same time identify them more closely to the royal family and separate them more completely from the remainder of the nobility, the four families of Seymour, Grey, Howard, and Fitzalan had provided training in the ancient languages for their daughters. With the subsequent failure of Henry VIII's line, the nobility, except in the special case of Arbella, lost interest in classical training for their female progeny.

Even though only two fashionable women can be identified as third-generation Latin scholars, both modern and contemporary writers have persisted in praising the members of Elizabeth's court for their great fluency in languages. Evidence taken from William Harrison's work, *The Description of England,* published in 1577 and greatly enlarged in 1587, can be cited as indisputable proof of this linguistic brilliance. In his book Harrison boasted that both the men and women at court had a "sound knowledge" of Greek and Latin and were "no less skillful" in Spanish, Italian, and French. Unquestionably, he greatly overestimated the linguistic abilities of both sexes. While most of them did not have a "sound knowledge" of Greek, very few were fluent in either Spanish or Italian. In 1584, just a few years before the appearance of Harrison's second edition, the Spanish Ambassador wrote to his superiors that Sir Francis Walsingham, could speak Italian more readily than the other members of the Privy Council, implying by his statement that most of the English councilors had little or no skill in that language.[51]

Even though it exaggerates their skills, Harrison's statement does have some validity. Many courtiers did learn Latin and a smattering of Greek at grammar school and University and were often tutored in at least one vernacular tongue, usually the French, although a few scholars may also have learned the Spanish or Italian. By James' reign, partly because of the belief that Italy was vice-ridden and partly because of the long-standing contacts of the English with Huguenots, French was without question the most popular foreign language.[52]

While Harrison's remark about the linguistic abilities of women was overstated, it is interesting to note that in a later paragraph on that same page of the *Description* he made a more specific and revealing comment about female scholarship at court:

> I could in like sort set down the ways . . . our antient ladies of the court do shun and avoid idleness . . . some in continual reading either of the Holy Scriptures or histories . . . and divers . . . in translating of other men's into our English and Latin tongue, whilst the youngest sort in the meantime apply their lutes, citerns, prick song, and all kind of music. . . .[53]

In 1577 when he first differentiated between their activities, Mary Sidney, at the age of sixteen, was a member of the "youngest sort," spending her leisure moments in the playing of musical instruments. There were several second-generation humanists, including the Queen, who by the standards of the day, qualified as Harrison's "antient" women.

Although many of these "antient" classicists, among whom can be counted Lady Berkeley, Lady Lumley, Lady Burghley, Lady Russell, and Lady Bacon, were not in regular attendance on Elizabeth in 1577, they were often present on special occasions. In addition, a foreign-born lady with Latin skills served as a royal lady-in-waiting: in 1565 Helena Ulfsdotter Snakenborg had visited England in the train of the Swedish Princess Cecilia and had remained behind after the departure of her mistress to become the third wife of William Parr, Marquess of Northampton, and to serve as a confidante of the Queen. Harrison may also have remembered that before their disgrace and death both the learned Jane Seymour and her friend, Katherine Grey, had been royal maids of honor. Finally, there were sometimes present at court two third generation women who knew Latin but not Greek; in the 1570s Lady Oxford was often a guest with her mother and in 1587, the year of Harrison's second edition, Lady Arbella Stuart arrived on one of her infrequent visits.[54]

There is no doubt that among courtiers as well as among gentlewomen classical scholarship that could meet the high standards of Sir Thomas More and Roger Ascham was on the wane in the 1580s and the 1590s. A friend of Sidney, Fulke Greville, Lord Brooke, later remembered that out of concern for the calibre of education in the universities and among her diplomatic corps, the Queen had attempted to prevent this decay. Her efforts, if the writer Henry Peacham is any judge, were singularly unsuccessful, for in 1622 he sadly referred to the "ignorant times" of his day when numerous English gentlemen toured the continent with almost no knowledge of Latin. No evidence exists to indicate that the Queen had any corresponding concern for the decay of classical learning among her gentlewomen or even for upgrading the elementary educational level of her youthful maids of honor.[55]

Among the other social classes in England, only a few women knew Latin. While there may have been more Protestant women of the lesser aristocracy than Jane Anger and Anne Cecil to receive training in this language, in the absence of any contemporary comment about their scholarship, it is improbable that they achieved any great fluency. Since Latin was used in clandestine Catholic services, it is likely that a number of recusant women had at least an elementary introduction to this language in their households. Because of the secrecy surrounding the private lives of the recusants in England, it is more difficult to discover information about their instruction than it is of the Catholic women who were educated at nunneries on the continent. Nevertheless, in addition to Magdalen Pridieux, one recusant woman, Elizabeth Grymeston, who received her Latin instruction in the kingdom, can be definitely identified. She was born in 1560 to Martin Bernye and Margaret Flint of North Erpingham, Norfolk and was married to Christopher Grymeston of Smeeton in Yorkshire. The only evidence of her skills has survived in a book she wrote to offer words of advice and comfort to her son, the sole survivor of her eight children. In the work, *Miscelanea, Meditations, Memoratives,* which was issued in four different editions after it was published posthumously in 1604, she frequently quoted from Latin and Greek texts, both pagan and Christian. Although these quotations are incorrect enough to justify the speculation that they were lifted from an intermediary source, they were incorporated into her book in such a way as to warrant the conclusion that she was able to read these languages, an ability that was almost unique in her generation, for only she and Magdalen Pridieux indisputably had some knowledge of the Greek language.[56]

While there is more extant information about the education of Englishwomen abroad than in their native land, it is still possible to identify only a few Latinists on the continent. Most of these learned women were associated with St. Ursula's, a Flemish Augustinian convent at Louvain where Margaret Clement had been prioress since 1569. While it is true that her niece, Magdalen Pridieux, received some religious instruction at the convent, she had probably already studied Greek and Latin with her learned mother. Another scholar at St. Ursula's was Jane Wiseman, called Mary after she was professed. Her instruction had been supervised by her recusant father, who had regularly exhorted his children, including Mary and her three sisters, in Latin every Friday. After his death, his widow's example in aiding Catholic priests despite the danger of fines, imprisonment, or capital punishment, inspired the four daughters to become nuns. The two youngest, Mary and Bridget, decided to join St. Ursula's even though their two older sisters, Anne and Barbara, were already professed at Syon Monastery, then located in Rouen. From the available documentation, it is possible to identify only Mary among the Wiseman sisters as a Latin scholar. Not only did she translate the homilies, sermons, and expositions of the Psalms at St. Monica's, the affiliation of St. Ursula's where she transferred as prioress in 1609, but she was also able to compose Latin letters. Despite the reverence for clerical Latin that persisted in the Catholic faith, there is almost no evidence that the other English nuns of this generation devoted themselves to advanced studies in this language. One exception was Anne Clitherow, a daughter of the Catholic female martyr of York, who after she had joined St. Ursula's, reputedly learned the tongue so well that she "understood it perfectly."[57]

Because the Countess of Pembroke, unlike Lady Arbella, Lady Oxford, Magdalen Pridieux, Jane Anger, Elizabeth Grymeston, and Mary Wiseman, was not a Latin scholar, it is necessary to review the status of Tudor humanism for the purpose of more clearly defining its meaning for women of the third generation. The first great proponent of women's education in England, Sir Thomas More, had insisted that women be trained in the classics as a character-forming exercise with an emphasis that was both religious and ethical, and as a means of preparing them to perform scholarly and domestic functions. Their scholarly goal had been to write classical compositions, to emend faulty versions of the ancient texts, and to make accurate translations into English, and their domestic goal had been to use their knowledge to enhance the intimacy of their relationships with the members of their nuclear family. Although the women of the second generation were divided in the emphasis that they placed upon the study of Christian texts and upon the need for training in vernacular languages, the general focus of their activity, the translating of ancient works into their native tongue, still reflected the tenets of More's Christian humanism. While Lady Burghley and Queen

Elizabeth, for example, differed widely in their preference for pagan and Christian works and in their domestic roles, as adults they both devoted their leisure time to rendering the classics into English for their personal inspiration and guidance.

In the third generation the humanism for women that More and Vives advocated may have disappeared altogether. Grymeston and Pridieux, the two women who read Greek and Latin pagans as well as Christian writers left no record of their skill in translations or compositions. Mother Wiseman, only a Latinist, was the sole female scholar to complete a great number of translations and to compose Latin letters, but she seems to have devoted her skills selectively to religious subjects. While her education served to strengthen her Christian commitment, she was not able to utilize it for the domestic goals outlined by More and Vives since she had no husband or children. In addition, there is no evidence that either she or the other women of her generation who studied ancient languages created any works of merit, as had their predecessors, Lady Bacon and Lady Basset. Although it is true that Lady Arbella and Lady Oxford wrote some light verse, neither woman was noted for experimentation with literary forms, for translations of either vernacular or ancient works, or for serious compositions in any language.[58] Furthermore, not one of these Latinists gained reputations as patrons of the new vernacular literature, although Lady Arbella and Lady Oxford were, indeed, the recipients of a few book dedications. It is possible that this negative appraisal which is based primarily on the absence of information is too severe, but with almost no extant examples of their work and with the overwhelming silence of their contemporaries about their literary and scholarly talents, it seems to be a realistic conclusion.

If the ability to read classical rather than a variety of vernacular languages had been absolutely essential to participation in the Elizabethan literary movement, it would have been impossible to identify any woman as a major contributor. While indisputably a knowledge of Latin and Greek literature offered a wide range of literary experiences and gave the confidence of a disciplined mind to those who mastered the technique of classical composition, others unskilled in ancient languages could absorb a wide variety of moral lessons and historical facts by studying this literature in translation. It is also evident that through a rigorous and thorough review of continental works in their native versions, it was possible for scholars to fill the void of language experience and intellectual discipline caused by their ignorance of the classical tongues. The translation into English of the literature of any foreign language, not just the ancient ones, could provide an apprenticeship in the uses of language important to a successful experimentation with literary form and content.

As the emphasis of her generation's scholarship was largely that of the reinterpretation of classical and religious values to meet the needs of her society, Lady Pembroke was able to participate on many levels of the new literary movement. Guided by the achievements of her brother, she began her writing career with the versification of the Psalms, a project that she pursued for more than two decades slowly improving her style through the numerous revisions that she made. Continuing to follow his intellectual leadership, she translated a play of Garnier that appeared in print with her version of a work by Du Plessis de Mornay, an important French Protestant. Through her patronage of scholars as well as her publication of Sidney's manuscripts, she helped to popularize his work and his literary ideals. Honored by many of the greatest authors of her day for her versification as well as for her support of their literature, she cannot be patronized by the suggestion that for her sex and time she was a learned woman, since the numerous extant copies of her "imitations" prove that by any standard she excelled as a poet.

While the Elizabethans read and admired Castiglione's description of a court lady, they did not expect gentlewomen to perform any public task more onerous than attendance on the Queen or any poetic effort more profound than the writing of light verse. Even the Duchess of Urbino to whom Lady Pembroke was compared had played an indirect role in the entertainment at her court. Without apology to her literary associates or to her readers, Lady Pembroke not only personally joined the male-dominated world of serious literary composition and publication but also gave it decisive creative leadership and direction. Her efforts generally evoked praise from her contemporaries because of the widely perceived notion that she was completing the goals set by her deceased brother. Many of those who complimented her verse, as did Spenser, linked her skills and abilities closely to those of Sidney. Even Henry Constable, who was not a close acquaintance, wrote:

> Thy minde all say like to thy brother is,
> What need I say more to honoure it?
> For I have praysed thyne by praysing his.[59]

She remains the only identifiable woman of this generation with outstanding literary talent, but because she was not skilled in classical languages, she cannot be identified as a humanist. Following her leadership, women of the next more scholarly generation would continue to write remarkable vernacular pieces, but they would also be joined by women classicists with the ability to translate ancient texts and to create original Latin compositions.

NOTES

1. See Lewis Soens, ed., *Sir Philip Sidney's Defense of Poesy* (Lincoln, Nebr., 1970).

2. Ian Maclean, *The Renaissance Notion of Women* (New York, 1980), p. 24; Joseph B. Collins, *Christian Mysticism in the Elizabethan Age* (Reprint, 1967), pp. 10 and 105; Helena Shire, *A Preface to Spenser* (London, 1978), p. 82.

3. Ian Maclean, pp. 24 and 55-85.

4. Richard Puttenham, *The Arte of English Poesy,* (New York, 1971), pp. 51 and 208; L. G. Black, "A Lost Poem by Queen Elizabeth I," *Times Literary Supplement* (May 23, 1968), p. 535; Leicester Bradner, ed., *The Poems of Queen Elizabeth I* (Providence, R.I., 1964), pp. xii and 26; Lisle Cecil John, *The Elizabethan Sonnet Sequences* (New

York, 1964), p. 17; Sir John Harington, *Nugae Antiguae,* 2 vols. (Reprint, 1966), I, 109 and 140.

5. Roy Strong, *Splendour at Court: Renaissance Spectacle and Illusion* (London, 1973), p. 52 and *The Cult of Elizabeth* (London, 1976), pp. 15 and 46; Elkin Calhoun Wilson, *England's Eliza* (Reprint, 1966), pp. 135, 336, and 394; George P. Rice, *The Public Speaking of Queen Elizabeth* (New York, 1951), pp. 68 and 85.

6. Anthony Esler, *The Aspiring Mind of the Elizabethan Younger Generation* (Durham, N.C., 1966), pp. 51 and 114; Malcolm W. Wallace, *The Life of Sir Philip Sidney* (Cambridge, 1915), p. 147; C. T. Onions, ed., *Shakespeare's England,* 2 vols. (Oxford, 1917), II, 191.

7. Roger Howell, *Sir Philip Sidney, The Shepherd Knight* (London, 1968), p. 7; Arthur Collins, *The Letters and Memorials of State,* 2 vols. (London, 1746), I, 348.

8. Baldessare Castiglione, *The Book of the Courtier,* trans. Sir Thomas Hoby, intro. W.H.D. Rouse (New York, 1966), pp. 16 and 32; John Buxton, *Sir Philip Sidney and the English Renaissance* (New York, 1954), p. 37; Roberto Weiss, *The Spread of Italian Humanism* (London, 1964), p. 79.

9. Baldessare Castiglione, pp. 189-250; see also Joan Kelly-Gadol, "Did Women Have a Renaissance?" *Becoming Visible: Women in European History,* ed. Renate Bridenthal and Claudia Koonz, (Boston, 1977), pp. 137-164.

10. Baldessare Castiglione, pp. 20-21; Nicholas Breton, *The Pilgrimage to paradise* (London, 1592), dedication.

11. *The Queenes Majesties entertainment at Woodstocke, 1575* (London, 1585).

12. Frances Campbell Young, *Mary Sidney, Countess of Pembroke* (London, 1912), p. 26; *Report on the Manuscripts of Lord De L'Isle & Dudley, Preserved at Penshurst Place,* H.M.C., 6 vols. (London, 1925-1934), I, 247, 264, and 268 and II, 381.

13. Marjorie Keniston McIntosh, "Sir Anthony Cooke: Tudor Humanist, Educator and Religious Reformer," *Proceedings of the American Philosophical Society,* CXIX (1975), 240; C. H. Conley, *First English Translators of the Classics* (Reprint, 1967), p. 117; Richard Mulcaster, *Positions (1581)* (New York, 1971), p. 30; Joseph H. Marshburn, *Murder and Witchcraft in England, 1550-1640* (Norman, Okla., 1971), p. 33; Protestant strictures against the study of Latin were often directed against women. See, for example, Thomas Salter, *A Mirrhor mete for all Mothers, Matrones, and Maidens, intituled the Mirrhor of Modestie . . .* (London, 1579).

14. Richard Bruch, *Epigrammatum hecatontades duae* (London, 1627), dedicatory letter; John Owen, *Epigrammatum libri tres* (London, 1607), p. 49.

15. J.C.A. Rathmell, ed., *The Psalms of Sir Philip Sidney and the Countess of Pembroke* (New York, 1963), pp. xvii-xxvii; Frances Campbell Young, *Mary Sidney,* p. 151; Joseph Ritson, *Bibliographica Poetica* (London, 1802), p. 239; for the best interpretation of her work, see G. F. Waller, ed., *The Triumph of Death and Other Unpublished and Uncollected Poems of Mary Sidney, Countess of Pembroke* (Salzburg, Austria, 1977), pp. 9, 10, 37, and 43; and "The Text and Manuscript Variants of the Countess of Pembroke's Psalms," *Review of English Studies* N.S. 26:101 (1975), 8-18; for another opinion, see Noel J. Kinnamon, "Melle de Petra: The Sources and Form of the Sidneian Psalms," *Dissertation Abstracts International,* XXXVII (1977), 5143A-5144A; for information about Clément Marot's influence see Ann Lake Prescott, *French Poets and the English Renaissance* (New Haven, 1978), pp. 1-36.

16. G. F. Waller, *The Triumph of Death,* pp. ii; and *Review of English Studies,* pp. 8-18; J.C.A. Rathmell, p. 311.

17. G. F. Waller, *The Triumph of Death,* pp. ii, 46 and 52-63; J.C.A. Rathmell, pp. ix-xxviii; Joseph Ritson, p. 329; she also wrote a companion poem in the dedication to Elizabeth called "To the Angell spirit of the most excellent Sir Phillip Sidney"; Sir John Harington, *Nugae,* II, 172 and 407-410.

18. Gervase Babington, *A Briefe Conference betwixt mans frailitie and faith* (London, 1584); and *A Profitable Exposition of the Lords Prayer* (London, 1588).

19. Sir John Harington, *Nugae,* II, 407, note 4; Joseph Ritson, p. 239; J.C.A. Rathmell.

20. Anthony Esler, p. 115.

21. C. S. Lewis, *English Literature in the Sixteenth Century Excluding Drama* (Oxford, 1954), p. 331; Roger Howell, p. 168; A. C. Hamilton, *Sir Philip Sidney* (Cambridge, Mass., 1977), p. 171; Kenneth T. Rowe, "The Countess of Pembroke's Editorship of the *Arcadia*," *Publication of the Modern Language Association,* LIV (1939), 126; at least one of her contemporaries was unhappy with the 1593 edition of the *Arcadia*; see Frances A. Yates, *John Florio* (Cambridge, 1934), pp. 200-204.

22. G. F. Waller, *The Triumph of Death,* pp. iii, 11-12 and 15; Hoyt T. Hudson, "Penelope Devereux as Sidney's Stella," *Huntington Library Bulletin,* VII (1935), 91-129; Jean Robertson, ed., *The Countess of Pembroke's "Arcadia,"* (New York, 1973), pp. 296-297; Roger Howell, p. 164; Lisle Cecil John, pp. 8 and 18; Frances Berkeley Young, "The Triumph of Death," *Publication of the Modern Language Association,* XXVII (1912), 51.

23. Alice Luce, *The Countess of Pembroke's Antonie* (Weimar, 1897), pp. 24 and 28; Theodore Spenser, "The Elizabethan Malcontents," *John Quincy Adams Memorial Studies,* ed. James G. McManaway, Giles E. Dawson, and Edwin E. Willoughby (Washington, D.C., 1948), pp. 524-525; Alfred Horatio Upham, *The French Influence in English Literature* (Reprint, 1965), p. 5.

24. Frances Campbell Young, *Mary Sidney,* pp. 144-147; Alexander M. Witherspoon, *The Influence of Robert Garnier on Elizabethan Drama* (New Haven, Conn., 1924), pp. iii, 13, 80, and 184; Lewis Soens, p. 45; V. W. Beauchamp, "Sidney's Sister as Translator of Garnier," *Renaissance News,* X (1957), 9; Alice Luce, pp. 33-34; Francis R. Johnson, "Shakespearian Imagery and Senecan Imitation," *Joseph Quincy Adams Memorial Studies,* p. 38; recently, M. E. Lamb, "The Myth of the Countess of Pembroke: The Dramatic Circle," *Yearbook of English Studies,* XII (1981), pp. 194-202 has argued persuasively that Lady Pembroke did not set out to reform the stage and that caution must be used in making references to her "circle" and to her "influence."

25. Frederick Samuel Boas, *Sir Philip Sidney, Representative Elizabethan* (London, 1955), p. 38; G. F. Waller, *The Triumph of Death,* pp. 53, 61, and 63 and "Mary Sidney's '. . . Two Shepherds,'" *American Notes & Queries,* IX (1971), 100-102; Francis Davison, *A Poetical Rhapsody,* ed. Edward Hyde Rollins (Cambridge, Mass., 1931), pp. 15-17; Edmund Spenser, *The Works of Edmund Spenser,* 8 vols. (Baltimore, 1947), VII (1), 186.

26. Nicholas Breton, *A Pilgrimage,* dedication, and *A Divine Poem divided into two Partes: The Ravisht Soule and the Blessed Weeper* (London, 1601), dedication; Edwin Miller, *The Professional Writer in Elizabethan England* (Cambridge, Mass., 1959), p. 45.

27. Samuel Daniel, *The Complete Works,* 5 vols. (London, 1885), I, xvi-xxii; *The Tragedy of Cleopatra* (London, 1593), dedication; and *Delia* (London, 1592), dedication; George K. Brady, *Samuel Daniel: A Critical Study* (Urbana, Ill., 1923), p. 3; Joan Rees, *Samuel Daniel, A Critical and Biographical Study* (Liverpool, 1964); Sidney Lee, *The*

French Renaissance in England (Oxford, 1910), p. 444; Lisle Cecil John, p. 18; see also David M. Bergeron, "Women as Patrons of English Renaissance Drama," *Patronage in the Renaissance,* ed. Guy Fitch Lytle and Stephen Orgel (Princeton, 1981), pp. 285-290.

28. Roger Howell, p. 157; Edmund Spenser, VII(i), 185; VII(ii), 161 and 284; and VIII, 142.

29. John Buxton, p. 24; Thomas Nashe, "Christ's Tears," *The Works of Thomas Nashe,* 5 vols. (Reprint, 1958), II, dedication, quoted by Violet A. Wilson, *Society Women of Shakespeare's Time* (London, 1924), pp. 137-138; Victorinus Trigelius, *Proceedings In The Harmonie of King Davids Harp,* trans. Richard Robinson (London, 1595); F. P. Wilson, "Some Notes on Authors and Patrons in Tudor and Stuart Times," *John Quincy Adams Memorial Studies,* p. 556; David M. Bergeron, pp. 274-290.

30. Clara Gebert, ed., *An Anthology of Elizabethan Dedications and Prefaces* (Reprint, 1966), p. 25; Richard Puttenham, p. 209; one other contemporary noblewoman, Elizabeth Knyvett, the wife of Thomas, third Earl of Lincoln, published in 1622 *The Countess of Lincoln's Nursery,* (London, 1622).

31. Anne Dowriche, *The French Historie,* (London, 1589), was not included here because of its essentially religious preoccupation; Anne Wheathill, *A handfull of holesome (though homelie) hearbs* (London, 1584), dedication; Isabella Whitney, *A sweet Nosegay or pleasant Posye* (London, 1573); Margaret Tyler, *The mirror of princely deeds and knighthood* (London, 1578); Jane Anger, *Jane Anger her Protection for Women* (London, 1589).

32. Geoffrey Whitney, *A Choice of Emblems,* ed. Henry Green (Reprint, 1967), pp. vii-xi; Isabella Whitney, *The Copy of a Letter lately written in meeter by a yonge Gentelwoman to her unconstant Lover* (London, 1567); for a recent, sympathetic review of Whitney, see Betty Travitsky, *The Paradise of Women: Writings by Englishwomen of the Renaissance* (Westport, Conn., 1981), pp. 117-127.

33. E. D. MacKerness, "Margaret Tyler: An Elizabethan Feminist," *Notes & Queries,* CXC (1964), 112-113; Thomas Whythorne, *Autobiography,* ed. James M. Osborn (London, 1962), p. 140.

34. Helen A. Kahin, "Jane Anger and John Lyly," *Modern Language Quarterly,* VIII (1947), 31-35.

35. Elizabeth S. Bier, "Education of English Women under the Stuarts," M.A. thesis, University of California at Berkeley, 1926, pp. 47-50; Margaret Roper had no surviving granddaughters through the female line; for a reference to one of More's great-grand-children through the male line, see Timothy J. McCann, "Catherine Bentley (More's great granddaughter) and Sussex," *Moreana,* XI (1974), 40-45.

36. Catherine Thysmans alias Tishem had four children by Wouter de Gruytere. Only the sex of one, Janus Gruter, has been identified. See Leonard Forster, *Janus Gruter's English Years* (Leiden, 1967), p. 2.

37. B. W. Beckingsale, *Burghley: Tudor Statesman, 1520-1598* (New York, 1967), p. 58. "William Lewin," *Dictionary of National Biography;* Joseph Ritson, p. 380; John Strype, *Annals of the Reformation,* 4 vols. (Oxford, 1824), II-i, 178 and IV, 473-476.

38. *Calendar of the Manuscripts of Salisbury of the Most Honourable the Marquis of Salisbury, Preserved at Hatfield House, Hertfordshire,* H.M.C., 2 vols. (London, 1883), I, 404 and 432; John Strype, *Annals,* III-ii, 129-130; Conyers Read, *Lord Burghley and Queen Elizabeth* (New York, 1960), p. 128.

39. Conyers Read, *Mr. Secretary Cecil and Queen Elizabeth* (New York, 1955), p. 436;

Eleanor Brewster, *Oxford, Courtier to the Queen* (New York, 1964), p. 184; Jan Van Dorsten, "Literary Patronage in Elizabethan England: The Early Phase," *Patronage in the Renaissance,* pp. 191-206.

40. *Calendar of the Manuscripts of Salisbury,* II, 220.

41. Amos Miller, *Sir Henry Killigrew: Elizabethan Soldier and Diplomat* (Leicester, 1963), p. 227; Vyvyan Jago, "Some Observations on a Monumental Inscription in the Parish Church of Landulph, Cornwall," *Archaeologia,* XVIII (1817), 91.

42. Jeremiah Holmes Wiffen, *Historical Memoirs of the House of Russell,* 2 vols. (London, 1833), I, 501; *Calendar of the Manuscripts of Salisbury,* IX, 251 and 350; Roy Strong, *The Cult of Elizabeth,* p. 25.

43. *Calendar of the Manuscripts of Salisbury,* VII, 267 and X, 121; Horatia Durant, *The Somerset Sequence* (London, 1951), pp. 45-52.

44. *Calendar of the Manuscripts of Salisbury,* VII, 267; Andrew Kippis, *Biographica Brittanica* (London, 1778), p. 99.

45. John Smyth, *The Berkeley Manuscripts. Lives of the Berkeleys,* ed. Sir John Maclean, 2 vols. (Gloucester, 1883), II, 336 and 382; Scipio Lentulo, *An Italian grammar written in Latin, turned into English by H. Grantham* (London, 1574), dedicatory letter.

46. P. M. Handover, *Arbella Stuart: Royal Lady of Hardwick* (London, 1957), p. 62; Ian McInnes, *Arabella* (London, 1968), p. 76; Leonard Howard, *A Collection of Letters and State Papers from the Original Manuscripts of Princes and Great Personages in the Two Last Centuries* (London, 1765), p. 303.

47. Sir John Harington, *A Tract on the Succession to the Crown,* ed. Clements R. Markham (London, 1880), p. 45; P. M. Handover, *Arbella,* p.134; *Calendar of State Papers Venetian,* IX, 529 and 565.

48. *Calendar of the Manuscripts of Salisbury,* XII, 583.

49. P. M. Handover, *Arbella,* p. 67; Ian McInnes, p. 29; David N. Durant, *Arbella Stuart, A Rival to the Queen* (London, 1978), p. 60; Rachel R. Reid, "The Political Influence of the 'North Parts' under the Later Tudors," *Tudor Studies,* ed. R. W. Seton-Watson (London, 1928), p. 229; Thomas Wilson, "The State of England," *Camden Miscellany,* vol. XVI, ed. F. J. Fisher, Camden Society, third series, vol. LII (London, 1936), pp. 2-3.

50. P. M. Handover, *Arbella,* p. 62; Sir John Harington, *Succession,* p. 46; John Bruce, ed., *Letters of Queen Elizabeth and King James VI of Scotland,* Camden Society, vol. XLVI (London, 1849), p. 72; Helen G. Stafford, *James VI of Scotland and the Throne of England* (New York, 1940), pp. 200-220 and 254.

51. William Harrison, *The Description of England,* ed. George Edelen (Ithaca, N.Y., 1968), pp. xv and 228; *Calendar of State Papers Spanish, Elizabeth,* III, 461.

52. Henry Peacham, *The Complete Gentleman,* ed. Virgil B. Heltzel (Ithaca, N.Y., 1968), p. 162.

53. William Harrison, p. 228.

54. John Nichols, *The Progresses and Public Processions of Queen Elizabeth,* 3 vols. (London, 1823), III, 18, 37, and 128; Ian McInnes, p. 81; C. A. Bradford, *Helena, Marchioness of Northampton* (London,1936), p. 45; Gunnar Sjogren, "Helena, Marchioness of Northampton," *History Today,* XXVIII (1978) 597-604.

55. Henry Peacham, p. 7; Fulke Greville, p. 223; a relative of one maid of honor, Lady Bridget Manners, who was described as "barren" of education, wrote that the Queen was well pleased with her when she arrived at court in 1588. See *The Manuscripts of his*

Grace the Duke of Rutland, H.M.C., 4 vols. (London, 1888-1905), I, 187, 191, and 256.

56. Jane Anger here is identified as a Protestant because there is no internal evidence in the text of her *Protection* to warrant her description as a Catholic; Philip Gawdy mentioned that a sister had a "smacke of the lattin." See I. H. Jeayes, ed. *Letters of Philip Gawdy of West Harling, Norfolk, and of London to Various Members of his Family, 1579-1616* (London, 1906), p. 66; even though Amelia Lanier's book was published in 1611 under the title of *Salve Deus Rex Judeorum,* she had no classical training; Ruth Hughey, "Cultural Interests of Women in England from 1524 to 1640 Indicated in the Writings of Women," Ph.D. dissertation, Cornell University, 1932, pp. 66-77; and "Elizabeth Grymeston and her *Miscellanea," The Library,* fourth series, XV (1934), 71-91; Charlotte Kohler, "The Elizabethan Woman of Letters," Ph.D. dissertation, University of Virginia, 1936, pp. 295-301; Elizabeth Grymeston, *Miscelanea, Meditations, Memoratives* (London, 1604); Sir Samuel Egerton Brydges, *Censura Literaria* (Reprint, 1966), V, 39-42; Mary R. Mahl and Helen Koon, *The Female Spectator* (Bloomington, Ind., 1977), pp. 52-54; see also Henry Foley, ed., *Records of the English Province of the Society of Jesus,* 7 vols. (London, 1875-1880), II, 445.

57. For a discussion of the Catholic nunneries, see Chapter 9; Margaret Roper had no granddaughters through the female line and records of her sisters' granddaughters through the female line are not available; Catherine S. Durrant, *A Link Between Flemish Mystics and English Martyrs* (London, 1925), pp. 230 and 422; John Gerard, *Narrative of Gunpowder Plot,* ed. John Morris, 2nd ed., (London, 1872), p. xliv, note 1.; Sir Henry Ellis, "Account of the Convent of English Nuns formerly settled at Louvain in South Brabant," *Archaeologia,* XXXVI (1855), 74-77; Dom Adam Hamilton, *The Chronicle of the English Augustinian Canonesses Regular of the Lateran at St. Monica's in Louvain,* 2 vols. (London, 1904), I, 22 and 33.

58. Harold St. Maur, *Annals of the Seymours* (London, 1902), p. 487; there is some question as to whether the sonnets John Soowthern attributed to the Countess of Oxford and to Queen Elizabeth were actually written by them. See John Soowthern, *Pandora,* ed. George B. Parks (New York, 1938), and Leicester Bradner, p. 26; Ruth Hughey, p. 48.

59. *The Poems of Henry Constable,* ed. Joan Grundy (Liverpool, 1960), p. 154.

8

Elizabethan Reformers

Since Protestantism has been a splendid kaleidoscope of beliefs and values from its inception, its fervent apostles appear in retrospect to have held in common only one opinion, a commitment to the eradication of Roman Catholicism. One important reason for the emergence of these differences was the regional and national variations imposed by governmental enactments, as in England where the Church was established by secular legislation rather than by religious decree. In 1559 this kingdom's national Church was authorized by two parliamentary statutes, one recognizing Queen Elizabeth as its Supreme Governor and the other mandating a uniform system of service and ceremony.

It was not until 1571 that Parliament enacted the Thirty-Nine Articles, a statement of faith that was heavily indebted to the Swiss reformed traditions. Throughout the Reformation English Protestants had maintained close ties with Huldreich Zwingli at Zurich and John Calvin at Geneva and their intellectual heirs, Heinrich Bullinger and Théodore de Béze, respectively. Because the English establishment was recognized as a true church by these leaders, most reformers believed that separation from its communion was a sin. The subsequent conflicts which gave rise to Puritanism, a dissident movement within the Elizabethan Church, arose over trivial rather than essential matters.[1]

It will be possible to assess the role of women in this Church and in its opposition only after guidelines have been established by which Puritanism may be distinguished from other varieties of Protestantism. This is a crucial step because there has long been a scholarly disagreement as to the precise meaning of Puritanism. After a statement of these definitions and a study of the activities of a few women reformers, a comparative review will be made of the social esteem of women in Protestant and Catholic cultures.

Although traditionally the word, Protestant, has been interpreted in a comprehensive way to include all members of the Church of England, its use here will be limited to those who were reformed. Before turning to their views, which are the major focus of this Chapter, it will be helpful for future reference to give some brief description of the other members. While these conforming unbelievers shared a mutual disinterest in theological issues, the diversity of their beliefs requires that they be divided into three subgroups: The lukewarm, who were prepared to attend any Christian establishment, the Church-Papists, who would have preferred a Catholic settlement, and the profane, who were ignorant of Christian teaching and often steeped in pagan superstitions. As every dedicated reformer was well aware, the unbelieving clergy and lay people greatly outnumbered the genuine Protestants. It was over the question of how to govern the Church in which they constituted a distinct minority that the reformers soon split into two major factions.[2]

As the exiles returned to join forces with churchmen who had remained in seclusion during Mary's reign, their many public defeats began with the new Queen's decision to assume the office of Supreme Governor of the Church. With the passage of the Act of Supremacy in 1559, the reformers lost the initiative in religious matters for Elizabeth generally refused to sanction parliamentary debates or public discussions about controversial Church issues. Not only did she require her priests to accept the lay supremacy, but she also expected them to use the Catholic vestments and ceremonies mandated by the Act of Uniformity. To some reformers an even greater grievance was her encouragement of the symbolism that associated her with the Virgin Mary. By 1600 the poet, John Dowland, could refer to her successful use of this symbolism in his Second Book of Airs:

> Vivat Eliza! for an Ave Mari!
> Long Live Eliza! instead of Hail Mary.[3]

Clearly, the Queen's goal was to ease the great mass of lukewarm, profane, and Papist subjects into her state Church by appealing to traditional practices, for she assumed that Protestant doctrine would be more palatable with the sugar coating of medieval vestments, ceremonies, and imagery.

It was the mandatory use of the Catholic portions of the prayerbook that generated bitter quarrels between the clergy and the episcopacy. Some of the churchmen, here called Anglicans, freely acknowledged the right of the Supreme Governor to require conformity on these non-essential matters while other clergy, here called Puritans, protested her decision to override individual consciences on trivial issues, such as vestments and services. Puritans argued in vain for the removal from the prayerbook of churching for women and of midwifery baptism. In neither case did the arguments arise from a more enlightened view of womanhood. They objected to the first of these two services because of its resemblance to the Jewish rite of purification and because of its popular association with pagan superstitions, such as the taboo preventing the reintroduction of new mothers into society until after their churching. Opposition to midwifery baptism arose from general Protestant hostility to the female administration of any sacrament and from fears that maintaining this service would lead the ignorant to conclude that infants were spiritually damned if they died before baptism. Many reformers also believed that Catholic parents were secretly having midwives of their faith baptize the healthy as well as the sick newborn infants.[4]

After the early Elizabethan bishops, following the lead of Matthew Parker, Archbishop of Canterbury, had moved reluctantly to enforce conformity in non-essential matters, some disgruntled churchmen began to respond by calling for the abolition of episcopacy. The attacks of these reformers had special significance when they were made in Parliament or at Cambridge University. The Queen was able to suppress legislative challenges to her authority, but it was more difficult for her to have members of the academic and clerical world silenced. A few, like Thomas Cartwright, the Lady Margaret Professor of Divinity at Cambridge, finally had to be expelled from office after they gave lectures supporting Presbyterian rule.

On the grassroots level some churchmen began to seek assistance in theological and ministerial matters at district meetings called prophesyings. Fearing that they posed a threat to her authority, the Queen decided to demand their outright suppression. When Parker's replacement at Canterbury, Edmund Grindal, refused to implement her orders which he believed were detrimental to the well-being of the Church, he was suspended from office. In 1583 with Grindal's death a new generation of far less tolerant bishops assumed control of the Church. The conflict between Anglicans, who were led by John Whitgift, Grindal's successor, and the Puritans, who were angered by their failure to win concessions on episcopal and ceremonial issues, became intense and acrimonious. To undermine the authority of the bishops, some of the outraged Puritans began to participate in an informal presbyterian structure, called a classis. The success of the classical movement in developing into a shadow church within the established Church vindicated Elizabeth's earlier hostility to the prophesyings, for the classes grew out of the district exercises. With the use of *ex officio* oaths in the Court of High Commission Whitgift was able to suppress this movement.[5]

There were other dissident Protestant groups. In 1593 three men were executed for writing and publishing the anonymous Martin Marprelate tracts, a series of scurrilous attacks against Archbishop Whitgift, John Aylmer of London, and other bishops. Some of the Martinist writers were associated with Robert Browne, a well-known leader of the Separatist movement that was also suppressed by Whitgift. Except for denying that the Church of England was a true church, Separatist belief was virtually identical to Puritan thought.[6]

Both of Whitgift's predecessors differed from him in the degree of their sympathy for Puritan scruples and in the extent of their esteem for the episcopacy. Essentially "latitudinarian," the first two Archbishops had believed that episcopal rule was a "thing indifferent" and merely a convenient way of administering the Church. Faced with the threat of its extinction by radical appeals to the scriptures, Whitgift had become convinced even before his translation to Canterbury that its historical validity made episcopacy the "most fit" government for the English Church. In two of his works, *Of the Laws of Ecclesiastical Polity* and *A Preface,* Richard Hooker, an important theoretician of the Church of England, later expressed ideas that supported Whitgift's belief. Answering Puritan arguments that the scriptures were the only valid religious source, Hooker asserted that Church tradition and history as well as the Bible could be used as an authority for decisions affecting ceremonies and government.[7]

In efforts to differentiate among the reformers on grounds other than Church ceremony and government, some scholars, including Patrick Collinson, have maintained that the Puritans were the "hotter sort," who felt their religion more deeply than other Protestants. In response to this, it should be noted that Whitgift and his colleagues demonstrated an intense enthusiasm for the Church. If they had not had great determination, it is difficult to see how they could have suppressed the Presbyterian movement. While the Anglicans did have a genuine inner warmth for their beliefs, the zeal of the Puritans was more visibly strident. This difference largely reflects the gulf between Puritan idealists who were generating their demands from a vantage point outside the established power structure and Anglican administrators who were attempting to govern a large social and religious institution by guidelines outlined in parliamentary statutes. The contrasting attitude of these reformers toward the problem of the non-preaching clergy, characterized as "dumb dogs" by the Puritans, is a prime example of this difference in viewpoint. Although Whitgift believed that the essence of a true church was "the preaching of the word of God and the right administration of the sacraments," to the disgust of the Puritans he not only refused to remove the non-preaching parsons from their benefices but also demanded conformity to the prayerbook by reformers who had genuine scruples about its Catholic elements.[8]

Another issue that has clouded the history of the English Reformation is the popular and literary assumption that the Puritans were more moralistic than the Anglicans. In fact, this pervasive mood or attitude toward life, which transcended doctrinal or theological beliefs and even national boundaries, was prevalent in most Tudor movements. From Sir Thomas More to Lord Burghley to Edward Dering, the Puritan preacher, this attitude held sway on such issues as gaming, dicing, and romance reading. In France from about 1630 these people were called *dévots*, a descriptive word that will sometimes be used here to avoid confusion.[9]

The Family of Love was also active in Elizabeth's reign until persecution forced it to go underground. A form of Anabaptism, its principal prophet in England was Henry Nicolas of Cologne, who translated three of his books into English in 1574 and 1575. Looked upon with horror as social and religious radicals by Anglicans, Puritans, and Roman Catholics, the Familists rejected infant baptism, considered personal revelation superior in authority to the Bible, and were Pelagians. Because secrecy was vital to their operations, little evidence has survived of their activities although, according to J. W. Martin, the group may have been "more widespread, better organized, and a greater source of concern" to the government than has previously been recognized.[10]

This survey of the Reformation was a necessary prelude to a discussion of the commitment of Englishwomen to Protestantism. Without it an attempt to identify their personal beliefs and to place their activities within the context of the Elizabethan period would have been difficult if not impossible. Even with it as a guide, their views cannot always be precisely determined partly because of lack of evidence but also because of the similarity of the ideal female model in Puritanism and Anglicanism. Despite the inferior nature of the evidence, some attempt must be made to assess the efforts of women reformers in England, for they were an active and vital force in every movement.

Among those who gathered in illegal assemblies, the women probably outnumbered the men. Unfortunately, there is little extant evidence about the female members of the Family of Love whose meetings were kept secret, but there are some records of women Separatists. The first firm information of Calvinist congregations meeting apart from the Church dates from 1567 when about one hundred men and women were seized at Plumbers' Hall in London for assembling to hear a sermon by their pastor, Ritchard Fitz. Scorned by the Puritans as well as the Anglicans, one Separatist woman, Anne Stubbe, wife to the writer, John Stubbe (whose hand was hacked off by the government in 1579 for publishing a statement against the proposed marriage of the Queen to Francis, Duke of Anjou) had the temerity to argue with Cartwright, the famous Presbyterian leader. In a letter to Cartwright, who was her brother-in-law, Stubbe explained that she refused to attend the Church of England because it had a great number of ministers "with no knowledge in the true faith," an allusion to its many "dumb dogs." Since he believed that it was a true Church, Cartwright responded: "Remember your frailty as a woman, and the small ordinary means of discerning exactly the truth. You have not the truth, because it is not taught you by some pastor under Christ."[11]

The most scandalous radical activity of the dissenters was the writing and the publishing of the Martin Marprelate tracts against episcopal rule. The success in publishing these secret, anonymous treatises in 1588 and 1589 depended largely upon the cooperation of women. One important member of this network of secrecy was a wealthy widow, Elizabeth Crane, who permitted the Martinist press to remain alternately at two of her homes between April and November, 1588. From May to August of the next year, the press was housed by Mrs. Roger Wigston, who "deliberately" kept her husband uninformed of its presence to protect him from arrest as an accomplice. Shortly after the press had been moved from the Wigston household, one of the Martinist publishers, John Penry, was seized while preparing still another edition. His capture led to the arrest of Elizabeth Crane and the Wigstons, but as Crane refused to answer any questions under oath, she was released while the Wigstons, who confessed, were imprisoned at her Majesty's pleasure. Mrs. Wigston was also fined £1,000 while Mr. Wigston paid 500 marks "for obeying his wife."[12]

While these court records provide information about Separatist activity, they seldom offer evidence of women whose only quarrel with the Church was the Catholic elements of its prayerbook. Most of the women indicted for violations which can be identified with Puritanism, as, for example, failing to participate in the churching service, were affiliated with the more radical reform groups.

Documents, such as letters, funeral sermons, and short biographies, with laudatory comments about the religious practices of women, also usually fail to give evidence of Puritanism, for the attributes which were commonly praised in this literature can be described generally as Protestant. They were lauded for participating in household and private devotions, for attending public services regularly and for heeding good preaching, for reading the scriptures daily, for supervising the religious education of the women of the household, for being charitable to their neighbors, for their humble, silent, and virtuous demeanor, and for accepting the spiritual leadership of their husbands. The women who could also be described as *dévots* were particularly admired. This silence about Church controversies may reflect the Protestant belief that it was the duty of women to seek the advice of their husbands in religious matters. Indeed, some married women, especially the wives of clergymen, may have found it convenient to adopt the views of their spouses, but independent evidence of female beliefs is essential to a firm identification of them as either Puritan or Anglican.[13]

Fortunately, there are some exceptions to the widespread failure of their contemporaries to discuss prayerbook controversies with women. In 1580, for example, Anthony Gilby, chaplain to Katherine, Lady Huntingdon, wrote a dedicatory letter to her in which he freely attacked the use of the wafer bread and the practice of kneeling at worship, two well-known Puritan complaints about the Anglican communion service. This epistle was published with his English translation of the Latin Psalms of Béze, the original of which had been dedicated to Lady Huntingdon's husband, a Yorkist claimant to the throne. It is reasonable to assume that Gilby chose to discuss those topics because as a member of her household, he was aware that Lady Huntingdon agreed with his opinions on those issues.[14]

In addition to the praise of letters and the indictments in courts, information about the religious views of women is available in diaries and journals. Some Protestants began to keep written accounts of their daily activities as part of their self-examinations on religious matters, a practice that they had adopted in its oral form from medieval Christians. While it was the custom of a wide range of reformers, including the Queen, to undergo self-examinations, it was unusual for them to maintain records of their assessments. Joining scholars who have believed that it was the Puritans who initiated this religious diary keeping as a substitution for the confessional, M. M. Knappen, the editor of two Puritan diaries, has concluded:

> An attitude predominately ethical, involving the individual in a methodical struggle for the Pietistic delight in a correct state of mind resulting in the fulfillment of all duties, both contemplative and active, is a better description of the Puritan character as illustrated by these documents.

The so-called Puritan character that emerges from these diaries was nothing more than a manifestation of the Protestant commitment to salvation. It was the "Pietistic delight in a correct state of mind" that led both Anglicans and Puritans to record their daily assessments and meditations.[15]

Of the three surviving diaries written by Elizabethan women, one belonged to Margaret Dakins Hoby who happened also to be a Puritan. Born in 1571 and reared in the home of Katherine, Lady Huntingdon, Dakins received a traditional training that was heavily influenced by Puritan thought. As the sole heiress of Arthur Dakins of Yorkshire, she was a much sought-after bride in her intermittent years as a single adult. After the death of Walter Devereux, a brother of the second Earl of Essex, whom she had married in 1589, she became the wife of Thomas Sidney, brother to the celebrated poet. When she was widowed for the second time in 1595, she agreed with reluctance to wed Thomas Posthumous Hoby, the impoverished younger son of Lady Elizabeth Russell, because she believed that his relatives at court, including Sir Robert Cecil, would be able to assist her in legal disputes about her inheritance.[16]

Married in 1596 the Hobys resided at Hackness in Yorkshire where from 1599 to 1605, she kept a record of her daily activities. While its modern editor believes that she began the journal to record her religious exercises, it is interesting to note that in her last entries she frequently failed to mention her daily devotions. Ending in 1605 about twenty-eight years before her death, the chronicle is a somewhat dry recitation of routine events, revealing "no real capacity for self-knowledge or ability in self-analysis," for the most introspection that Hoby allowed herself was an occasional assertion that she had not been attentive enough to the services.[17]

Since the private prayers, the household exercises, and the catechizing of the servants which were described in her diary were the routine activities of pious Protestants, they do not provide evidence of her Puritanism. It is only when attention is turned from household to public worship that her beliefs become manifestly clear, for on April 14, 1605, she wrote that the prayerbook was read in their parish church for the first time. Usually a regular churchgoer, on the few occasions when she was too ill to attend services, she lamented that her absence had deprived her of both "the word and the sacraments." Finally, it is almost certain that she was a *dévot,* for she did not attend plays when she visited London, she read only Christian works, and she and her husband were shocked when guests gambled in their home.[18]

Another of these journals was written by an Anglican, Anne Clifford, the sole surviving child of George, third Earl of Cumberland, and his wife, Margaret Russell, the youngest daughter of the second Earl of Bedford. In 1609 when Anne was nineteen, she became the bride of Richard Sackville, the future Earl of Dorset, and after his death, married Philip Herbert, Earl of Montgomery and Pembroke. Beginning with an autobiographical sketch in 1603, her diary proper covers the period from 1616 to 1619. While it was probably written for the purpose of preserving for her heirs an account of her struggle to win the family estates, which her father had bequeathed to her uncle, it also has some information about her religious habits. A dedicated Anglican, Lady Pembroke was brought up by her mother as a staunch supporter of the Church. She read the scriptures daily, participated in private devotions, supervised the religious education of her household, re-endowed an almshouse founded by her mother, and repaired and rebuilt chapels on her property. Although a pious Christian, she was not a *dévot*, for she chose to participate in masques at the Jacobean court.[19]

The third surviving journal of an Elizabethan woman was compiled by Grace Sherrington, one of three co-heiresses of her father, Sir Henry, of Laycock Abbey, Wiltshire who had been a conspirator with Thomas, Lord Seymour of Sudeley, in 1549. Because Sir Henry had died in 1553 shortly after her birth, she was raised by her mother, who beat her severely to instill "precepts of virtue" in her and provided her with an education that included reading and writing English, playing the lute, casting up accounts, and doing needlework. In 1567 when she was about fifteen, Grace became the wife of Anthony Mildmay, only after his father, Sir Walter, the Queen's Chancellor of the Exchequer, had first bribed his reluctant son to agree to the union. The subsequent marriage was an unhappy one, for Anthony was consistently neglectful of her. When he died in 1617, some three years before her own death, she wrote that she had never challenged his "worst worde or deed" and that they had parted in love and Christian charity.[20]

Even though her journal is chronologically the earliest of the three which were kept by Elizabethan women, it was left to the last for analysis here because it is totally and completely different in form from the other two. Begun in 1570 and continued at least until the death of her husband in 1617, it was interspersed with brief autobiographical statements although the primary function of its approximately one thousand pages, a length that has prevented its complete publication, was to record a series of undated meditations. After the birth of her daughter, Mary, in 1582, Lady Mildmay wrote that she wanted her child to read four books: the scriptures, John Fox's *Martyrs,* the *Imitation of Christ,* and Wolfgang Musculus' *Common places,* all of which had been given to her by her mother, Lady Sherrington. It was with great enthusiasm that Lady Mildmay recommended to her daughter the *Imitation,* which she described as her "Jacobs Ladder." Probably written by Thomas à Kempis, this Catholic work continued to be immensely popular after the Reformation and had a great influence on Protestant movements as late as the eighteenth century. She may well have owned a Protestant translation that appeared in 1563, the same year that the *Martyrs* of Foxe and an English version of Musculus were first published. Even though it is likely that she used this version of the *Imitation,* which is notable for its exclusion of the fourth section on the Lord's Supper, her admiration for the *Common places* of Musculus, a Lutheran exile, led her to refer in her meditations to the sacramental elements as "flesh" and "blood."[21]

There is little information in the journal about her specific religious views, except that she was a Protestant. While she greatly admired her father-in-law, the founder of Emmanuel College, the future center of Puritanism at Cambridge, she left no evidence that she favored those beliefs, although she did bequeath money to the foundation. She also had an indirect association with Oxford University, for one of the four books that she particularly admired had been published by an Anglican of Merton College. John Man, the translater of Musculus' *Common places,* admonished his readers to be obedient "to all orders prescribed . . . in this Realme," and warned them that "it were a greate Tyrannie . . . for any one Author writing his opinion in things disputable, to desier to be precislie followed." It is also clear from her own remarks that Lady Mildmay admired qualities not usually defined as Puritan or indeed as strict Anglican. In her journal she wrote:

> But if everyone were instructed in theyr duties one towards another, with the feare of God in theyr harts, exercising those vertues of meekeness, temperance, patience, chastitie, love & obedience; the spirit of God would never leave them until a peace were concluded betwixt them.

Finally, although she was pious, she was not a *dévot,* for she attended plays at court and did not absolutely forbid pleasures of the flesh such as gaming.[22]

While there are some major differences in the style and content of their diaries, these three writers did have attributes in common. They were all educated by their mothers or female guardians, studied the scriptures daily, participated in private and household devotions, wrote only in English, and were Protestants. It is interesting that they almost certainly belonged to three different reform groups within the Church as outlined in this Chapter. Along with many other earlier Anglicans, Lady Mildmay, the eldest diarist, was probably "latitudinarian" while Lady Hoby, who was educated in the 1580s when dissident belief was the most strident in Elizabeth's reign, was a Puritan, and Lady Pembroke, the youngest diarist, was a strict supporter of the Church.[23]

Although she served as head of the Church for about forty-four years, Elizabeth, like many of her female subjects, left little evidence of her doctrinal opinions. It can be assumed that, since she consistently defended the prayerbook against parliamentary, clerical, and literary assaults, she was personally comfortable with its format for public worship. Because of her steadfast refusal to permit statutory approval of clerical marriages and of divorces with remarriage possible, it can also be concluded that she reserved for matrimony a status only slightly below its sacramental position in the Roman Church, a view that was not shared by Puritans, and, indeed, by many Anglicans.[24]

The Queen refused to legalize clerical marriages by parliamentary statute as had her brother, Edward VI, because she preferred that her churchmen remain celibate. As a result of her conviction, the wives of the clergy had to endure inferior social rankings and a precarious legal position during her reign. Even the reformers, themselves, were divided on this issue although not along Puritan or Anglican lines. While most did favor permitting clerical marriage, many Anglicans, including Archbishop Whitgift, as well as some Puritans, like Richard

Rogers of Braintree, Essex, had a "lingering belief in the superiority of the single life."[25]

Even though many of the continental Protestants had permitted divorces with remarriage possible in extreme cases such as desertion or adultery, in England the old canon law remained in force, permitting only annulments of invalid marriages and a mensa et thoro separations of other unions. While some of the early Anglican churchmen would have permitted divorces with remarriage possible if the Queen had approved, most came to adopt her attitude. The issue tended to split along Puritan and Anglican lines although a few churchmen, like Joseph Hall, privately disagreed with the official policy on this issue.[26]

The continuation of the medieval divorce regulations caused immense financial hardship for women. The a mensa et thoro separations left them in vulnerable legal positions, for they were still technically wives without the power to make contracts or to purchase goods on credit. While all of their personal property, including their earnings, belonged to their husbands absolutely, wives could also not alienate their real estate without the permission of their estranged spouses. To avoid this tyranny, the Court of Chancery in 1581 did begin to apply the doctrine of the separate use to the question of land disposal, a solution that was not very helpful, for even in the late seventeenth century, when most of the basic principles of this doctrine were fully developed, these cases were sometimes bogged down in expensive delays. It was not until the passage of the Matrimonial Causes Act in 1857 that women could obtain divorces that left them entirely free of the control of their husbands.[27]

Except for the issue of marriage insolubility, there is no evidence of a general disagreement between Elizabethan Anglicans and Puritans on social issues affecting women. Indeed, in a recent study of English villagers of the early modern period, Margaret Spufford could find no economic, social, educational, or geographical correlation with religious views. It was neither a Puritan nor an Anglican but a Protestant ethic with which the great mass of Tudor women interacted. In the following study of a few issues that are vital to women, most especially family relationships, education, and witchcraft, evidence will be offered to dispel the long-held notion that Puritans held unique social attitudes toward women. After this review, attention will be turned to the popular assumption that Protestant women had greater social esteem than contemporary Catholic women.[28]

James T. Johnson and other scholars have argued that Puritanism fostered a new emphasis upon loving relationships between husbands and wives, but this was a concept that English Protestantism generally adapted from the tenets of Christian humanism. The Anglican position was officially stated in a Church homily that called for a "perpetually friendly fellowship" between spouses and concluded that wives who tried to please their husbands would find them more attentive and supportive in the home. The Protestants optimistically assumed that, if parents obtained the consent of their children before disposing of them in wedlock, marital alliances would be formed in which this mutual affection would readily grow and develop. While emphasizing the need for companionship, reminiscent of that which Adam and Eve shared before their expulsion from Paradise, the Puritans and Anglicans were careful to warn spouses against surrendering to lust in their carnal dealings. Many clergymen, as Richard Greaves and Richard T. Vann have recently pointed out, even warned spouses against enjoying sexual relations.[29]

There was in fact no Puritan family, only a Protestant ideal in which the father, who was sometimes referred to as a bishop, was expected to assume charge of all religious matters, making of his home a "spiritualized household." The family was the key to the social implementation of the Protestant program for the encouragement of lay participation in religious matters and for the limitation of priestly authority in domestic affairs. This shift in emphasis from the priest in the parish to father in the household is evident in the changing attitudes toward the presence of clergy in noble homes. In the pre-Reformation days of the sixteenth century, Margaret, Countess of Richmond, had employed several priests in her household but in the seventeenth century, the Countess of Pembroke chose to maintain no chaplains in residence.[30]

The Protestant family was a concept that most civil authorities could favor. Viewing households as the grassroots social institution, reformers claimed that the obedience owed by family members to the father or husband on the local level was analagous to that owed by the subject to the governor on the central level. In 1583 the newly installed Archbishop of Canterbury, John Whitgift, elaborated on this theory at St. Paul's Cathedral, informing the congregation that the obedience owed by the subject to the magistrate was like that owed by the wife to her husband, the child to his father, and the servant to his master. By contrast a Catholic catechism of the same period compared the Biblical commandment requiring children to honor their parents to the reverance due from all of God's creatures to "Our Prelates, Bishops, Ghostly Fathers and other spiritual rulers and governers in the Christian Church, that have cure & charge of soules." There was no such exhortation in Protestant catechisms.[31]

Although this family structure, recently termed "restricted patriarchal nuclear" by Lawrence Stone, was idealized in Protestant literature, it failed to become the dominant social form. While it was not likely to be present among conforming unbelievers or non-churchgoers, it may not even have been implemented successfully on a widespread basis among the reformers, themselves. Surely, the household standards set by churchmen, such as Dr. John Dove, were beyond the human capacity of most husbands to achieve. According to Dove, an Anglican who preached on this subject in 1601 at Paul's Cross, men had "more perfection," were more knowledgeable, and had more religious understanding than women because the male sex had been created in the image of God while the female sex had been created only in the image of man. It was, he explained, the husband's duty to conceal the infirmities of his wife and to "swallow up" the many indignities caused by her weakness, a pattern of behavior surely adopted only by long-suffering men married to equally long-suffering wives. The impact on women of this failure to popularize the "restricted patriarchal nuclear" family is a topic that will be addressed in more detail later in this Chapter.[32]

One of the many duties of the Protestant father was to oversee the devotions of the household and the religious education of its members. While he had the final responsibility for leading them in standard prayers and statements of faith and for teaching them to read the scriptures, his wife might ordinarily attend to the elementary education of the women and occasionally function as his deputy. It is interesting to note that Levin Schucking was forced to conclude that even though, as he believed, the position of women was generally improved in Protestant England, he could find no evidence that the woman's role as her husband's deputy in any way enhanced her esteem as a mother. His proof was in part the extant religious literature on family matters that either ignored the role of the mother altogether or treated her as a relatively unimportant family member.[33]

Because of its emphasis upon scripture reading, Protestantism has long been credited with boosting the literacy level of its adherents, but this conclusion needs to be reconsidered. Recent studies by David Cressy indicate not only that there was probably an educational recession in Elizabeth's reign but that the literacy rate of women, in particular, was extraordinarily low. Of female deponents in the diocesan court of Norwich between 1580 and 1604, for example, about ninety-five percent could not sign their names. This sampling unfortunately was composed of a mixture of women from all classes because it is impossible to identify their status unless their husband's names were specifically mentioned. The female rate was lower than that of the poorest male group for only about eighty-five percent of the laborers could not sign their names. Less than one percent of aristocratic men did not have that skill.[34]

There are some problems with accepting this and similar studies as indications of English literacy. First, it is not clear that the skills of a small group of people functioning as deponents and in other legal capacities can be applied in a general way to the population of a particular area, or, indeed, to that of the rest of the kingdom. Secondly, it is difficult to interpret what these people's ability to sign their names really meant. Some who had this skill probably could not write and perhaps not even read, while others who lacked this skill undoubtedly were able to read. Since it was scripture reading that the Protestants advocated, these statistics seem hardly relevant to a general discussion of the reformed impact on education.[35]

Although historians have been unable to determine a method by which reading ability can be quantified, it is reasonable to assume that far more people could read than could write or sign their names. Even conceding a higher reading rate, the conclusion that Protestantism had a significant impact upon educational achievement still must be challenged. There is abundant evidence that numerous people in this predominately oral society simply relied upon extensive memorization for their study of the Bible. A servant of John Bruen of Cheshire, who had learned the scriptures by heart, for example, was known as a "godly instructor and teacher of young professors." As long as doubts have been raised about the implementation in Elizabethan England of the "restricted patriarchal nuclear" family, it seems logical to question whether its accompanying household instruction was as widespread as has been believed.[36]

While some women may have learned to read solely because of the encouragement of Protestant theologians, it is indisputable that a huge percentage, perhaps as many as ninety-five percent, did not know enough about writing to sign their names. Apparently, the evidence in contemporary publications that writing was a proper skill for them to learn had very little impact on the content of their education. In addition to publishing a few secular works, several women, including the Queen, had a variety of religious compositions and translations printed. Even one or two Protestant schoolmasters, such as Richard Mulcaster, began to advocate that women be taught to read and to write in their households. In his *Positions,* printed in 1581, he suggested, after first admitting that the "bringing up of young maidens in any kynd of learning" was really only "an accessory by the way," that girls should be given as comprehensive and as demanding an academic education "as shall be needefull" to challenge their abilities and to meet their family's needs. Despite the appearance of this and other publications, the available evidence indicates that there was no widespread social commitment to teaching women the skill of writing.[37]

Although a few of the daughters of well-to-do parents did occasionally attend a petty school or even a grammar school for elementary training, most were limited to the educational opportunities available in their households. One important reason for the low female literacy rate was the Protestant failure to provide special schools for women who did not receive instruction in the home or who needed supplementary training. Only one reformer, Thomas Becon, had the foresight to argue that such institutions should be founded. In 1559 he proposed the establishment of public schools in which "honest, sage, wise, discreet, sober, grave and learned matrons" could teach young women to be virtuous and sober-minded, to be obedient to their husbands, to be loving to their children, and to be discreet and chaste housewives. Ignoring even a discussion of the most rudimentary academic training such as reading and writing, Becon's plan did not gain widespread approval partly because all-female institutions were too closely associated in Protestant thought with Catholic nunneries and female celibacy. While reformers were ready to admit that some men had the gift of celibacy, they were quick to deny that it was a gift natural to women. In this belief they adopted the view of medieval Catholics who had not considered virginity to be "an affirmation" of the being of a woman but her assumption of the "nature of the male."[38]

When more research is done on literacy rates in Catholic lands as well as in Protestant countries, it will probably be concluded that the educational level of the people of preindustrial societies depended less on the version of Christianity that they espoused than on other factors. Some recent research by John Bossy of Catholic communities on the continent indicates there was vigorous action on the part of local authorities to provide elementary instruction at the parish level. It is also instructive to note that seventeenth century Catholic movements, unparalleled in Protestant countries, led to the foundation of numerous teaching congregations for poor girls. Although the Protestant women of England did endow a few almshouses for their sex, most of their educational funds were donated to institutions for men. In 1589, for example, Frances Sidney, the widow of Thomas Radcliffe, third Earl of Sussex, bequeathed funds to endow Sidney Sussex College at Cambridge.[39]

While women had only secondary or supporting roles in Protestant theories on marriage and education, they held the leading or starring roles in reformed attitudes toward witchcraft, a crime that was more brutally punished in Protestant England than in the medieval period. Among all of the criminal laws the ones most pernicious and most selective in their enforcement were those regulating witchcraft, for over ninety-five percent of the defendants were women, mainly those who were old, poor, and powerless. Although at one time Puritans were blamed for the increased activity against witchcraft, it is now the accepted conclusion that their attitudes as a group are indistinguishable on this issue from those of other Protestants.[40]

Because the belief in witchcraft has been a universal one, transcending historical periods, national boundaries, and religious beliefs, scholars have increasingly turned to sociological studies for assistance in their investigation of this phenomenon. In Elizabethan England, for example, Keith Thomas and Alan Macfarlane have suggested that changes after the Reformation in attitudes toward the dispensing of charity led increasing numbers of people to accuse their poor, begging female neighbors of witchcraft. While social changes are important considerations, more attention needs to be directed toward the decision to transfer this crime from ecclesiastical to common law jurisdiction. As part of their laitization of the Church, the Henrician schismatics had decided in 1542 to make witchcraft a royal offense. Because records of cases heard under the authority of this statute, later repealed by the government of Edward VI, are unfortunately no longer extant, modern historians are limited to comparing the small number of cases in Church courts of the medieval and the early Tudor period with the much greater number that were heard in royal courts after 1563 when a second statute against witchcraft was passed. This is a crucial gap in the documentation, for it would be helpful to ascertain whether the number of trials in the Henrician period increased after the 1542 statute gave jurisdiction in this crime to royal courts.[41]

After the succession of Elizabeth, many Protestants (including Edmund Grindal who complained, "Our ecclesiastical punishment is too slender for so grevious offences . . .") welcomed the passage of the 1563 statute on witchcraft. While it is unlikely that the subsequent increases in judicial activity against this crime was the result of widespread solicitation on the part of royal officials, it is possible that access to the trial procedures of the common law was a major cause of these increased public confrontations. It is indicative of the reputation for thoroughness of the royal system that the first case in Essex under the 1563 statute was transferred there from an ecclesiastical court even though the Church continued to have concurrent jurisdiction on this offense. The difference in how witches were brought to justice in the two systems is relevant to the question of why the number of trials increased. In Church courts, unlike the royal courts, the defendants could testify in their own behalf, could undergo purgation rather than jury trial, and if convicted, could do penance and gain their freedom. In the more severe royal courts, the women were tried by all-male juries, were prejudiced by the right of hostile witnesses to testify about unnatural phenomena, and if convicted, were sentenced to one year's imprisonment and four appearances in the pillory for the first offense and given capital punishment for the second offense. It was not until juries refused to convict for this crime in the late Stuart period that the wave of trials came to an end. Even though they could no longer give public testimony against their neighbors in court, the English country folk retained a fear of witchcraft that led them to lynch old women for this offense until the late nineteenth century, about one hundred and fifty years after the last statute making it a crime was abolished in 1736. By transferring the jurisdiction over this superstition to state courts in 1563, the Protestants had made it possible for a society that had long believed in witchcraft to punish an unprecedented number of its alleged adherents. Given this perspective, even if the fear of this phenomenon did increase in the Reformation era, it still seems plausible to suggest that access to the common law courts was a contributing factor to the popularity of these trials.[42]

There were other public and private customs which had a selectively negative impact upon women. While requiring the female sex to be punished for the imaginary offense of witchcraft, the law maintained a loophole by which men who were literate could be relieved of penalties for commiting major offenses. Although it is true that beginning with the reign of Henry VII, several parliamentary statutes were enacted to limit the number of crimes in which benefit of clergy could be claimed, even in its reduced form, this privilege was not granted fully to women until the late seventeenth century. In addition, while most reformed churchmen frowned upon the practice of wife-beating, it remained so common in London that because of its noise a civic regulation forbade it after nine in the evening. It was apparently impossible to enforce a rule suspending this barbaric habit altogether even though it was officially condemned by the Church homily on matrimony.[43]

Even in the Church, itself, customs were continued which perpetuated the secondary social standing of the female sex. Not only could women hold almost no ecclesiastical office, but they were also relegated to special pews, a seating arrangement that was continued in some parishes until the nineteenth century. Even the foremost constructive thinker of the Church, Richard Hooker, in his discussion of the marriage ceremony, made the following comment about women: "the very imbecility of their nature and sex doth bind them, namely to be always directed guided and ordered by others. . . ."[44]

It is now necessary to review the assumption that Elizabethan women enjoyed greater social esteem than other European women. While contemporary reports have lacked unanimity on this issue, most recent historians, including Natalie Davis and Richard T. Vann, are in agreement that women enjoyed more liberty in Calvinist countries, like England, than in Catholic cultures. The evidence for this interpretation depends largely upon speculation about the impact of the Protestant decision to reject clerical celibacy with its implicit negative attitudes toward women. Following a brief investigation of this issue, the questions of why numerous women chose to join Protestant movements and of why the reformers were unable to implement the "restricted patriarchal nuclear" family in England will be addressed.[45]

Although the Protestant extension of marriage to the clergy was a recognition that only a few of the male sex had the gift of celibacy, it is not clear in England, at least, that this concession was accompanied by a significant "downgrading" of the Catholic concept that men had a "greater capacity for sexual discipline" than women. In contrast to the Catholic religion in which women remained free to become nuns while clergymen continued to take vows of celibacy, English-women were limited theologically to the vocation of matrimony while reformed churchmen were permitted a choice. They could enjoy respectable status as bachelors, as did John Whitgift, or they could choose to marry as did Edward Dering. When the Queen, who remained a highly visible but ineffectual role model for virginity, failed unsuccessfully to convince her clergymen to stay single, she refused to grant proper social and legal recognition to their wives, a policy supported by many of her subjects. The hostility to clerical marriage with its implicit assumption that the wives of parsons were sexual offenders lingered among English parishioners throughout the Tudor period.[46]

Traditionally, women had been drawn to Christianity by its promise of spiritual equality and by its offer of an earthly identity separate and distinct from that of their fathers and husbands. By their private confessions to priests, by their vows of celibacy, and by their mystical yearnings for "full union" with God, Catholic women had for centuries been disregarding family relationships. In this sense, "a woman never belonged wholly to her husband, was never completely defined in terms of her sexuality, for there was always the prior bond of the soul to God. . . ." In contrast, the Protestants, by supporting the family structure known as "restricted patriarchal nuclear" sought to define women entirely in terms of their sexuality. They insisted that the only natural state of women was as wives, whose duty included recognizing their husbands, already their legal guardians, as their spiritual advisers.[47]

In practice, this household standard was not widely adopted in England, a failure that can be credited both to the unwillingness of a vast number of male unbelievers to convert to Protestantism and to two inherent qualities in the internal make-up of the religion, itself: its diversity and its anti-clericalism. One insurmountable problem for reformed husbands was the existence of competing Protestant movements to which an Anglican woman seeking religious fulfillment might turn. While admonishing wives within their own groups to heed their spouses, these Separatist, Presbyterian, and Familist competitors did not hesitate to encourage a dissatisfied Anglican women to adopt their formula for salvation even if it meant ignoring the advice of her Anglican mate. Because of the Catholic elements in its prayerbook, the Church of England from its origins was resisted by various groups which women in defiance of their male relatives could and did join on the basis of a higher commitment to God.[48]

The second inherent quality of Protestantism that helped to undermine the widespread adoption of the "restricted patriarchal nuclear" family was, ironically, its anti-clerical bias. When laymen acquired important religious functions in a system that de-emphasized the power and authority of a male clerical elite, many laywomen, whose medieval ancestors had dared to seek mystical unions with God, began also to aspire to similar positions of authority. As females had traditionally been an important and vital element in splinter Christian groups, religious leaders who wished to gain followers began to permit if not to encourage women to perform ministerial functions. It is possible that Queen Elizabeth's role as lay head of the Church also served these women as a female model. By the 1640s and 1650s numerous Englishwomen were involved in organizing congregations in which they held pastoral and teaching positions, a result of the Reformation that neither John Calvin nor Thomas Cartwright nor John Whitgift would have tolerated.[49]

The final assessment must be that if, indeed, Englishwomen had greater esteem than other Christian women of this period, Protestantism only inadvertently encouraged that development because its goal was to grant women less freedom by withdrawing them into the family and away from the spiritual influence of the local parish priest or of the nunnery leadership. It was the failure to implement the "restricted patriarchal nuclear" family within the framework of a successfully enforced monopoly Protestant religion that may have led to an improved social position for Englishwomen, but even this interpretation must remain tentative until valid comparative studies of women of a wide variety of Reformation and Counter-Reformation cultures are completed. This assumption may well not stand up under intensive research any better than the long-held truism that because of their need to read the scriptures, Protestants manifested a greater interest in education than other Christians. Ultimately, it will surely be concluded that questions of women's social esteem, of their instruction, and of many other issues vital to their well-being were less related to the theology of Protestantism than to the dynamics of its outward struggles against unbelievers and the Roman Church and its internal search for a final, authoritative definition. In both endeavors it remained as it began, a splendid kaleidoscope of beliefs and values united only in opposition to the Devil's disciples and the Antichrist.

NOTES

1. The name, Puritan, was not adopted until late in the Elizabethan period. Early dissidents were often called precisionists; see Richard Greaves, *Society and Religion in*

Elizabethan England (Minneapolis, 1981), pp. 3-14; a dialogue about Puritan and Anglican definitions can be found in Paul Christianson, "Reformers and the Church under Elizabeth I and the Early Stuarts." *Journal of Ecclesiastical History,* XXXI (October, 1980), 463-482; and in the same issue, Patrick Collinson, "A Comment: Concerning the Name Puritan," 463-482.

2. Thomas H. Clancy, "Papist-Protestant-Puritan: English Religious Taxonomy, 1565-1665," *Recusant History,* XIII (1976), 239-253; R. C. Richardson, *Puritanism in North-West England: A Regional Study of the Diocese of Chester to 1642* (Manchester, 1972), p. 3; at least one contemporary doubted the wisdom of using Protestant to incorporate all churchgoers; see Sir John Harington, *A Tract on the Succession to the Crown* (London, 1880), pp. 5-7; in a sermon of 1619 Samuel Hieron argued that the "lukewarmness" of some churchgoers was worse than the "poperie" or "profaneness" of others. *The Sermons of Master Samuel Hieron* (London, 1620), p. 39.

3. Quoted by Frances Yates, *Astraea: The Imperial Theme in the Sixteenth Century* (London, 1975), p. 78.

4. James Vaux, *Church Folklore, A Record of Some Post Reformation Usages Now Mostly Obsolete,* 2nd ed. (London, 1902), p. 112; *The Sermons of Edwin Sandys,* ed. John Ayre (Cambridge, 1842), p. 328; Richard Hooker, *Of the Laws of Ecclesiastical Polity,* 2 vols. (New York, 1958), II, 259; W.P.M. Kennedy, *Elizabethan Episcopal Administration,* 3 vols. (Milwaukee, Wisc., 1924), I, cxii; R. H. Michel, "English Attitudes toward Women, 1640-1700," *Canadian Journal of History,* XIII (1978), 45.

5. W. J. Sheils, *The Puritans in the Diocese of Peterborough, 1558-1610,* Northampton Record Society, vol. XXX (Northampton, 1979), pp. 24-90; see also Patrick Collinson, *Archbishop Grindal, 1519-1583* (London, 1979); for a study of a classis, see Roland G. Usher, ed., *The Presbyterian Movement in the Reign of Queen Elizabeth as Illustrated by the Minute Book of the Dedham Classis, 1582-1589,* Royal Historical Society, third series, vol. VIII (London, 1905); Patrick McGrath, *Papist and Puritans under Elizabeth I* (New York, 1961), p. 159.

6. Michael R. Watts, *The Dissenters* (Oxford, 1978); Champlin Burrage, *The Early English Dissenters,* 2 vols. (Reprint, 1967); and John Waddington, *Congregational History* (London, 1874); see also William Pierce, *An Historical Introduction to the Marprelate Tracts* (London, 1908) and Donald J. McGinn, *John Penry and the Marprelate Controversy* (New Brunswick, N.J., 1966).

7. Roland Usher, *The Reconstruction of the English Church,* 2 vols. (New York, 1910), I, 70; W.D.J. Cargill Thompson, "Anthony Marten and the Elizabethan Debate on Episcopacy," *Essays in Modern English Church History in Memory of Norman Sykes,* ed. C. V. Bennett and J. D. Walsh (New York, 1966), pp. 47-56; Richard Hooker, I, 122.

8. Patrick Collinson, *The Elizabethan Puritan Movement,* (Berkeley, Calif., 1967), pp. 26-27; Millar Maclure, *The Paul's Cross Sermons, 1534-1642* (Toronto, 1958), p. 72; the phrase, "dumb doges," was also used by medieval friars. See Irvonwy Morgan, *The Godly Preachers of the Elizabethan Church* (London, 1965), p. 1; Norman Sykes, *Old Priest and New Presbyter* (Cambridge, 1956), pp. 9 and 39.

9. Ronald S. Crane, *The Vogue of Medieval Chivalric Romance during the English Renaissance* (Menasha, Wisc., 1919), pp. 11-17; for a recent discussion of the social morality of the *dévots* as it related to women's education, see Judith Taylor, "From Proselytizing to Social Reform: Three Generations of French Female Teaching Congregations, 1600-1720," Ph.D dissertation, Arizona State University, 1980, pp. 200-205;

for a discussion of this morality as a European phenomenon, see H. R. Trevor-Roper, "The General Crisis of the Seventeenth Century," *Crisis in Europe, 1560-1660,* ed. Trevor Aston (New York, 1967), pp. 85-102.

10. Peter Milward, *Religious Controversies of the Elizabethan Age* (London, 1977), p. 33; Ernest Belfort Bax, *The Rise and Fall of the Anabaptists* (New York, 1966), p. 357; John Strype, *Annals of the Reformation,* 4 vols. (Oxford, 1824), II-ii, 282-287; J. W. Martin, "Elizabethan Familists and other Separatists in the Guildford Area," *Bulletin of the Institute of Historical Research,* LI (1978), 90-93 and "Elizabeth Familists and English Separatism," *Journal of British Studies,* XX (1980), 53-73; Jean Dietz Moss, "Variations on a Theme: The Family of Love in Renaissance England," *Renaissance Quarterly,* XXXI (1978), 188-195.

11. M. M. Knappen, *Tudor Puritanism* (Chicago, 1939), p. 212; William Pierce, pp. 22 and 25; Champlin Burrage, II, 19; Michael R. Watts, p. 21; John Waddington, p. 19.

12. William Pierce, pp. 152 and 181-207; Eric St. John Brooks, *Sir Christopher Hatton: Queen Elizabeth's Favorite* (London, 1946), p. 340; Donald J. McGinn, pp. 97-111.

13. See, for instance, Samuel Clarke, *The Lives of Sundry Eminent People in this Later Age* (London, 1683) and *The Second Part of the Marrow of Ecclesiastical History* (London, 1650). In neither of these works did the celebrated Puritan minister differentiate in the private and public demeanor of the Anglican and Puritan women he praised for their virtue.

14. Claire Cross, *The Puritan Earl: The Life of Henry Hastings, Third Earl of Huntingdon* (New York, 1966), pp. 4-25; Théodore de Béze, *The Psalmes of David, Truely Opened and explaned,* trans. Anthony Gilby (London, 1580), dedication.

15. Patrick McGrath, p. 337; Keith Thomas, *Religion and the Decline of Magic— Studies in Popular Belief in Sixteenth and Seventeenth Century England* (London, 1971), p. 93; William Haller, *The Rise of Puritanism* (Paperback Reprint, 1972), p. 96; Richard Shacklock, *The Hatchet of Heresies* (Antwerp, 1565), dedication; M. M. Knappen, *Two Elizabethan Diaries* (Gloucester, Mass., 1966), p. 16.

16. Dorothy Meads, ed., *Diary of Lady Margaret Hoby* (London, 1930), pp. 4-5.

17. Ibid., pp. 34, 47, and 93.

18. Ibid., pp. 106, 118, and 270.

19. V. Sackville-West, *The Diary of Anne Clifford* (London, 1923), pp. ix-xxix. It is likely that many such diaries were kept, for as early as 1516 Erasmus suggested to a friend, who had trouble with his memory, to keep one. See *Erasmus and His Age: Selected Letters of Desiderius Erasmus,* ed. Hans J. Hillerbrand (New York, 1970), p. 103. See also George C. Williamson, *Lady Anne Clifford,* 2nd ed. (London, 1967); and R. T. Spence, "Lady Anne Clifford, Countess of Dorset, Pembroke, and Montgomery (1590-1676): A Reappraisal," *Northern History,* XV (1979), 43-65; Martin Holmes, *Proud, Northern Lady. Lady Anne Clifford, 1590-1676* (London, 1976), pp. 16-17 and 35; Edward Rainbow, Bishop of Carlisle, *A Sermon Preached at the Funeral of Anne, Countess of Pembroke, April 14, 1676* (London, 1677), pp. 18, 55, and 59; Amelia Lanier, daughter to Baptista Bassano and Margaret Johnson, married Captain Alfonso Lanier and in 1611 published *Salve Deus Rex Judeorum,* a work honoring many women but especially the Countess of Cumberland. Despite the book's interesting title, she did not know Latin. For information about Lanier, see A. L. Rowse, *Sex and Society in Shakespeare's Age: Simon Forman, The Astrologer* (New York, 1974), p. 99.

20. The Diary of Grace Mildmay, Northampton Public Library, p. 81; Rachael Weigall, "An Elizabethan Gentlewoman: The Journal of Lady Mildmay, circa 1570-1617, Un-

published," *Quarterly Review*, CCXV (1911), 119-138; Stanford Lehmberg, *Sir Walter Mildmay and Tudor Government* (Austin, Tex., 1965), pp. 77-78.

21. The Diary of Grace Mildmay, pp. 3 and 29; F. A. Wright and T. A. Sinclair, *A History of Later Latin Literature* (London, 1931), pp.359-360; David Crane, "English Translations of the *Imitatio Christi* in the Sixteenth and Seventeenth Centuries," *Recusant History*, XIII (1975-1976), 79-83.

22. Rachael Weigall, pp. 126-138; The Diary of Grace Mildmay, pp. 27, 32, 35, 61, and 73; Wolfgang Musculus, *Common places of Christian Religion* . . . , trans. John Man (London, 1563), Letter to the reader.

23. J. Cargill Thompson, pp. 47-56.

24. William P. Haugaard, *Elizabeth and the English Reformation* (New York, 1968), p. 201; Charles George and Katherine George, *The Protestant Mind of the English Reformation, 1570-1640* (Princeton, 1961), p. 265; M. M. Knappen, *Two Elizabethan Diaries*, p. 21.

25. See also William P. Haugaard, "Elizabeth Tudor's Book of Devotions: A Neglected Clue to the Queen's Life and Character," *Sixteenth Century Journal*, XII (1981), 79-106.

26. *The Works of the Right Reverend Joseph Hall, D.D.*, 10 vols. (Reprint, 1969), VII, 379.

27. Courtney Kenny, *The History of the Law of England as to the Effects of Marriage on Property and on the Wife's Legal Capacity* (London, 1879), p. 14; J. H. Baker, *An Introduction to English Legal History* (London, 1971), pp. 45-46 and 258-261; Sir William Holdsworth, *History of English Law*, 17 vols. (London, 1924), V, 310-311.

28. Margaret Spufford, *Contrasting Communities: English Villagers in the Sixteenth and Seventeenth Centuries* (London, 1974), p. 352.

29. James T. Johnson, "English Puritan Thought on the Ends of Marriage," *Church History*, XXXVIII (1969), 429-436; and Edmund Leites, "The Duty to Desire: Love, Friendship, and Sexuality in some Puritan theories of Marriage," *Journal of Social History*, XV (1982), 383-408; Margo Todd, "Humanists, Puritans, and the Spiritualized Household," *Church History*, IL (1980), 18-34; *The second Tome of Homilies* (London, 1577), p. 476; one writer on marriage argued that parents must get children's consent but must not marry them as they desire. See Charles Gibbon, *A Work worth the Reading . . . Wherein is Contayned, five profitable and pithy Questions, very expedient, as well for Parents to perceive howe to bestowe their children in Marriage* . . . (London, 1591), p. 7; Richard T. Vann, "Toward a New Life Style: Women in Pre-Industrial Capitalism," *Becoming Visible: Women in European History*, ed. Renate Bridenthal and Claudia Koonz (Boston, 1977), p. 199; Richard Greaves, pp. 228-235.

30. Margo Todd, pp. 18-34; one author on Puritanism saw so little difference between Anglican and Puritan views on the family that he relied heavily on the works of the Anglican minister, Jeremy Taylor, for his Puritan evidence. See Levin Schucking, *The Puritan Family* (New York, 1969); Thomas Wats, *The Entrie to Christianitie* (London, 1589), p. 26; Edwin Sandys, pp. 261-264.

31. John Strype, *The Life and Acts of John Whitgift*, 3 vols. (Oxford,1822), III, 74; Richard Greaves, p. 331; Richard Mulcaster, *Positions (1581)* (New York, 1971); p. 30; Laurence Vaux, *A Catechisme or Christian Doctrine*, English Recusant Literature, vol. II (Menston, Yorkshire, 1969), pp. 44 and 56.

32. Lawrence Stone, *The Family, Sex, and Marriage in England, 1500-1800* (New York, 1977), pp. 7 and 141; Kathleen M. Davies, "The Sacred Condition of Equality. How Original Were Puritan Doctrines of Marriage?" *Social History*, V (1977), 563-580;

for an example of a family in which the wife was the more religious of the marriage partners, see *The Reverend Oliver Heywood, His Autobiography,* ed. J. H. Turner (London, 1822), p. 19; Dr. Dove quoted by G. B. Harrison, *The Elizabethan Journals,* 2 vols. (Garden City, N.Y., 1965), III, 180; at least in Kent a large percentage of people were non-churchgoers. See Peter Clark, *English Provincial Society from the Reformation to the Revolution: Religion, Politics and Society in Kent, 1500-1640* (Hassocks, Sussex, 1977), p. 156.

33. Levin Schucking, pp. 87-88; for a rebuttal to this argument, see Betty S. Travitsky, "The New Mother of the English Renaissance," Ph.D. dissertation, St. John's University, 1976.

34. Wallace Notestein, "The English Woman, 1580-1650," *Studies in Social History,* ed. J. H. Plumb (New York, 1955), pp. 102-107; David Cressy, "Levels of Illiteracy in England, 1530-1730," *Historical Journal,* XX (1977), 19-23; and "Literacy in Pre-industrial England," *Societas,* IV (1974), 233-240; and *Literacy and the Social Order* (Cambridge, 1980), 128 and 145; Margaret Spufford, *Small Books and Pleasant Histories* (London, 1981), p. 19 estimated that between 1580 and 1700 only 11% of the women could sign their names.

35. Imogen Luxton, "The Reformation and Popular Culture," *Church and Society in England, Henry VIII to James I,* ed. Felicity Heal and Rosemary O'Day (Hamden, Conn., 1977), p. 74.

36. David Cressy, *Historical Journal,* pp. 19-23; and *Literacy,* pp. 1-167; Imogen Luxton, p. 74.

37. Several works were published in Thomas Bentley, *The Monument of Matrones* (London, 1582); see also Lady Elizabeth Tyrwhitt, *Morning and Evening Prayer* (London, 1574); Anne Wheathill, *A handfull of holesome hearbes* (London, 1584); Anne Dowriche, *The French Historie* (London, 1589); and Lady Katherine Knolles, *A heavenly Recreation* (London, 1569); this literature is discussed in Ruth Hughey, "Cultural Interests of Women in England from 1524 to 1640 Indicated in the Writings of Women," Ph.D. dissertation, Cornell University, 1932; Richard Mulcaster, pp. 133 and 168-187; Richard L. Greaves, *The Puritan Revolution and Educational Thought: Background for Reform* (New Brunswick, N.J., 1969), p. 54.

38. Thomas Becon, *The Catechism,* ed. John Ayre (Cambridge, 1844), pp. 376-378; Rosemary Ruether, ed., *Religion and Sexism* (New York, 1974), p. 234.

39. Judith Taylor, pp. 200 ff.; see Chapter 9 for a discussion of Mary Ward's schools; see also Christopher Haigh, *Reformation and Resistance in Tudor Lancashire* (London, 1975), p. 311 and John Bossy, "The Counter Reformation," *Past and Present,* XLVII (1970), 63-70.

40. E. William Monter, "Pedestal and State: Courtly Love and Witchcraft," *Becoming Visible,* p. 133; Keith Thomas, p. 499.

41. Keith Thomas, pp. 436-563; Alan Macfarlane, *Witchcraft in Tudor and Stuart England* (New York, 1970), pp. 8, 159, 187, 197, and 200.

42. Keith Thomas, pp. 245 and 438 ff.; Alan Macfarlane, p. 216; Philip Tyler, "The Church Courts at York and Witchcraft Prosecutions, 1567-1640," *Northern History,* IV (1969), 86 and 98; R. A. Marchant, *The Church Under the Law: Justice, Administration, and Discipline in the Diocese of York, 1560-1640* (Cambridge, 1969), p. 4; Ralph Houlbrooke, *Church Courts and People During the English Reformation* (Oxford, 1979), pp. 39-40; these penalties were for witchcraft that causes bodily harm. There were more stringent penalties for this crime if it led to death. See George Lyman Kittredge, *Witchcraft*

in Old and New England (Reprint, 1972) pp. 328-373; Alan R. Young, "Elizabeth Lowys: Witch and Social Victim, 1564," *History Today*, XXII (1972), 879; see *The Lady Falkland: Her Life From a MS. in the Imperial Archives at Lille,* ed. Richard Simpson (London, 1861), pp. 5-6 for an interesting confrontation with a confessed witch.

43. Felix Makower, *The Constitutional History and Constitution of the Church of England* (New York, 1895), p. 403; Sir James Fitz James Stephen, *A History of the Criminal Law of England,* 3 vols. (Reprint, 1964), I, 461-62; *Homilies,* p. 489; Cecily Wedgwood, *The King's Peace* (New York, 1969), p. 42; there were many more discriminatory and civil laws against women. For example, they continued to be burned for petty treason. See John Bellamy, *The Tudor Law of Treason* (Buffalo, 1979), p. 207; women did have the privilege of benefit of womb, but it only delayed execution until after childbirth had been accomplished; Penry Williams, *The Tudor Regime* (Oxford, 1979), p. 226.

44. James Vaux, pp. 30-32; Richard Hooker, I, 79 and II, 393.

45. In *De Republica Anglorum,* Thomas Smith argued that the women of France had more liberty than those in England, quoted by Ruth Kelso, *Doctrine for the Lady of the Renaissance* (Urbana, Ill., 1956), p. 267; for the views of foreigners in England, see for example, William B. Rye, ed., *England as Seen by Foreigners* (New York, 1967); Richard T. Vann, p. 211; Natalie Davis, *Society and Culture in Early Modern France* (Stanford, Calif., 1975), pp. 88 ff.; for a different view, see Traugott L. Richter, "Anti-feminism in English Literature, 1500-1660," Ph.D. dissertation, Northwestern University, 1934, pp. 74-75 and 251-256.

46. Natalie Davis, pp. 88-89.

47. Rosemary Ruether, p. 286; Robert Lerner, *Heresy of the Free Spirit in the Later Middle Ages* (Berkeley, Calif., 1972), p. 229.

48. See Jasper Ridley, *John Knox* (New York, 1968), pp. 132 and 263.

49. Claire Cross, " 'He-Goats before the Flocks,' a Note on the Part Played by Women in the Founding of some Civil War Churches," *Popular Belief and Practice,* ed. G. J. Cuming and Derek Baker (Cambridge, 1972), pp. 195-200; see also Christopher Hill, *The World Turned Upside Down* (New York, 1972); Keith Thomas, "Women and the Civil War Sects," *Past and Present,* XIII (1958), 46-62; E. M. Williams, "Women Preachers in the Civil War," *Journal of Modern History,* I (1929), 561-569; and Phyllis Mack, "Women as Prophets During the English Civil War," *Feminist Studies,* VIII (1982), 19-38. See also Jerome Nadelhaft, "English Woman's Sexual Civil War: Feminist Attitudes toward Men, Women, and Marriage, 1650-1740," *Journal of the History of Ideas,* XLIII (1982), 555-579.

9

The Catholic Women of Elizabethan England

In 1559 the parliamentary changes in the Church of England did not result in a widespread boycott of its services by Catholics because the government made it easy for them to conform. By law they were able to secure immunity from religious persecution merely by attending a vaguely familiar Sunday morning service that contained nothing specifically anti-Catholic. Often the parish incumbent who had been celebrating mass remained in office to preside over scripture readings, the reaffirmation of a creed that was reminiscent of the Roman one, and the saying of prayers which had largely been translated from medieval texts. Receiving conflicting advice from Roman pastors about the desirability of conformity, a majority of the English faithful for at least a decade after Elizabeth's succession chose to attend schismatic services to avoid social and religious ostracism. Although it failed to refer specifically to this controversial practice, the Papal Bull of 1570 that excommunicated and deposed the Queen finally served to convince some Catholics to shun Sunday worship. Others simply continued to obey the religious laws publicly while hearing mass privately.[1]

In 1568 William Allen endowed a seminary at Douai to train young Englishmen as missionary priests. This foundation was an important first step in achieving the goal of supplying replacements for the clandestine Marian priests whose deaths from natural causes had deprived the English of Catholic clergy. Between 1574 and 1580, when they were first joined by a few members of the Society of Jesus, about one hundred of Allen's students had returned home taking with them the message of the Counter Reformation against attendance at heretical services. Although they were not able to reconvert the kingdom, their strong stand on this issue slowly worked to coalesce the English faithful into a cohesive unit for religious action and survival as a minority sect.[2]

While the number of Jesuits in Elizabethan England remained small, probably less than twenty, their very presence created controversy, since many secular clergymen believed that the Jesuits, as members of a religious order, should be cloistered. The most active campaign to limit their activities was prompted by the appointment in 1598 of George Blackwell as the kingdom's first archpriest.

Outraged by the Papal decree that required Blackwell to consult with the Superior of the English Jesuits, some secular churchmen, known as Appellants, successfully secured the repeal of the directive in 1603. Within twenty years they had won the appointment of a bishop from among their group to replace the archpriest.[3]

Although greatly affected by these clerical disputes, the lay Catholics were usually not personally involved in them. These loyal worshippers can be divided into three major groups: the nobility of the old feudal North who in 1569 tried to restore the Roman faith by challenging the Queen's authority, the recusant peerage and their relatives who gave shelter to both the Jesuits and the Douai graduates, and the small independent "seigneurial" families who sometimes heard mass and received the sacraments from priests in the homes of their wealthier neighbors. Although the twelve-pence fine levied for absence at Sunday morning worship generally served to limit the recusants to members of the aristocracy, the peripatetic missionaries were able to find refuge in the households of craftsmen and skilled workers in a few towns such as York and Durham.[4]

In this Chapter the efforts of Englishwomen on behalf of the Roman faith will be integrated into a study of the Catholic struggle for survival against a persecuting government and into an analysis of its search for a definition of its proper political and social goals. The role of these women as rebels in 1569, as members of wealthy households in which the mass continued to be celebrated, and as recusants generally will be explored in some detail. Finally, a survey of some of the female institutions that were founded on the continent and a comparison of the social esteem of English Catholic and Protestant women will be made.

Angered by the policies of Sir William Cecil, a number of courtiers joined with a few Catholic lords of the North in a conspiracy to force Queen Elizabeth to assent to a marriage between her prisoner, Mary, Queen of Scots, and Thomas Howard, fourth Duke of Norfolk. With the support of the northern nobility, led by Charles Neville, sixth Earl of Westmoreland, and Thomas Percy, seventh Earl of Northumberland, Norfolk planned to replace Cecil as adviser to Elizabeth and to persuade her to limit the English succession to his betrothed, the Scottish Queen. In November, 1569 the Earls stumbled into a revolt that was so disorganized it was suppressed within six weeks. While both of them immediately found refuge in Scotland, Northumberland was captured and returned to England for trial in 1572 and Westmoreland fled to the continent where he lived as a Spanish pensioner until his death in 1601.[5]

Rachel Reid and other historians have usually described the Earls as less enthusiastic than their wives about the rebellion. This statement is far less true of Jane, Lady Westmoreland, a sister of Norfolk, than it is of Anne, Lady Northumberland, who actually fled into exile with her husband. Despite Lady Northumberland's flight, it has been Lady Westmoreland, who has most frequently been accused of promoting this futile effort. According to Sir George Bowes, a royal commissioner investigating the outbreak, when Lady Westmoreland learned that many of the conspirators were planning to desert her husband, she "braste owte agaynste them with great curses, . . . for their unhappye counseling, as nowe, there cowerd flyghte." It was shortly after this altercation that the Rising was set in motion by the march of the rebel forces on Durham.[6]

Angered by her outburst, Northumberland was eager to blame Lady West-moreland for the entire fray after his capture and return to England in 1572. He charged that when he had suggested dispersing the troops and leaving everyone to provide for himself, she had fulminated that he and his advisers would be "shamed for ever" and would have to "seeke holes to creep into." Without her public abuse, he hinted to his interrogators, the subsequent march on Durham would never have occurred. Upon being informed of this version of her comments, the Countess sent a letter of denial to William, Lord Burghley, suggesting that had she been able to reply directly to Northumberland, her "playn and trewe defences should have put hym to sylence, whose wrytng wyll remayn a perpetuall wytness of my evyll behaviour."[7]

Her protest that his writing would remain a "perpetual wytness" against her was prophetic, for even though there is no other evidence of any complicity on her part in the planning of the revolt, most scholars have not questioned the truthfulness of Northumberland's accusations. Although Lady Westmoreland probably had approved of her brother's scheme to marry the Queen of Scots, there is no evidence that she had ever been an active advocate of that alliance. Like Norfolk, she was by inclination a Protestant, and if her opinion had been sought at the outset, she probably would have encouraged the rebels to drop all activity on behalf of the Scottish marriage. The most reasonable interpretation of her outburst is that it occurred because she could not conceal her anger when she learned that after first encouraging her husband in treasonable activities, his fellow conspirators had then proposed cowardly to forsake him. Following the suppression of their Rising, Lady Westmoreland was exonerated by a royal investigation and granted an annual allowance that was increased from £200 to £300 in 1577 to help her provide for her four girls.[8]

While Lady Westmoreland remained in England, Lady Northumberland lived in exile. The daughter of the second Earl of Worcester, she chose to join her husband in the rebellion and to flee with him into Scotland even though she was in the early stages of pregnancy. While he was subsequently captured and returned to England, she escaped to the continent to become a Spanish pensioner and to continue her efforts on behalf of the Scottish Queen. Her actions indicate that, unlike Lady Westmoreland, she had been entirely supportive of her husband's involvement in the Rising.[9]

Following the 1569 revolt, there were at least four more unsuccessful con-spiracies on behalf of Mary, Queen of Scots, but their support did not center in northern England, for the last bastion of feudal independence had crumbled with the defeat and flight of the Earls. In 1572 Elizabeth appointed Henry Hastings, the third Earl of Huntingdon, as Lord President of the Council of the North. Known as the "hammer of the northern Catholics," he became by virtue of this office the most powerful nobleman in the region. Like other Tudor rebellions, the Rising of 1569 had done "as much to strengthen as to restrain the Crown," for it had given Elizabeth's government an excuse and an opportunity to destroy the northern feudal power that had been so closely identified with Catholicism.[10]

After the execution of Queen Mary in 1587 there was no obvious Catholic successor. While some southern nobles preferred Arbella Stuart to her cousin, James VI, the heir of the Scottish Queen, others favored the claims of Isabella, the daughter of Philip II of Spain and the wife of Cardinal Archduke Albert of Austria. In 1593 Robert Doleman (a pen name for English Jesuit Robert Persons), and some of his associates, discussed this dispute in a publication entitled *A Conference about the Next Succession to the Crowne of England.* Although Doleman failed to make an outright declaration in the Infanta's favor, his book served to encourage her candidacy by pointing out the flaws in the other claims. At the English court the prominence of Robert Devereux, the second Earl of Essex, who had become an ally of James VI, led even Sir Robert Cecil to show an interest in the Infanta as successor, but after Essex's death in 1601, Cecil and his advisers promoted the King of Scotland's candidacy. Although Arbella continued to have some support among the recusants, a majority of them openly endorsed the ascension of James to the English throne in 1603 and later disassociated themselves from the Gunpowder Plot, an abortive attempt by a few extremist Catholics to blow up this King and his ministers on the opening day of the second session of his first Parliament in 1605. Before the end of his reign, Catholics loyal to his government had been able to convince their Church to acknowledge them as members in good standing, but their struggle in England for emancipation and for full recognition of their allegiance was not won until the nineteenth century.[11]

Despite the attempts of a few clergymen and their associates to undermine the Protestant rule, the secular and the Jesuit priests were concerned primarily with ministering to the spiritual needs of the loyal English recusant population. In fact, the controversies that affected most Catholics were religious rather than political, for as representatives of the Counter Reformation, the missionaries sought to update devotional observances in their native land. Their attempt to limit fast days, to prevent attendance at heretical churches, to introduce new methods of prayer and to effect other reforms led to disputes with the more traditional Marian clergy and their lay supporters. Like the Protestants, the post-Tridentine English Catholics were often in disagreement over non-essential religious practices.[12]

To be successful in England the missionaries needed the support of the aristocracy, especially the peerage. As the nobility were usually exempted from taking the oath of supremacy to the Queen, their ability to practice their faith free from governmental interference depended largely upon convincing her of their personal loyalty. A few noble recusants, among them Anthony Browne, first Viscount Montague, and his wife, Magdalen, were able to demonstrate effectively to her Majesty that their devotion to the Roman cause was not incompatible with their allegiance to her government. In 1591 the Queen was even pleased to honor their home with a visit despite their well-known refusal to obey her religious laws.[13]

Born in 1539 to William, fourth Lord Dacre of Gilsland, and his wife, Elizabeth Talbot, daughter to the Earl of Shrewsbury, Lady Montague had been educated by her mother and had at the age of sixteen won an appointment as Maid of Honor to Queen Mary. At Court she had captured the attention of Lord Montague and with the permission of the Queen had become his second wife. Married to him for thirty-six years, the Viscountess "served him as her lord" and bore him four surviving children. According to Richard Smith, who became her confessor after she was widowed in 1592, she supervised a pious Catholic household of eighty persons at her home near Hastings, popularly referred to as "Little Rome" by her neighbors. Here Father Thomas More, the great-grandson of the martyr, and two other resident priests, provided pre-Tridentine services that included three daily masses. Her proven allegiance to Elizabeth served to protect her in an informal way from imprisonment, but after the succession of James in 1603, she was granted a public letter freeing her officially from all religious "molestation." Until her death in 1609, she provided a shelter for Allen's missionaries and maintained a private chapel in her home for the worship of scores of her neighbors.[14]

The Howards were less fortunate than the Brownes. In 1572 the fourth Duke of Norfolk, like his father Surrey the poet, was beheaded for challenging the power of the Tudor dynasty. While his conviction for treason prevented his heir, Philip, by his first wife, Mary Fitzalan, the learned daughter of the twelfth Earl of Arundel, from becoming the fifth Howard to hold the ducal title, that son was permitted to inherit the earldom of his maternal grandfather. About a year before Norfolk's execution, Philip was married at the age of fourteen to his stepsister, Anne Dacre, a co-heiress of Thomas, fifth Lord Dacre of Gilsland, and his wife, Elizabeth Leybourne, who had become the Duke's third bride after the death of Dacre in 1566. Raised as a Protestant, Philip attended Cambridge University and then went to court to lead a life that was "prodigal" and "dissipated."[15]

Because she had been educated by her maternal grandmother as a "religious good Catholick," his young wife, Anne, was able to resist the attempts of her stepfather, Norfolk, and his sister, Lady Westmoreland, to dissuade her from privately adhering to the Roman faith. After Norfolk's death, the ill-usage of Philip, who had deserted her for the royal court, prompted her to seek shelter at the home of his maternal grandfather Arundel. With the encouragement of the Earl's learned daughter, Jane, and her husband, John, sixth Lord Lumley, Anne's inclination for the religion of her youth was strengthened. Following Arundel's death in 1580, she was reconciled with Philip and gave birth to a daughter in 1583 and a son in 1585.[16]

Before their second child was born, the new Earl of Arundel and his Countess had received communion as members of the Roman Church from William Weston, a Jesuit priest. A short time later his lordship resolved to flee abroad to escape the "constant danger to his material and spiritual welfare," but when his plans were discovered by the government in 1585, he was incarcerated in the Tower where for the next few years he remained isolated from his family. Charged with having a mass celebrated for the success of the Armada in 1588, he was convicted of treason but was kept in prison until his death in 1595 from natural causes. While Lady Arundel dedicated the remainder of her life to her faith, it has been her husband's death that has inspired the Church, for in 1970 he was canonized.[17]

After his arrest the Countess assumed control of their children and of their household. At the death in 1599 of her daughter, Elizabeth, whose education in Latin and French she had supervised, Lady Arundel consoled herself with the knowledge that her child had ascended into heaven. As the Countess had adopted a practice of avoiding contact with most of her heretical relatives, she was greatly disappointed to learn of the adult conversion of her son, Thomas, to Protestantism. Reportedly, she found the death of her daughter easier to bear than the apostasy of her son. In the spirit of the *dévots,* she enforced rules against idleness and drunkenness in her household and also encouraged participation in daily devotions, including two masses and diligent self-examinations.[18]

One of her most important advisers was Robert Southwell, who had returned in 1586 as a Jesuit priest to his native land where he had first sought shelter with a trusted Catholic peer, William, third Lord Vaux. While he was at his lordship's home, Southwell was nearly captured in a raid that occurred during his celebration of mass. At the age of eleven, Frances Burrows, a member of the household, saved him from arrest by bravely defying the pursuivants despite their threats of bodily harm for her refusal to assist them. Shortly after this narrow escape, he accepted the invitation of Lady Arundel to reside at her home in the Strand and to use a house of hers in Acton, Middlesex. With her husband's conviction in 1589, the Countess was evicted from her London home and unable to provide further housing for the priest, although until her death in 1630 she continued to aid him and the Catholic cause whenever she could. She endowed the English College of the Society at Ghent, gave an £80 dowry to a relative who wished to join St. Ursula's convent at Louvain, and arranged for the posthumous publication of the *Epistle of Comfort* by Southwell, "one of the truly great religious writers of the Elizabethan period." Written about 1587, only a few years before his martyrdom, his *Epistle* was based on letters he had sent to comfort her husband during his imprisonment. In the book his readers were reminded that the Church was increased rather than diminished by persecution and that martyrdom was an honorable estate for it was a "sure sign" of membership in "God's Flock."[19]

The family with whom Southwell had first sought refuge had already been punished for disobeying the religious laws, as its head, Lord Vaux had suffered imprisonment for aiding Edmund Campion, the first Jesuit to be executed in England. Undaunted by the threat of reprisal, the Vaux family continued to give assistance to the missionaries. Soon after his arrival in 1586, Henry Garnet, the new Jesuit Superior, found shelter in the Leicestershire home of his lordship's widowed daughter, Eleanor Brooksby. Living with Brooksby was her younger sister, Anne, who decided to adopt the Jesuit cause as her vocation from her first meeting with Garnet, a fortunate decision for the Society, as a few years later it was her efforts alone that saved their entire mission from destruction. In 1591 when following their usual practice all of the Jesuits were assembled together to renew their vows, Anne bravely succeeded in delaying some government searchers long enough for the priests to disperse and to escape. Her close association with Garnet led the royal government to arrest her as well as him for complicity in the Gunpowder Plot of 1605. Although through the confessional, Father Garnet had been made aware of the plot to blow up the King and his ministers, neither he nor Vaux was a party to the conspiracy. In an attempt to discredit them both, their interrogators accused the two of "moral misconduct," but, in fact, she had decided that she could better serve her religion by taking private vows and administering to the needs of the Church through obedience to Garnet than she could by professing in a convent abroad. After her release and his execution, she continued to aid the Jesuit cause by housing other priests, like John Gerard, and by supporting one of their schools for boys. Her lifelong devotion to her faith was recognized in at least two book dedications written by eminent Jesuits.[20]

From 1580 the heightened government persecution caused the members of small, independent families, whether they were recusants or schismatics, to turn increasingly to households of the Catholic peerage and their relatives for religious leadership. Generally the faith was able to survive in areas where the social and economic influence of the recusant nobility, who sheltered and supported the seminary priests, proved to be particularly strong. Because public mass was forbidden, a noble household thus became by default "a parish by itself," a circumstance that gave the laity opportunities to control the quality and content of religious services and to prevent the clergy from widespread participation in politics. On the continent where it had greater freedom than in England, the post-Tridentine Church was attempting to enforce parochial conformity by abolishing the private celebration of mass, by encouraging priests to catechize and to educate children in the parish, and by limiting the importance of family gatherings in the administration of sacraments, such as baptism.[21]

That the services were performed privately in England made it possible for women to influence religious practices. Those bereft of husbands through widowhood or imprisonment could take charge, as did Lady Arundel and Lady Montague, of household devotions. Other women who were married to husbands with a lukewarm faith were able to assume the spiritual leadership of their families. Catholicism like Protestantism had numerous women with greater fervency than their husbands, a circumstance to which Persons referred in 1580 when he wrote of men whose wives were threatening to leave them if they attended heretical services. In addition, information from a variety of sources indicates that many women remained home as recusants while their husbands chose to conform. Although a few of these men were, no doubt, reformers, some were surely sympathizers of the Roman faith. Evidence for concluding that numerous church-going husbands were actually schismatics can be found in autobiographical statements of young Jesuit novices. While several English students admitted that their conforming fathers privately supported the recusant habits of their mothers, only a few were aware of any dissatisfaction with such recusancy.[22]

A household with a recusant wife was one in which the support system of the faith was readily available to a schismatic husband. The family could maintain close contact with other Catholics, could marry their children to members of their religion, and could have access to private services and to the assistance of priests. Although they were aware that for these personal reasons, some conforming husbands tolerated and even encouraged the recalcitrance of their spouses, royal officials were slow to require wifely attendance at Church because of two major problems. First, it was useless to fine the women since all of their property was controlled by their churchgoing husbands and second, it seemed improper to deprive law-abiding gentlemen of conjugal rights by imprisoning their wives. As the women made up a large proportion of the recusant population, the government finally was forced to require that male heads of households insist upon conformity from all of their dependents. When numerous women still refused to attend public services, some of them were imprisoned and a statute was approved making it legal to penalize their husbands £10 a month for harboring recusants. Neither of these actions met with any great success, and after the discovery of the Gunpowder Plot, even more stringent laws were enacted in a futile attempt to decrease the number of female recusants. In 1606 the dower rights of Catholic widows were limited and access to public office was denied to men with spouses of this faith.[23]

Recusant women who were married to reformers rather than to schismatics had a special household ministry to perform, as it was possible for them by living an inspiring and Godly life to convert their husbands to Catholicism. Dorothy Constable proved to be one of many successful domestic missionaries, for after her marriage in 1597 to a reformer, Roger Lawson, she won over him and most of the household to her religion. Raised as a Protestant, Grace Babthorpe's decision to become a Catholic had a similar effect upon her spouse and his relatives. Her husband not only converted to her faith but also joined her in supporting the cause so vigorously that they were both forced to flee to Louvain where following his death in 1617 she was professed at St. Monica's.[24]

Even when both spouses were loyal Catholics, the women had a major input into religious practices. It was they who made the preparations for the fasts and celebrations of their faith and who often instructed the members of the household in catechisms and in Latin prayers. In addition, they retained a remarkable degree of religious independence, for while submission to their husbands as their lords in worldly matters was expected, wives were not required to seek advice about their salvation or to ask spiritual questions of anyone other than a clergyman. Indeed, the popular English catechism of Laurence Vaux strongly urged obedience on the part of both men and women to the church pastors. This authoritarian difference may partially explain why schismatic husbands challenged the decision of royal officials to hold them responsible for the recalcitrance of their wives.[25]

The government had moved slowly to limit recusancy among women because simple heresy was not its major concern. The Catholics most feared by the royal officials and the ones for whom capital punishment was usually reserved were the missionaries and the laypeople who aided them. Viewed as political agents of a deposing Papacy, the clergy were more severely affected by the persecution than any other single group, for slightly more than two-thirds of the 189 Elizabethan martyrs were from their class. Only fifty-eight laymen and three laywomen were executed, a death statistic that contrasts sharply with that of the Marian persecution in which the majority of the victims were poor laypeople, including a significant number of women.[26]

All three of the Catholic female martyrs, two of whom were executed at Tyburn and one in York, have been canonized by the Roman Catholic Church. They were accused of giving aid and comfort to the seminary priests, a charge of which they were all guilty. The least well known of the three, Margaret Ward, a gentlewoman, was executed at Tyburn in 1588 after several days of torture for providing Father Richard Watson with a rope and a ladder that made possible his escape from Bridewell Prison. The other woman to hang at Tyburn was Anne Line of Essex, who had been born a Protestant but who had converted to Catholicism upon her marriage to a man of the Roman faith. Her husband subsequently fled to the Low Countries where he lived as a Spanish pensioner until his death in 1594. Left behind in England, Line overcame many illnesses including dropsy and migraine headaches to dedicate her life to the Jesuit cause. She kept house for John Gerard until 1597 when she moved into a London flat provided for her by the Jesuits in which she gave religious instruction to children. Adjoining her dwelling were two other buildings, one for the use of a resident chaplain and the other for the shelter of traveling priests; it was in this complex that the pursuivants discovered her early in February, 1601. Because her body had been gravely weakened by her illnesses, she had to be carried in a chair to her trial at Old Bailey where she was convicted of harboring priests. In late February "with great joy" she kissed the gallows, said her prayers, and died bravely.[27]

Although the survival of Catholicism was greatly dependent upon aristocratic support, it had strong adherents in some northern towns such as Durham and York. The most famous of the three women martyrs, Margaret Clitherow, was a citizen of York, a town second only to London in its number of victims largely because of the zealous activities of the Lord Presidents of the North, beginning with the administration of the Earl of Huntingdon. Like many other recalcitrant women of this town, Margaret was married to a Protestant tradesman. In 1571 at the age of fifteen, she had become the wife of John Clitherow, a butcher and churchwarden, who was a widower of about twice her age. It was not until some three years after their marriage that she had been converted to Catholicism, a religious commitment that was deep and sincere. According to Father John Mush's account of her life that was written in 1586, she had a "singular reverence to the priesthood" and served as a powerful religious example to her family and friends. Besides her private morning and evening devotions, she prayed one hour with her children every day and fasted regularly.[28]

On several occasions between 1577 and 1584 she was incarcerated in prison where she fasted four days a week, learned how to read and to write English, and studied Catholic works selected to aid her in her meditations. Each time she was released, she immediately returned to her former practice of sheltering clergymen and of inviting friends to the celebration of mass at her home. When she was arrested for harboring priests in March, 1586, she deliberately prevented the government from setting her trial date by refusing to enter into the record a plea of innocent or guilty, a refusal that was based on her fervent wish to protect the jurors from having her death on their consciences. It was a decision that led to the implementation of *peine forte et dure,* a common law procedure that required victims to be tortured with weights until they died or agreed to plead. Accordingly, she was stripped naked and laid down with her back on the ground; a linen cloth was spread across her body on which was placed a door that was piled high with as much weight as she could bear. On the third day of this torture, she was pressed to death.[29]

Widely circulated in manuscript, Father Mush's story of her ordeal was eagerly read by contemporary Catholics. Among those greatly inspired by her heroism was Jane Wiseman, a widow of Braddocks, Essex, who longed to join Clitherow in a similar death. When in 1598 after years of harboring priests in her home, Wiseman was arrested, she, too, refused to plead, but the Queen intervened to prevent this determined woman from also undergoing *peine forte et dure*. Wiseman remained in prison until the succession of James I when she and a few other women were pardoned. That she had been a tremendous inspiration to those who knew her and a powerful role model for her own children there is no doubt, for all four of her daughters professed in nunneries on the continent.[30]

While hundreds of young men went abroad for religious training, only a few young women were offered a similar educational opportunity. One reason parents hesitated to send their daughters to the continent was the paucity of institutions that could receive them. The Bridgittine house of Syon, the only English nunnery to survive the Reformation, had undergone harrowing experiences in exile. Between 1559 and 1580, when its nuns finally departed for Rouen, they had been forced to move their headquarters to three different Flemish locations. Despite these difficulties, a few intrepid young women continued to join the house; among them were Barbara and Anne, the two eldest of Jane Wiseman's daughters, one of whom was later elected its abbess and the other its prioress. After fourteen years in Rouen, the nuns moved to Lisbon where the convent remained until it was transferred to England in the nineteenth century.[31]

The Flemish Augustinian convent of St. Ursula's at Louvain with its boarding school for young ladies proved to be the most popular haven for Tudor women although even it received only about thirty English novices. In 1548 Elizabeth Woodford, an ex-nun of Burnham Abbey in Buckinghamshire, became the first

Englishwoman to join these canonesses. Three years later Margaret and Helen, the two youngest children of Sir Thomas More's dependents, John Clement and Margaret Gigs, were sent to Woodford for their religious training. In 1557 after Helen's return home, her sister, Margaret, was professed at the convent, a commitment that inaugurated a distinguished career, for in 1569, at the age of thirty, she was elected its prioress. As the leader of the Flemish canonesses, Mother Margaret helped them to survive floods, plague, and religious warfare, but after almost thirty years in office, she had to relinquish her position because of blindness. Her resignation disappointed her twenty-four compatriots who had joined the house under her leadership, for they were reluctant to accept the authority of the Flemish religious who succeeded her.[32]

In 1609 Mother Clement and six compatriots founded an Augustinian convent for Englishwomen in Louvain, called St. Monica's. While four canonesses, among them Anne Clitherow, a daughter of the York martyr, chose to remain at St. Ursula's, the other twenty Englishwomen, including Frances Burrows, who had as a child saved the life of Southwell, and Mary and Bridget, the two youngest daughters of Jane Wiseman, decided to transfer to the new house. Its first elected prioress was Mary Wiseman, who was later honored in a book dedication for her "singular learning." Initially a boarding school for ladies was maintained at St. Monica's, but in modern times its professed have chosen to devote themselves entirely to the Adoration of the Blessed Sacrament. During the French Revolution they relocated in their homeland while the colony they had founded at Bruges in 1629 was returned to the town of its origin after dwelling in England from 1794 to 1803.[33]

The support of Mother Clement for an English Augustinian house may well have been prompted by the example of a Benedictine convent established at Louvain in 1598 by eight of her compatriots. The leader of the group that founded the Abbey of the Glorious Assumption of our Lady, the first all-English nunnery on the continent, was Mary Percy, daughter to the exiled Countess of Northumberland. Because of her youth, Mary, who was later praised in three book dedications for her nobility, piety, and goodness, could not be elected the first superior of the house but she was chosen as its second abbess. While most laywomen in England were somewhat isolated from the clerical disputes of their faith, the professed on the continent, especially in this nunnery, became intimately involved in the power struggle between the Appellants and the Jesuits. Political controversies in the Brussels house, which were ultimately won by the Appellants' supporters, led to the establishment of an anti-Jesuit affiliation at Cambrai in 1623 and a pro-Jesuit one at Ghent in 1624. After the outbreak of the French Revolution these nuns were forced to retire to England.[34]

In the early Stuart period many other houses for Englishwomen were endowed on the continent, none of which was more controversial than Mary Ward's Institute. The daughter of recusant parents, Ward had been born in Yorkshire in 1585 and had been sent at the age of five to the home of her Catholic grandmother with whom she had lived until she was about ten years old. During those formative years she had not only studied Italian, but had also learned Latin well enough to write it fluently and to read the literature of the Church Fathers. Throughout her life she was keenly aware of the religious persecution of her family and friends, including the imprisonment of her grandmother and of Grace Babthorpe, a relative with whom she resided during her teenage years.[35]

In 1606 when she was twenty-one years old, Ward sought advice about her religious vocation from the leaders of the English Jesuit College at St. Omer. She may have been drawn to this town by a desire to observe for herself the educational methods of this famous school. Established in 1593 by Robert Persons, St. Omer's followed policies first set out by Ignatius Loyola, the founder of the Society, and updated in 1599 by its fifth General, Claudio Aquaviva. The first male religious order to assign a large number of its members exclusively to the teaching of youth, the Jesuits adopted this ministry as a means of attaining the "glory of God and the salvation of souls." Although their curricula, which combined medieval philosophical speculation with humanistic studies, were remarkable, it was their instructional methods that won the greater attention. By offering a graduated order of advanced studies, by respecting the varying capacities of students, and by insisting upon class attendance, they gave direction and structure to the educational process. While the students sometimes suffered corporal punishment, they were usually motivated to learn by more pleasant techniques such as the promise of holidays and the freedom to write and to produce drama for the public.[36]

Some of the Jesuits suggested to Ward that she ought to join the local Walloon Order of St. Clare's, whose lay sisters went into town daily to beg under the Third Rule of St. Francis. As one of their lay sisters, Ward suffered this humbling experience for one year before rejecting it as her vocation. Leaving the convent in 1607, she journeyed to Gravelines where she used her dowry to found an English house of St. Clares under the Second Rule of St. Francis. Here her interests in education and in the methods of the Society of Jesus became immediately evident, for besides planning a boarding school, she asked the Jesuits of St. Omer's to act as her spiritual directors. Although subsequent disputes with the newly elected abbess led Ward to return to her homeland, the convent she endowed survived to be relocated in England during the French Revolution.[37]

By 1609 she was back at St. Omer with five women compatriots who had taken vows with her to devote their lives to good works, especially to female education. Intending not only to found a boarding school for young ladies, but also a free day school for poor girls, the first to be established by Englishwomen living in community, Ward hoped to adopt for her new order the Institute of the Blessed Virgin Mary, a female Rule based on the constitutions of the Society of Jesus. It was to include three extraordinary provisions: obedience to a Superior who was to be held responsible directly to the Pontiff, non-enclosure, and semi-religious dress. Even if the disapproving General of the Society of Jesus had favored a female branch of his order, her decision to pattern the Institute after his organization would still have aroused opposition. Partly because of their exemption from episcopal obedience, a status that Ward was seeking for the Institute, the Jesuits were widely distrusted and sometimes feared. In her own country where Catholicism was struggling for survival, the Appellants were locked in a battle with the Jesuits for control of the recusant population, a duel that from 1603 the secular clergy had been winning. Without support from the episcopate or from most of the Jesuits, Ward's chances for success depended almost exclusively upon her own personal contacts with members of the Papal curia.[38]

The other two provisions were equally controversial. It was her contention that the only viable way to provide instruction to girls of the lower classes was to give them access to free day schools and to permit their teachers to move out of the convent into the towns to acquaint themselves with the daily lives of their charges. Since one aim of this education was religious conversion, these personal contacts were viewed as essential to the Institute's success, but Ward's plans for community involvement contradicted the canon of the Council of Trent, recently enforced upon other female teaching congregations, such as the Ursulines, that required all women in orders to follow strict enclosure. As this requirement was extended to the pupils as well as to their teachers, its enforcement precluded the operation of free day schools for poor students. In addition, there were many who believed that the Jesuit instructional methods, particularly the production of public plays, were inappropriate for women.[39]

The decison of Ward not to adopt conventual dress presented another public relations problem, for it infuriated many of the Catholic faithful, especially in England, where she and her associates traveled in the disguise of gentlewomen to avoid capture by pursuivants. Even her semi-religious habit that allowed for the free movement that was impossible in the traditional garb of the religious, evoked "surprise and disgust" in many circles. When Ward dared to wear the costume to Rome for a personal audience with Pope Gregory XV, her appearance alienated many who might otherwise have supported her efforts.[40]

While awaiting a Papal decision on her new Rule, Ward and her followers, popularly known as Jesuitesses, founded ten houses of their order. Some of their schools were immediately successful: the one at Vienna, for example, soon had an enrollment of five hundred pupils. Despite this favorable reception, Church politics and preconceived notions of the proper role of the female religious finally combined to deprive Ward of her dream. In 1631 instead of approving her Rule, an action that would have given her official authority to raise funds and to enforce discipline over the Institute's houses that were scattered from England to Italy, Pope Urban VIII issued a Bull of Suppression and ordered her arrested as a heretic. Undaunted by her two months in prison, Ward decided to continue her ministry since the Bull had not specifically forbidden women, who lived together under private vows, to provide for the educational needs of young girls. Continuing to maintain branches at Munich and London, she drew the professed from the other convents together into a new mother house at Rome. Her Second Institute proved to be more lasting than the first, for about sixty years after her death in 1645, her followers were able to gain the privileges of a Congregation of the Church, although they were forbidden to recognize her as their foundress, a decision that was not overturned until 1909 when there were over two hundred houses with six thousand members teaching seventy thousand young girls in boarding and day schools.[41]

In 1609 exactly sixty years after the Protestant clergyman, Thomas Becon, had foreseen the need for free educational facilities for women, Mary Ward was the first English person to achieve that goal although the persecution drastically limited the Institute's activities in her homeland. While Protestantism has been credited with encouraging basic literacy because of its insistence on Bible study, in the late Reformation period in England it failed to offer practical means by which poor women could gain the skills of reading and writing. Later, after the death of James I, some reformers did begin to formulate serious plans for girls' schools but societal hostility to female communities prevented the implementation of these schemes. Among the authors of these projects were Lady Lettice, Viscountess Falkland, and Mary Astell, two staunch royalists and defenders of the Church of England.[42]

Because of the deplorable state of women's education, the schools of Ward's Institute, unlike those of the Society of Jesus, were at first forced to focus on elementary subjects. It was only after the girls had learned the customary Latin vocabulary for worship and had gained the skills of reading and writing that some of them were given the opportunity to study Latin grammar, composition, and rhetoric. By contemporary standards this was a radical program, as the traditional boarding schools in houses such as St. Monica's did not attempt to teach grammar. According to its set of directions dated in 1697, every morning for one and one-fourth hours the girls were to study two languages, Latin for their religious exercises and French, and every afternoon for two hours they were to devote themselves to needlework, painting, and music. Following afternoon vespers, they turned again to French and to the memorization of prayers and the catechism. In addition, they also learned other elementary subjects such as writing and arithmetic. Except for Church Latin, St. Monica's curriculum was not greatly dissimilar to that offered to young Catholic ladies in their homes in England. That Ward, herself, was aware of the revolutionary character of her educational program with its advanced Latin training, is evident from comments in some of her extant letters. In 1627, for example, she was forced to deny to an anxious correspondent that the learning of Latin by girls would lead to their loss of virtue. She hoped, she continued, to make the knowledge of that language "so common to all as there will be no cause of complaining." Since there is almost no extant evidence of her educational efforts in England, a detailed study of them is impossible, but in Chapter 10 a review will be made of her classical skills and of those of the Englishwomen of her generation.[43]

It is now necessary to compare and to contrast the social standing of Catholic and Protestant women of England. An entrenched Protestant assumption is that its focus on marriage and the family rather quickly led to a heightened social esteem for reformed women. In fact, the belief that the divine plan for humanity had limited woman to matrimony and that their husbands had been granted authority over them in religious matters as well as in worldly concerns can be more easily defined as a social demotion for women. The Protestant advocacy of the "spiritualized household" officially established a secondary religious status for wives by requiring them to apply to their husbands rather than to priests for spiritual assistance. It was primarily because this household ideal broke down amidst the competition of reformed sects and the widespread indifference of men that in practice many married women were able to assert their religious independence and even to assume some of the spiritual authority that had been transferred from churchmen to laymen by the reformers.[44]

Catholic women participated in marriages which, according to the extremely popular English catechism of Laurence Vaux, were in some respects similar to the Anglican companionate version:

> Matrimonie, which is a signe of the conjunction of Christ & the Church, his spouse, is a Sacrament, whereby man and woman joyned togather in marriage do enter into an undivided society or feloship of life, and grace is given therein, both honestly and Christianly to procreate children and to bring them up godly and also to avoyde filthy lust and incontinence.[45]

While the Anglicans had dropped matrimony from their list of sacraments, they had retained the Catholic requirement that spouses of valid unions remained lawfully wedded until their death. In practice, a more significant difference in these two faiths was their disagreement about sexual abstinence, for, unlike the Protestants, the Catholics believed that it was possible and even desirable for husbands and wives to overcome sexual temptations. Contending that God had recognized celibacy as the perfect human state, they permitted consenting partners to dwell together in continence, a marital relationship outlawed by the reformers.

By the tenets of their religion Catholic women were also not bound to seek spiritual advice from their husbands, for their faith had no concept comparable to the "spiritualized household" of the Protestants. While Catholics were expected to reverence and to obey the pastors of their Church, this authoritarian structure broke down in England because of the persecution. Consequently, women and men of this faith were able to take advantage of the private focus of religious worship to establish a control over the insecure and fugitive priesthood similar to that already gained by Protestants over their ministers. As a result, it is unlikely that the social and religious standing of most Catholic married women in Elizabethan England was in practice radically different from that of their Protestant counterparts.[46]

A greater difference in the social esteem of the women of these two faiths can be found among those who were single. Despite the example of their celebrated Virgin Queen, Protestant women were expected to marry, and those who did not were denied the respect of their communities. With their reluctance to believe that women could remain celibate, reformers continued to hold traditional biases against female communal life, not doubting that the word nun was synonymous with the word whore. The Counter Reformation had by contrast renewed the Catholic dedication to celibate life for women. Many of the professed in the English convents on the continent had clearly taken the vows in response to the "dynamic force" of the persecution. They were often the children of mothers or of mother-substitutes who had provided them with strong religious role models, for the Countess of Northumberland, Margaret Clitherow, Jane Wiseman, and Margaret Gigs Clement all had daughters who lived in convents abroad. Serving as a great inspiration to the people of their faith, they established and maintained their houses in foreign countries under difficult and trying circumstances.[47]

Although Catholic women were permitted to live in honorable celibacy, it was assumed that they would have more difficulty than men in restraining their emotions. Because of this perceived weakness, the Council of Trent had insisted on strict enclosure of the professed in an attempt to protect them from worldly temptations. When Mary Ward sought to win the right to mingle freely in the communities in which her poor students lived, it was partly this widespread prejudice that defeated her. In neither the Catholic nor the Protestant reform movements were women recognized as equal to men in their ability to deal with their sexuality.

The social experience of professed women was quite different from that of their sex at home. Although single laywomen in England did visit together at Church and on social and family occasions, they were usually separated from each other in households. The major exception to this isolation was at court but attendants of the Queen were more famous for their competition for royal favors than for their communal cooperation. Because in theory the place of married women was at home, caring for their families, wives, too, were prevented from organizing together to accomplish social changes. While it is true that many women did suffer for their faith during the various Tudor persecutions, unless they were professed, they did so by individual action or under male leadership. By contrast, in convents and especially in teaching congregations, women were taught to work with one another for religious and sometimes for social endeavors. By their interaction with each other, they were able to develop leadership qualities and by their efforts, their failures as well as their successes, they were able to foster a community feeling of self-worth, of self-esteem, and of pride in being female. Women of the Counter Reformation who gained respect for themselves as women found it a natural step to direct their attention toward the social rehabilitation of the impoverished young of their sex whose plight had generally been neglected or ignored.

It can even be argued that this kind of community interaction transformed Mary Ward into the first known English feminist. Insisting on establishing a Rule that permitted her to function as a female Jesuit in all capacities except the priestly one, Ward was a leader and not a follower like Anne Vaux, the assistant of Father Garnet. The women of her Institute wore clothes that permitted them to travel unhampered by the bulk of traditional garments from London to Vienna to Munich and even to Rome for an audience with the Pope. They claimed for themselves the right not only to teach poor female children but to proselytize the people living in their students' communities, a vocation dangerously approaching the ministerial office. Determined to direct her order with a minimum of outside interference, Ward had the courage to demand that as its Superior she should have only one male supervisor, the Pontiff himself. While she was willing to recognize that her sex had to operate under some restrictions, she would admit to only four specific ones, none of which hindered her in her drive to accomplish her teaching goals. In a speech she made to her women of St. Omer in 1617 she spoke clearly and forcefully about female limitations and potential:

> I confess wives are to be subject to their husbands, men are head of the Church, women are not to administer sacraments, nor preach in public churches, but in all other things, wherein are we so inferior to other creatures that they should term us 'but women?' For what think you of this word, 'but women?' but as if we were in all things inferior to some other creature which I suppose to be man! Which I dare to be bold to say is a lie.

She continued with an anecdote that gives insight into the depths of her self-confidence and self-esteem:

> There was a Father that lately came into England whom I heard say that he would not for a thousand of worlds be a woman, because he thought a woman could not apprehend God. I answered nothing but only smiled.[48]

In late Tudor and early Stuart England, the Reformation resulted in a heightened social status for some women, a change that had not been anticipated by its leaders. The anti-clericalism of Protestantism and its propensity to split into factions or sects inadvertently freed many married women from religious obedience to their husbands as well as to priests. The decision of the Elizabethan government to support the new worship and to persecute members of the Roman faith had a similar effect upon Catholic women. While the hunted missionary priests had to rely upon the generosity of the lay aristocracy for support, losing in the process much of their clerical independence, Catholic women proved capable of adopting new religious roles for themselves in the home. Finally, by forcing into exile single people who wished to pursue traditional celibate vocations, Protestantism made it possible for them to become acquainted with and to adapt to their use the standards and the methods of the Counter Reformation. Winning social approval and gaining immeasurable self-esteem for their accomplishments, these women, among whom the most prominent was Mary Ward, were the first of their compatriots to give expression to and to practice feminist doctrine. Ironically, it was the unmarried women of the victorious faith who lost esteem. Left without religious justification for their rejection of matrimony, their membership in a society in which economic and social discrimination against women was widespread and pervasive made it increasingly difficult for them to develop a sense of community value and of self-worth.

NOTES

1. William R. Trimble, *The Catholic Laity in Elizabethan England* (Cambridge, Mass., 1964), pp. 102-103; Evelyn Waugh, *Edmund Campion* (London, 1947), p. 112; Albert Joseph Loomie, *The Spanish Elizabethans: The English Exiles at the Court of Philip II* (New York, 1963), p. 4.

2. John T. Cliffe, *Yorkshire Gentry from the Reformation to the Civil War* (London, 1969), p. 171; Adrian Morey, *The Catholic Subjects of Elizabeth I* (Totowa, N.J., 1978), pp. 99-117; Hugh Aveling, *The Handle and the Axe* (Colchester, Essex, 1976), pp. 59-68.

3. John Bossy, *The English Catholic Community, 1570-1850* (Oxford, 1976), pp. 38-42; M.D.R. Leys, *Catholics in England, 1559-1829* (New York, 1961), pp. 51-52; Hugh Aveling, *Handle*, p. 68.

4. John Bossy, "The Character of Elizabethan Catholicism," *Past and Present*, XXI (1962), 39-41; H. G. Alexander, *Religion in England, 1558-1662* (London, 1968), p. 106; Mervyn James, *Family, Lineage, and Civil Society: A Study of Society, Politics, and Mentality in the Durham Region, 1500-1640* (Oxford, 1974), p. 138.

5. Rachel R. Reid, "The Political Influence of the 'North Parts' under the Later Tudors," *Tudor Studies*, ed. R. W. Seton-Watson (London, 1928), pp. 221-222; Thomas Wilson, "The State of England," ed. F. J. Fisher, *The Camden Miscellany*, Vol. XVI, Camden Society, vol. LII, third series (London, 1936), pp. 2-3; Anthony Fletcher, *Tudor Rebellions*, 2nd ed. (London, 1973), pp. 92-106.

6. Rachel Reid, *The Rebellion of the Earls,* Transactions of the Royal Historical Society, vol. XX, new series (London, 1906), pp. 194-197; Sir Cuthbert Sharp, *Memorials of the Rebellion of 1569* (London, 1810), pp. 33-34.

7. Cuthbert Sharp, pp. 198, 207, 212, and 307; Rachel Reid, *The Rebellion of the Earls,* p. 177; Edward B. De Fonblanque, *Annals of the House of Percy From the Conquest to the Opening of the Nineteenth Century,* 2 vols. (London, 1887), II, 42.

8. Gerald Brenan, *A History of the House of Percy,* 2 vols. (London, 1902), I, 275; Henry Howard, *Indications of Memorials, paintings and engravings . . . of Howard Family* (London, 1834), pp. 24-28 and Appendix VIII; Cuthbert Sharp. pp. 104, 145, 175-179, 307, and 309; Henry Graville Howard, 14th Duke of Norfolk, *The Lives of Philip Howard, Earl of Arundel, and of Anne Dacres, His Wife* (London, 1857), p. 175.

9. Gerald Brenan, I, 358-360; Cuthbert Sharp, pp. 343-348; Edward B. De Fonblanque, II, 125.

10. S. J. Watts, *From Border to Middle Shire, Northumberland, 1586-1625* (Leicester, 1975), p. 78; John T. Cliffe, p. 2; Penry Williams, *The Tudor Regime* (Oxford, 1979), p. 350; Claire Cross, *The Puritan Earl: The Life of Henry Hastings, Third Earl of Huntingdon* (New York, 1966), p. 226.

11. Rachel R. Reid, "The Political Influence of the North Parts," p. 229; P. M. Handover, *Arbella Stuart: Royal Lady of Hardwick* (London, 1957), pp. 123-129; Albert Joseph Loomie, p. 45; Robert Doleman, *A Conference about the Next Succession to the Crowne of England,* English Recusant Literature (Menston, Yorkshire, 1972); Arnold Pritchard,

Catholic Loyalism in Elizabethan England (Chapel Hill, N.C., 1979), p. 18; see the comments of Jane Owen about loyalism in *An antidote against purgatory* (1634), English Recusant Literature, vol. 166 (Menston, Yorkshire, 1973), p. 190.

12. Bernard Basset, *The English Jesuits* (New York, 1968), pp. 46-47; Adrian Morey, pp. 174-179; Sir Tobie Matthew, *The Life of Lady Lucy Knatchbull,* ed. Dom David Knowles (London, 1931), p. ix; Arnold Pritchard, pp. 8-10.

13. W. K. Jordan, *The Development of Religious Toleration in England,* 4 vols. (Cambridge, Mass., 1932-1940), I, 103.

14. Richard Smith, *The Life of the Most Honourable and Vertous Lady, the La. Magdalen Viscountess Montague,* trans. Cuthbert Fursdon, English Recusant Literature (Menston, Yorkshire, 1970), pp. 1-12 and 27-43; Robert B. Manning, *Religion and Society in Elizabethan Sussex* (Leicester, 1969), pp. 157-161; John Bossy, *The English Catholic Community,* p. 112.

15. Henry Graville Howard, pp. 6-15; see also F. W. Steer, *The Life of Saint Philip Howard* (London, 1971); Gerald Brenan and Edward P. Statham, *The House of Howard,* 2 vols. (New York, 1907), II, 461-488.

16. Henry Graville Howard, pp. 168-202.

17. Arnold Pritchard, p. 42; William Weston, *An Autobiography from the Jesuit Underground,* trans. Philip Carman (New York, 1955), p. 12; Christopher Devlin, *The Life of Robert Southwell, Poet and Martyr* (New York, 1956), pp. 131-132. See also J. H. Pollen, ed., *Unpublished Documents Relating to the English Martyrs, 1584-1603,* Catholic Record Society, 2 vols. (London, 1908 and 1919), II.

18. Henry Graville Howard, pp. 202-262; see also Mary Hervey, *The Life, Correspondence & Collections of Thomas Howard, Earl of Arundel* (Cambridge, 1921), pp. 12-14.

19. Christopher Devlin, pp. 108, 124, 131-132, 141, 197, 199, and 290; Henry Graville Howard, pp. 209, 215, 271, and 293; Joseph B. Collins, *Christian Mysticism in the Elizabethan Age* (Reprint, 1976), p. 170; John H. Pollen, *Acts of the English Martyrs* (London, 1891), p. 212; Robert Southwell, *An Epistle of Comfort,* ed. Margaret Waugh (Chicago, 1966), pp. 5, 11, 90, and 228; for some verses of Lady Arundel, see the Rev. Alexander Dyce, *Specimens of British Poetesses* (London, 1877), pp. 43-44.

20. Philip Caraman, *Henry Garnet and the Gunpowder Plot* (London, 1964), pp. 37, 350, 369, and 422; Christopher Devlin, p. 235; John Bossy, *The English Catholic Community,* p. 205; Henry Foley, ed., *Records of the English Province of the Society of Jesus,* 5 vols. (London, 1875-1880), II, 316; Leonard Lessius and Fulerius Androtius, *The Treasure of Vowed Chastity in secular Persons also the Widdowes Glasse,* trans. I. W. (St. Omer, 1621), dedication; Pedro de Ribadeneira, *The Life of B. Father Ignatius of Loyola,* trans. M. Walpole (St. Omer, 1616), dedication; Godfrey Anstruther, *The Vaux of Harrowden* (Newport, Monmouth, 1953), pp. 183-202; Bernard Basset, p. 124.

21. John Bossy, "The Character of Elizabethan Catholicism," p. 41 and "The Counter Reformation," *Past and Present,* XLVII (1970), 57-58 and 63-70; Robert B. Manning, pp. 158 and 239.

22. For the Persons quote, see Philip Caraman, ed., *The Other Face: Catholic Life under Elizabeth I* (New York, 1960), p. 61; John Bossy, *The English Catholic Community,* pp. 156-157 and 170; John Strype, *Annals of the Reformation,* 4 vols. (Oxford, 1824), II-i, 497; Brian Magee, *The English Recusants* (London, 1938), p. 2; Henry Foley, I, 68, 143, 166, 295, and 403; II, 589; III, 148 and 192; IV, 18, 204, 285, and 403-404.

23. John Bossy, *The English Catholic Community,* p. 154; Elliot Rose, *Cases of*

Conscience: Alternatives Open to Recusants and Puritans Under Elizabeth I and James I (Cambridge, 1975), p. 113; David Mathew, *Catholicism in England, 1535-1935* (London, 1936), p. 54; Hugh Aveling, *Northern Catholics* (London, 1966), pp. 170-183; K. R. Wark, *Elizabethan Recusancy in Cheshire* (Manchester, 1971), p. 83; Mervyn James, p. 140; Adrian Morey, p. 153; Godfrey Anstruther, p. 218.

24. Sister Joseph Damien, "These Be But Women," *From the Renaissance to the Counter-Reformation. Essays in Honor of Garrett Mattingly*, ed. Charles H. Carter (New York, 1965), pp. 371-392; William Palmes, *The Life of Mrs. Dorothy Lawson of St. Anthony's near Newcastle-on-Tyne* (Newcastle-upon-Tyne, 1851), pp. 13-43; C. S. Durrant, *A Link between Flemish Mystics and English Martyrs* (London, 1925), p. 252.

25. For a contemporary example of a woman instructing her son in Latin vocabulary, see Henry Foley, II, 445; John Bossy, *The English Catholic Community*, p. 111; Laurence Vaux, *A Catechisme or Christian Doctrine*, English Recusant Literature (Menston, Yorkshire, 1969), p. 56; Vaux was a priest who died in prison and was not an associate of Lord Vaux. See Godfrey Anstruther, p. 151 and Patrick McGrath, *Papists and Puritans under Elizabeth I* (New York, 1967), p. 62; Elliot Rose, p. 112.

26. Arthur Joy Klein, *Intolerance in the Reign of Elizabeth, Queen of England* (Reprint, 1968), p. 50.

27. Nuns of Tyburn Convent, *The One Hundred and Five Martyrs of Tyburn*, intro. Don Bede Camm (London, 1917), pp. 12 and 31; Christopher Devlin, p. 175; Henry Foley, I, 414 ff.; Philip Caraman, *Henry Garnet*, pp. 67 and 278; Richard Challoner, *Memoirs of Missionary Priests and Other Catholics of Both Sexes* (London, 1924), pp. 142-143 and 257; *The Manuscripts of his grace the duke of Rutland*, H.M.C., 4 vols. (London, 1888), I, 369.

28. Mervyn James, p. 138; Henry Foley, III, 261; Hugh Aveling, *Catholic Recusancy in the City of York, 1558-1791*, Catholic Record Society (London, 1970), pp. 47, 58, and 59; Mary Claridge, *Margaret Clitherow* (Fordham, N.Y., 1966), pp. 26 and 42; John Morris, ed., *The Troubles of Our Catholic Forefathers Related by Themselves*, third series (London, 1877), p. 379.

29. John Morris, *Troubles*, pp. 85 and 375-379 and 391-394; Mary Claridge, pp. 70, 85-90, 143-144, and 151.

30. Mary Claridge, p. ix; Henry Foley, II, 578; Philip Caraman, *The Other Face*, pp. 84 and 326; Herbert S. Burke, *Historical Portraits of the Tudor Dynasty and the Reformation Period*, 4 vols. (London, 1879-1883), IV, 116.

31. Henry Foley, III, 27; Luca Pinelli, *The Mirrour of Religious Perfection* (St. Omer, 1618), dedication; Edward Petre, *Notices of the English Colleges and Convents Established on the Continent*, ed. F. C. Husenbeth (Norwich, 1849), p. 77; see also George J. Aungier, *The History and Antiquities of Syon* (London, 1840); John Hungerford Pollen, *The English Catholics in the Reign of Queen Elizabeth* (Reprint, 1971), p. 248; Peter K. Guilday, *English Catholic Refugees on the Continent* (London, 1914), p. 56; J. B. Wainwright, "Queen Mary's Religious Foundations," *Downside Review*, VIII (1908), 143.

32. Dom Adam Hamilton, *The Chronicle of the English Augustinian Canonesses Regular of the Lateran at St. Monica's in Louvain*, 2 vols. (London, 1904), I, 25-31; C. S. Durrant, pp. 165-208, 371, and 420.

33. Dom Adam Hamilton, pp. 64-86; C. S. Durrant, pp. 118-221, 230-236, 371, and 422; after she became a nun, Mother Mary changed her name from Jane to Mary; Antonio de Molina, *A Treatise of Mental Prayer*, trans. by a Jesuit (St. Omer, 1617), dedication.

34. George Oliver, *Collections Toward Illustrating the Biography of the Scotch, Eng-*

lish, and Irish Members of the Society of Jesus (London, 1857), pp. 531-534; Peter K. Guilday, I, 15 and 256-257; Jean Pierre Camus, *A Spiritual Combat,* trans. Miles Car., English Recusant Literature (London, 1974), dedication; Albertus Magnus, *The Paradise of the Soule,* English Recusant Literature (Menston, Yorkshire, 1972), dedication; Vicenzo Puccini, *The Life of the Holy and Venerable Mother Suor Maria Maddalene D. Patsi,* trans. G. B., English Recusant Literature (Menston, Yorkshire, 1970), dedication; Hugh Aveling, *Handle,* pp. 92-94; see also Joseph Hansom, "The English Benedictine Nuns of Brussels and Winchester, 1598-1856," *Catholic Record Society Miscellany,* IX (1915), 174-203; David Lunn, *The English Benedictines, 1540-1688* (New York, 1980), pp. 198-202.

35. T. A. Mann, "A Short Chronological Account of the Religious Establishments Made by English Catholics on the Continent," *Archaeologia,* XIII (1800), 251-273; Dom Adam Hamilton, I, ix-xi; Peter K. Guilday, I, 21; for biographical information, see Mary C. E. Chambers, *Life of Mary Ward,* 2 vols. (London, 1882), I and II.

36. William V. Bangert, *A History of the Society* (St. Louis, 1972), p. 28; Martin P. Harney, *The Jesuits in History* (New York, 1941), pp. 26, 177, 192-217.

37. Peter K. Guilday, I, 297; Mary C. E. Chambers, I, 112-118.

38. Mary C. E. Chambers, I, 236-255, 287-290, and 366; Peter K. Guilday, I, 175-176.

39. Peter K. Guilday, I, 175-176; C. S. Durrant, p. 196; A.C.F. Beales, *Education Under Penalty* (London, 1962), pp. 203-204; Mary C. E. Chambers, I, 287-290; for an excellent study of teaching congregations see Judith Combes Taylor, "From Proselytizing to Social Reform: Three Generations of French Female Teaching Congregations, 1600-1720," Ph.D. dissertation, Arizona State University, 1980.

40. Mary C. E. Chambers, I, 18; A.C.F. Beales, pp. 203-204; Peter K. Guilday, I, 181.

41. Mary C. E. Chambers, II, 333 and 403-423; Peter K. Guilday, I, 163-170 and 213; Hugh Aveling, *Handle,* p. 97; Leo Hicks, "Mary Ward's Great Enterprise," *Month,* CLI (1928), 137-146.

42. Thomas Becon, *The Catechism,* ed. John Ayre, Parker Society (Cambridge, 1844), pp. 376-378; for more information about Becon, see Chapter 8; for some references to a few establishments for poor girls, see Foster Watson, *The Beginnings of the Teaching of Modern Subjects in England* (Reprint, 1971), pp. xliv-l; John Duncon, *Lady Lettice, Vi-Countess Falkland,* ed. M. F. Howard (London, 1908), p. 28; Joan K. Kinnaird, "Mary Astell and the Conservative Contribution to English Feminism," *Journal of British Studies,* XIX (1979), 53-75.

43. Mary C. E. Chambers, II, 45, 237, and 249; C. S. Durrant, p. 424; for references to traditional training, see Dom Adam Hamilton, I, 241 and Henry Foley, II, 445; many of Ward's papers have been destroyed. See Hugh Aveling, *Handle,* p. 94.

44. Roger B. Manning, p. 173; for a discussion of Protestant attitudes, see Chapters 4 and 8. Margo Todd, "Humanists, Puritans, and the Spiritualized Household," *Church History,* XLIX (March, 1980), 18-34.

45. Laurence Vaux, p. 127.

46. An example of this attitude is the reported response of Margaret Clitherow when it was suggested to her that she seek the forgiveness of her reformed husband. She said: "I do not depend upon the judgement of men, but of God." See John Morris, p. 309; John Bossy, *The English Catholic Community,* pp. 31 and 111 and "The Character of English Catholicism," p. 40.

47. In his book, *The Anatomie of the English Nunnery at Lisbon* (Lisbon, 1623), p. 7, Thomas Robinson gave a scurrilous account of the moral misconduct of the Syon nuns. This statement is all the more ridiculous when their earlier history of hardship and travel is known. In 1618 Mother Barbara and her sisters were honored in a Jesuit dedication for their virtuous and austere life. See Luca Pinelli, *The Mirrour of Religious Perfection,* trans. I. Everard (St. Omer, 1618); see also William Fitch, *The Rule of Perfection* (Rouen, 1609), dedication; Hugh Aveling, *Handle,* pp. 91 and 100.

48. Mary C. E. Chambers, I, 409-410.

10

The Jacobean Generation

On March 24, 1603, Queen Elizabeth died after ruling for more than forty-four years. Noting the amiability of King James I, her successor, and the informality of his protocol, which sometimes led to confusion and social excesses at court, some of his subjects recalled her reign with nostalgia. Her godson, Sir John Harington, wrote: "In the Queen's days I never did see such a lack of good order, discretion and sobriety as I have now done. I wish I was at home." While a few did belittle his reign by contrasting his personal style with that of Elizabeth, it is unlikely that the majority of his courtiers found his padded clothes and vulgarity much more "grotesque" than the futile attempts of his predecessor to perpetuate her image as an ageless virgin. Like her, the new monarch was a scholar with skills in several languages. A gifted writer of prose, his negative attitudes about the use of tobacco were perceptive and despite his early belief in witchcraft, his growing skepticism provided a refreshing contrast to the gullibility of many of his subjects. His greatest advantage was his manhood, for as one royalist, Sir John Oglander, later commented about Elizabeth: "There was nothing wanting that could be desired in a prince, but that she was a woman."[1]

To analyze the achievements of the women scholars of the Jacobean generation and to place their accomplishments in perspective, a brief survey must first be made of the role of the King's consort, Anne of Denmark, in fostering dramatic productions at court. Next, a special study will be made of one of her attendants, Lucy, Countess of Bedford, the most celebrated patroness of the Jacobean age, for the purpose of assessing the literary talents of the court ladies. The individual works of the women who wrote in the tradition of Sir Philip Sidney and Mary, Countess of Pembroke, will also be reviewed to determine their association with classical scholarship. Finally, an investigation will be made of the status of Latin training for women at court and in the kingdom with particular emphasis upon the role of religion in encouraging, or, indeed, in discouraging a general knowledge of this language.

One of Queen Anne's favorite pastimes was participating with her ladies in Ben Jonson's and Samuel Daniel's masques, which had elaborate staging by

artists such as Inigo Jones. Reaching their fullest development under her patronage, the masques had been greatly influenced by the cult of chivalry which
had been popularized by the members of the Sidney circle. In essence, they were
dramatized dances choreographed around extraordinary spectacles such as Gods,
clouds, and stars all ascending radiantly into the heavens or sinking majestically
into the stage floor. While it was unusual but not unheard of for women to act
in plays, this royal pastime was harshly criticized by those who associated the
theatre with prostitution, a connection that had arisen because the public playhouses existed side by side with brothels and were owned by the same busi-
nessmen. Although one royal performer, Anne Clifford, Countess of Dorset,
admitted that the ladies' reputation had suffered because of their participation
in these masques, the Queen generally disregarded moralistic criticisms.[2]

Her Majesty's favorite royal attendant was undoubtedly Lucy, Countess of
Bedford. Born in 1581 to Anne Kelway and her husband, John Harington, later
first Baron Harington of Exton, Lady Bedford was a cousin of the Sidneys and
of Sir John Harington, the godson of Queen Elizabeth. In 1594 she had become
the wife of Edward Russell, the third Earl of Bedford, who had succeeded to
his grandfather's title in 1585 as an adolescent. The prominence of Lady Bedford
at Queen Anne's court cannot be explained only by her husband's noble standing.
Endowed with charm, wit, and intelligence, she was also aided in her social
ambitions by the special status conferred upon her family. Her access to royal
circles had been ensured by the decision of the King and Queen to place their
young daughter, Elizabeth, in the custody of Lord and Lady Harington, the
parents of Lady Bedford.[3]

Although Mary, the Dowager Countess of Pembroke, celebrated as the greatest
private patroness of Elizabeth's reign, continued to win literary compliments,
she was eclipsed in the Jacobean circles by this younger cousin. Among those
Lady Bedford patronized were Michael Drayton, John Donne (who named his
daughter after her), Ben Jonson, Samuel Daniel, John Florio, John Owen, George
Chapman, John Dowland, and Sir John Davies of Hereford. Several churchmen
also honored her in their works. With the Queen's death in 1619, Lady Bedford,
who had suffered from frequent bouts of illness, retired to her estate in Hertfordshire. While her regular attendance at court had surely limited the time
available to her for creative writing, even in retirement she failed to author any
original works, except for a few poems no longer extant, or to translate any
treatises, despite her fluency in several vernacular tongues. In 1598 her tutor,
John Florio, had boasted about her skills: "in Italian as in French, in French as
in Spanish, in all as in English, you understand what you reade, write as you
reade, and speake as you write."[4]

By the succession of James, as the example of Lady Bedford indicates, the
translation of classical works had ceased to be a normal pastime for women at
court perhaps because this activity had become too closely associated with ex-
cessive piety or with high scholarship. In fact, during his entire reign only one
new translation by a woman was printed, the version of John Poynet's work on

the Lord's Supper by Lady Elizabeth Cooke Russell in 1605. While the women of the fourth generation did not publish any translations at this time, two of them did have original English compositions printed. The experiences of Elizabeth, Lady Falkland, and Lady Mary Wroth, whose play and pastoral romance were removed from circulation after their appearance in 1613 and 1621, respectively, only served to discourage their female contemporaries from undertaking similar literary projects.[5]

Born in 1585, Elizabeth was the heiress of Laurence Tanfield, later the Chief Baron of the Court of Exchequer, and Elizabeth Symondes. In 1602 she became the wife of Sir Henry Cary, afterward first Viscount Falkland, and subsequently gave birth to eleven children, all of whom she nursed except for the eldest boy, Lucius, who lived with her parents. After Lady Falkland's death in 1639, one of her daughters wrote a memoir of her mother's life. Although the dates given in the manuscript are sometimes slightly inaccurate, there is reason to believe that its basic facts are correct, especially as it was carefully edited by another one of the Cary children. In her youth, her daughter noted, Lady Falkland had taught herself the French, Spanish, Italian, Latin, and Hebrew languages and had later studied without any great success Transylvanian and Gaelic. Before her marriage to Sir Henry, these linguistic talents had attracted some notice. In his *Heroical Epistles* printed in 1597, Michael Drayton had complimented her French and Italian skills, and the next year to please her great uncle, Sir Henry Lee, the royal Champion, Elizabeth had translated into English Abraham Ortelius' *Le Miroir du Monde,* which was subsequently published in Amsterdam. Finally, in *England's Helicon,* a collection of lyrical and pastoral poems printed in 1600, she was referred to as "Learning's delight."[6]

For several years following her marriage, Lady Cary seldom saw Sir Henry who had chosen her as his spouse primarily because she was her father's sole heiress. After residing with her family for about one year after the wedding, she moved into her husband's home to live with his mother while he was on a military assignment in the Low Countries. Despite the hostility of her mother-in-law, Lady Katherine Cary, to her academic exercises, Elizabeth wrote some verses and two plays. None of these pieces except for the *Tragedy of Mariam,* a French-Senecan play published in 1613, is extant.[7]

Since there was more than one contemporary woman named Elizabeth Cary, including her sister-in-law, the wife of her husband's brother, Sir Philip, questions have been raised as to whether it was the future Lady Falkland who actually composed this tragedy. Unfortunately, her contemporaries made no direct reference to its published version, but the problem of authorship can be resolved in her favor on the basis of some comments by Sir John Davies of Hereford about the original manuscript. In 1612, the year before *Mariam* was printed, Davies dedicated his *Muses Sacrifice* to three ladies, two of them eminent peeresses, Lady Bedford and the Dowager Countess of Pembroke, and the other a gentlewoman, Lady Cary, who was identified as the wife of Sir Henry. Lauding her accomplishments, Davies referred to Lady Cary's writings, which were set in Palestine and Syracuse, and complimented her on her knowledge of holy tongues. It is likely that he was alluding to *Mariam,* a tragedy about the wife of King Herod of Palestine, and to a lost play with scenes in Sicily.[8]

The appearance in 1592 of *Antonie,* the Countess of Pembroke's version of Robert Garnier's tragedy, had heralded an interest in French-Senecan drama in England. By 1613 when Lady Cary's play was published, there had been printed in English ten works similar to the *Antonie,* including *Cleopatra* in 1594 by Samuel Daniel. By honoring the literary ideals of her brother, the Countess had helped to create the literary climate in which *Mariam,* the first original play written in English by a woman, could be composed. The scenes of this play focus on the plight of two unhappily married women, one, Mariam, who was put to death because of the unwarranted jealousy of her husband, King Herod, and the other, Salome, who plotted the demise of her unloved spouse, Josephus.[9]

Mariam is probably the "most regular" of all of the classical plays published in England at this time. Written in rhymed quatrains, it had five acts, a chorus, no comic scenes, long expositions, and almost no action, for even the death of its heroine occurred offstage. As the writing of drama requires a long apprenticeship in the practical as well as the intellectual aspects of the craft, her completion of two plays in an unquestionably hostile environment is an astonishing achievement. Unsuitable for public entertainment, *Mariam* was written as an intellectual exercise for the pleasure of a few intimate friends, and when it was unexpectedly published, its author had the copies withdrawn from circulation.[10]

Lady Falkland's daughter later stated that the play had been stolen from the chamber of a friend and printed without her mother's permission, a story that has been challenged because *Mariam* was entered in normal fashion in the Register of the Stationers', the Company that licensed publications. As the other family information revealed by this daughter is reliable and can usually be corroborated by independent evidence, it is inconsistent to argue that in this particular instance she was mistaken. Indeed, it seems likely that the play was printed in a hasty, if not irregular, manner. The dedicatory verse addressed to Lady Cary's sister-in-law that had been written for the manuscript version of *Mariam* and not for its published form was surely a late insertion, for it is missing from a majority of the extant copies, an absence that indicates a hurried, disorganized, and perhaps secret printing. It is possible that the friend of the author, in whose custody the tragedy had been placed, carelessly showed it to Richard Hawkins, the publisher, when he indicated an interest in it because of the comments of Sir John Davies of Hereford. Without more evidence, it must at least be assumed that Lady Falkland's daughter was repeating information that she had heard from her mother about the manuscript's publication.[11]

It is likely, as Nancy Cotton Pearse has suggested, that the women of this play represented the ambivalent feelings of Lady Cary toward marriage: its heroine, Mariam, was a faithful but unsuccessful wife and its villainess, Salome, was an incorrigible homebreaker. For several years after Henry's return from the Low Countries in 1607 or 1608, Lady Elizabeth, like Mariam, was a dutiful but discontented wife, but in 1625 she made a decision that virtually destroyed her marriage. Leaving her husband in Ireland, their place of residence from 1622, the year of his appointment as its Lord Deputy, she traveled to England where she soon confessed her conversion to Roman Catholicism, a public confirmation of a long-standing private disenchantment with the Church of England. This act alienated her from her husband, her mother, and some of her children, although ultimately she was able to convert six of her offspring, including four daughters, who joined the English Benedictine monastery at Cambrai, and two sons, who entered holy orders.[12]

Within three years of her freedom, she had completed another play, *The History of Edward II*, which D. A. Stauffer has described as a "history . . . shaped by metrical drama" rather than a "poetic drama based upon history." In her introductory statement, Elizabeth, who had become Lady Falkland in 1620 at her husband's ennoblement, spoke of the "deep and sad Passion" that had led her to dramatize the life of this unfortunate King. Written in regular blank verse, its construction indicates that its author was acquainted with the Latin language. Ironically, when it was first published in 1680, it was attributed to Lord Falkland because the manuscript had been discovered among his papers, but on the basis of a statement in it signed with the initials, E. F., and of other internal evidence, Stauffer has conclusively identified it as her work.[13]

Separated from her husband during the last years of her life, she turned for solace to religious studies, translating several Saints' Lives and the works of Cardinal Jacques Davy Du Perron, a spiritual heir of Ronsard and a Catholic reformer. When she published her version of *The Reply of the Most Illustrious Cardinal of Perron to the Answer of the Most Excellent King of Great Britain* in 1630, she dedicated it to Queen Henrietta Maria, who was characterized as the woman "fittest to protect a womans worke." After copies of the book that was published in France were burned in her native land, Lady Falkland translated the entire works of Perron but never had them printed.[14]

That she had her French translation published in 1630 and that her family had permitted the printing of her youthful version of Ortelius in 1598 raises the suspicion that it had been her husband, Sir Henry, who had been angered by the appearance of *Mariam* in 1613. It is likely that the most controversial aspect of the publication had been the nature of the literary endeavor, itself. Except for a minor piece or two in collections of poetry, no non-religious original work of a woman had been printed in England for more than two decades. Further exacerbating this issue was that Lady Cary's original piece was a play, for moralists had long associated the theatre with sexual improprieties. In addition, the subject of her tragedy was not typical of the reading generally recommended to Protestant women at this time, for it dealt with the destructive nature of marriage and the wrongful deaths of innocent and loyal spouses. While Lady Elizabeth Cary was probably offended by the unauthorized appearance of her play, it seems reasonable to assume that her husband was outraged by the public exposure of his wife's dramatic talents. Although there is no evidence that she was reluctant to cancel its sale, it is still true that Sir Henry was quite capable of committing cruel acts to obtain her obedience. After her Catholic conversion in 1625, he deprived her of all financial support and of access to her children.[15]

The speculation that it was the antagonism of relatives that led to the *Mariam's* withdrawal is supported by an occurrence in 1633, the year of Lord Falkland's death. It may be only a coincidence, but an intriguing one, that William Sheares chose that year to print a volume of John Marston's plays and to dedicate it to Lady Falkland, who was living alone in poverty without funds to reward authors for their scholarship. After the appearance of *Mariam* in 1613, a public silence about her interest in drama with the exception of this dedication prevailed until long after her death. Like Lady Falkland, Marston was no longer a playwright, for he had retired from the theatre in 1608 when his production of *The Fawn* with its personal attacks on King James had resulted in the temporary closure of all London playhouses and in its author's imprisonment. Upon his release, he had entered holy orders and had held positions in the established Church.[16]

There is no evidence that Marston and Lady Falkland had ever been acquainted, but they did have at least two indirect connections. First, they had both written in the Senecan style, for his *Antonio and Mellida,* a piece included in the 1633 collection, is reminiscent of Roman tragedy and second, they were both former playwrights whose efforts had brought them some notoriety. Confessing in his introduction that his sole reason for honoring Lady Falkland was her intimate acquaintance with the Muses, Sheares failed to note any personal association between the two playwrights. In general terms, the publisher also lamented the aspersions that had been cast upon drama, thereby seeming to encompass in his discussion the fate of her literary efforts as well as those of Marston. When Marston, who was not informed in advance about this publication, learned of its appearance, he required that the volume be replaced with one that obliterated all references to his authorship. The second printing also omitted the prefatory letter, perhaps at the request of Lady Falkland, but it is more likely that the Anglican clergyman objected to the dedication of his writings to an apostate of his faith.[17]

At the conclusion of his dedication, Sheares referred to the international reputation of Lady Falkland's talents, a theme already addressed in 1622. Upon the departure of her ladyship and her family for Ireland, William Basse had written two congratulatory sonnets commenting on her scholarly fame. Among the women of this period who wrote in English her work was probably the most widely known outside her homeland, for not only had her books been published in England and in the Netherlands but also in France. In addition, Richard Beling dedicated to her his *A Sixth Booke to the Countess of Pembrokes Arcadia* which appeared in Dublin in 1624. Beling was only one of several writers to imitate the *Arcadia,* the most popular prose fiction in English until the eighteenth century.[18]

None of these imitators was as controversial as Sir Philip Sidney's niece, Lady Mary Wroth, who was forced to cancel the sale of her romance after it had been printed in an incomplete version in 1621. Born in 1586 to Sir Robert Sidney, the future Earl of Leicester, and Barbara Gammage, Mary had displayed a zeal for learning from an early age and had become an accomplished and cultured woman. She was honored in the writing of many outstanding authors, including George Chapman, William Gamage, George Wither, Sir John Davies of Hereford, Robert Jones, Joshua Sylvester, and Ben Jonson. In 1604 she married Sir Robert Wroth whom Jonson saluted in his poetry but whom he also characterized as a jealous husband. Personal tragedy struck Lady Wroth in 1614 when Sir Robert died, reportedly leaving her with a jointure of £1,200, debts of £23,000, and an infant son. An even worse financial crisis developed in 1616 after the death of her son caused his diminished inheritance to descend to his Uncle John Wroth. As she was left without support, it has been assumed that she had her work, *The Countess of Mountgomeries Urania,* published in 1621 to earn money as a professional writer. While the sale of books did not usually bring in profits to a writer, who remained dependent upon gratuities from patrons, the status of Lady Wroth could well have enabled her to make special arrangements with her publisher. In a 1978 study of the *Urania,* Margaret Witten-Hannah has rather convincingly argued that it was actually printed without its author's permission. This conclusion is based largely on the evidence of its lack of dedicatory letters and its unfinished state.[19]

The circumstances concerning the withdrawal of the *Urania* from sale are particularly germane to the question of whether Lady Wroth had approved of its appearance in print. The controversy that led to this decision arose because of her ingenuity in writing and her cleverness in characterization. Like other pastoral romances, the *Urania* is somewhat "longwinded" but it also has an interesting innovative technique. The main theme or plot is interspersed with "sub-plots" or minor stories that are prototypes of the novella and that contain "breathless dialogue." These love stories caught the imagination of Lady Wroth's readers, who studied them zealously to discover whether the characters bore any resemblance to real people. Her circle of friends became convinced that one novella did allude in a most unflattering way to Edward, Lord Denny, his deceased daughter, Honoria, and her husband, James, Lord Hay, later Earl of Carlisle.[20]

Even though Lady Wroth denied that the faithless wife depicted in this novella represented Lady Hay, Lord Denny wrote some scurrilous rhymes deprecating the author's virtue and characterizing her as a "Hermaphrodite." He refused to accept her private explanation that no resemblance to his family was intended, maintaining that it was "but a small recompence to be the onely chosen foole for a Maye game before all the world." His objections caused her to halt the book's sale six months after its appearance at the publishing house. It is interesting that although she, herself, asserted somewhat apologetically that the *Urania* had been published without her approval, she acted to suppress it only after the controversy with Lord Hay had developed. While it was still unusual for women to have their secular works printed, in the five years prior to the appearance of the *Urania,* four women had authored books, one of which had been extraordinarily successful. In contrast to Lady Wroth's satiric work, Dorothy Leigh's popular treatise, *The Mothers Blessing,* which went through sixteen editions between 1616 and 1640, was a pious tract about marriage and childcare. Had Lady Wroth chosen to write domestic literature like that of Leigh, her efforts would have been far less controversial. Indeed, Lord Denny lectured Lady Wroth on the subject matter of the *Urania,* reminding her that her learned aunt, the Countess of Pembroke, had translated Godly books and had not penned "lascivious tales."[21]

Like the *Arcadia,* the *Urania* was addressed to a relative, but instead of honoring a sister, Lady Wroth selected a friend, Susan Herbert, a more well-known public figure and also a Countess. She was the daughter of the learned Anne Cecil, Lady Oxford, and the wife of Lady Wroth's first cousin, Philip Herbert, first Earl of Montgomery, the younger son of Lady Pembroke and a great favorite at the Jacobean court. A cultured woman, Lady Montgomery had frequently attended Queen Anne and had been honored in Ben Jonson's poetry. An equally important consideration in Lady Wroth's decision to address the work to her may have been the knowledge that she was already known to literary circles in this capacity, for Robert Newton's *The Countess of Montgomeries Eusebia* had just been published in 1620. Urania was a significant name for the title and the shepherdess of Lady Wroth's romance. Not only is there a character named Urania in *Arcadia,* but it is also Lady Pembroke's alias in Edmund Spenser's *Colin Clouts Come Home Again.*[22]

It is unfortunate that the controversy with Lord Hay has generated more attention than the literary significance of the *Urania,* for the efforts of Lady Wroth were extraordinary, ranging from the writing of prose fiction to that of poetry. In addition to the fifty-nine sonnets and songs of the *Urania* proper, there are appended to it another eighty-three sonnets and nineteen songs composed in the name of its heroine, Pamphilia, to her beloved, Amphilanthus. These verses interpret traditional Petrarchan themes but with a slightly different focus as they are addressed by a woman to a man. Like her Aunt Pembroke, she also experimented with different rhyme patterns, drawing upon at least twenty distinct forms. The endeavors of Lady Wroth are clearly reminiscent of the creations of the Wilton circle of the 1580s and the 1590s. Her resurrection of these models, can be partially explained by her desire to identify her work with that of her more famous relatives. While this kind of prose and poetry was no longer in style among the most eminent poets and authors, including Ben Jonson, who disliked the sonnet form, it did remain popular with the reading public.[23]

Despite the similarities of her work to that of Sidney, there was a decidedly different tone to her writing. Rather than develop themes on the age of innocence, of youth, of high ideals, of morality, and of great expectations, she explored the age of disillusionment, of depression, of melancholy, of defeat, and of regret. Influenced by the "caustic muse of satire," she portrayed love that was flawed, betrayed, and jealous. Indeed, jealousy was a topic that appeared repeatedly in her sonnets, an emotion that, if Jonson's appraisal of her husband was correct,

she knew well from personal experience. In the following excerpt this tone is
evident in the advice she had an aged father give to his son:

> Love once I did, and like thee, fear'd my Love,
>   Led by the hatefull threed of Jealousie,
>   Striving to keep, I lost my liberty,
>   And gain'd my griefe, which still my sorrowes move.
>
> In time shun this, to love is no offence,
>   But doubt in Youth, in Age, breeds penitence.

After the withdrawal of the *Urania,* Lady Wroth spent the next forty years of
her life in obscurity, surviving with financial help from the crown and from
relatives.[24]

The public and private failures of Lady Falkland and Lady Wroth should not
obscure the significance of their undertakings. The first women to publish non-
religious original works in English of a serious literary nature, they built upon
the accomplishments of their predecessors, especially those of Lady Pembroke.
Both created original plays and romances by using poetic structures that the
Countess had popularized through the translation, versification, or publication
of the work of others. As valuable as the writing of Lady Pembroke is, it represents
a mode of expression long considered suitable and proper for women, for it was
primarily a conduit for the thoughts and ideas of male authors. On the basis of
this creativity it simply is not possible to suggest, as Roger Thomson had done,
that in the early Stuart period, there was a "decline from that golden age of
Renaissance flowering under the Tudors." Although *Mariam* and the *Urania*
have been less esteemed by critics than the Psalms of Lady Pembroke, the
challenges that Lady Falkland and Lady Wroth accepted for themselves were far
more risky.[25]

While the work of Lady Pembroke and Sir Philip Sidney had been written in
English, the language of the literary Renaissance, scholarly works continued to
be composed in Latin, for to write in the vernacular was to forego a reputation
among the intelligentsia abroad. None of the women of Lady Pembroke's generation had been capable of completing classical compositions in the style of Sir
Francis Bacon or of John Owen. Indeed, in the two decades after Elizabeth's
succession only a few women had Latin instruction, a result both of the inability
of the Queen, who had no children of her own, to popularize classical training
and of the negative attitudes of reformers to the use of Latin in the household.
There had been at court only two aristocratic women of the third generation with
these language skills: Anne Cecil, Lady Oxford, and Lady Arbella Stuart. With
the arrival of King James in 1603, an outright hostility to learned women became
evident. As late as 1633 the story was circulating that when the King had been
introduced to a lady who could speak Greek and Latin, he had retorted, "But
can she spin?" In addition to social ridicule, Ben Jonson, the most favored writer
of the Jacobean court made an abundance of unfavorable allusions to learned
women in his comedies.[26]

There were two royal women who were greatly affected by these negative attitudes: the Princess Elizabeth, who was seven years old at her father's ascension, and the Lady Arbella. While the training of the young Princess was deliberately limited to vernacular tongues, French and Italian, a restriction that symbolized the royal family's lack of interest in classical instruction for women, the learning of the King's cousin, Arbella, was viewed as rather odd and quaint. A chaste maiden without financial independence in a climate increasingly hostile to unmarried women, she was also the only female classicist at court. While all of the other Latin scholars, who had formerly been in attendance on Queen Elizabeth, were either deceased or too old-fashioned and aged to be a part of the Stuart regime, Lady Falkland, the sole learned representative at court of the new or fourth generation, was not present regularly until after the disgrace of Arbella in 1611. Whatever were the inner convictions that compelled Arbella to marry William Seymour clandestinely and to attempt a flight to the continent, acts which caused her to be imprisoned for the rest of her short life, she must have found attendance at the Jacobean court uncomfortable and bewildering.[27]

By the Stuart succession the vernacular tongues, especially French, had been recognized as those most appropriate for women to learn. In 1603 John Florio had even commented that French was the "language of Ladies." The classical training that made Lady Falkland unique among the women of her social class in the fourth generation also caused her to be considered somewhat eccentric. While her parents had offered her the customary language instruction in French, she had chosen to teach herself an assortment of tongues, including Latin. Like other aspiring dramatists of this period, she had realized the need to study Seneca, and had decided to read his works in their original versions. Although she did lose her fluency in Latin, her knowledge was deep enough for it to influence the verse construction of the play, *Edward II,* composed by her in 1628.[28]

While Lady Falkland ultimately converted to Catholicism, she must be counted here as a Protestant because her education was acquired in the early period of her religious life. Her parents like many other reformers did not provide her with elementary Latin instruction because it was identified with the Roman faith. From the beginning of the Reformation the conflicts between Catholics and Protestants had centered on the language in which their beliefs were expressed. In the new "spiritualized household" the reformers had all but eliminated the study of Latin in an attempt to prevent the saying of Catholic prayers and other devotions. While a few boys, particularly among the nobility, did continue to study grammar in their households, most were taught classical languages in public schools after they had received their basic religious instruction in English. In contrast, young women were not normally offered advanced academic challenges, a difference that was defended by the reformers for a variety of social reasons. A few may have feared that the girls would say magical incantations in Latin, for this language was still popularly linked to witchcraft, a crime for which women were more often convicted than men. Others contended that female students who read the Christian Fathers in their original tongues would be tempted to read the lascivious tales of Virgil and Ovid, a rather strange argument since many of the pagan classics were available in the vernacular. The most important consideration was the widespread belief that their classical learning would make women too proud to adopt a humble demeanor toward their husbands.[29]

Despite the general Protestant hostility to providing women with classical instruction, there were, including Lady Falkland, at least seven reformed women of the fourth generation with this training, a total of at least four more than in the previous generation. Some references to scholarly women of this younger age group are impossible to verify because no written work of theirs is extant. Besides the report that Elizabeth Legge, who moved to Ireland, knew Latin, Spanish, Irish, and French, it has been suggested that Rebecca Allen of Lindsey in Lincolnshire, the daughter of David Allen, a rector with Puritan sympathies, learned Latin, Greek, and Hebrew. Married to Thomas Rainbowe, a vicar, she is most well known as the mother of Edward Rainbowe, the future Bishop of Carlisle.[30]

In *The Lives of Sundry Eminent People in this Later Age* and in *The Lives of Thirty-two English Divines,* Samuel Clarke, an aged Puritan minister, included information on thirteen women. Only two of these women, all of whom he seemed to know personally and most of whom were Puritans, were identified as Latinists. The elder of the two, Lady Mary Armyne, born in the 1590s, had, the minister wrote, attained "some competent skill" in Latin and French. Even though the second scholar he praised, Lady Elizabeth Langham, was too young to qualify as a member of the fourth generation, a discussion of her achievements is included here largely to illustrate Puritan attitudes toward the advanced education of women. The academic accomplishments in which Lady Langham "so much exceeded her Sex" did not cause her to be "puffed up" with pride, for Clarke was able to recall with pleasure that she had been an ideal wife: "she would always lower her Sails to him her Lord and Head" who remained a "perfect Stranger and wholly unacquainted with all of those inconveniences, which some have fancied, to necessarily accompany a Learned Wife."[31]

In addition to Falkland, Legge, Rainbowe, and Armyne, there were three authors, Rachel Speght, Elizabeth Jocelin, and Lady Eleanor Audley, who left evidence of their knowledge of Latin. In 1615 Joseph Swetnam began another journalistic war over the nature of women in his publication, *The Araignment of Lewd, Idle, Froward, and Unconstant women.* Even though this book was an "awkward, rambling collection of stories," it was immensely popular, going through nine more printings by 1637. Among those who responded to it in 1617 were two anonymous female authors, Constantia Munda and Ester Sowernam, and one identifiable woman, Rachel Speght. It is entirely possible that the unknown authors, both of whom knew Latin, were actually men, a thought that surely occurred to the public, for Speght later complained that some readers believed that her father had been her ghost writer, a charge that she vehemently denied. Less than twenty years old in 1617 when her book, *A Mouzell for Melastomus,* appeared, Rachel was the daughter of Thomas Speght, a schoolmaster and the editor in 1598 of Chaucer's works. Although her occasional use of Latin was superior to that of Swetnam's, she revealed that her learning was nothing more than the "fruit of vacant houres, as I could spare from affairs befitting my Sex." In defending women from the slanders of Swetnam, she depended heavily on the scriptures although she also showed some familiarity with classical writings. Accepting reformed theories that women were the "weaker vessel," she maintained that they had been fashioned from finer material than men since they had been devised by God from human flesh rather than from the earth. Four years later in her book on death, *Mortalities Memorandum,* she confessed that the censure she had received for some of her statements in the *Mouzell* was "inevitable to a publique act."[32]

Elizabeth Jocelin's treatise, *The Mothers Legacie to her unborne Childe,* was published posthumously three years after the appearance of the *Mortalities.* She was the granddaughter of William Chaderton, Bishop of Chester and Lincoln, with whom she had lived most of her youth because of the separation of her mother, Joan Chaderton, from her father, Sir Richard Brooke. Born in 1595, Elizabeth, unlike her sisters, was given a classical education by her grandfather. At the age of twenty-one, she married Torel Jocelin, and having a premonition of her death in childbirth, wrote a book of advice as a "Legacy" to her child. The editor explained in the preface to her treatise that she had been well educated and that she had been endowed with an excellent memory that permitted her "upon the first rehearsall to repeat above 40 lines in English or Latin." In her dedicatory note to her husband, Jocelin discussed the education that would be most suitable for the child that she was carrying. If a boy, he should go to school, she thought, but if a girl, she should be taught good housewifery, reading, writing, and good works by her Grandmother Brooke. It was the opinion of this pious Anglican woman that her daughter did not need any further academic training, for there were already too many women with more learning than wisdom. As though she had made this negative comment because it was expected of her, she then stated:

> But where learning and wisedom meet in a vertuous disposed woman, she is the fittest closet for all goodness. Shee is like a well-ballanced ship that may beare all her saile. She is—indeed, I should but shame myself, if I should goe about to praise her more.

Deciding to leave the decision about her daughter's education to her husband, Jocelin then pleaded with him to take care that the child learned humility, for pride was a particularly onerous vice in a female. While there was a general fear that women would be too proud of their educational accomplishments to "lower [their] sails" to their husbands, Protestantism, seemed to be secure enough in its struggle against Catholicism for two of its clergymen, Allen, a Puritan, and Chaderton, an Anglican, to foster the classical training in their homes of two young female relatives.[33]

The most published Tudor or Stuart woman was the visionary, Lady Eleanor Audley. Born about 1590 to George, Lord Audley, Earl of Castlehaven, and Lucy Mervin, she became the wife first of Sir John Davies, the Attorney General for Ireland, who died in 1626, and second of Sir Archibald Douglas, who also predeceased her in 1644. Claiming as early as 1623 that she had been visited by the spirit of the Old Testament prophet, Daniel, she began to write and speak prophecies, apparently accurately foretelling the death of her first husband but incorrectly predicting the end of the world. The act which won her the most notoriety occurred in 1638 when after declaring that she was the Bishop of Lichfield, she sprinkled the hangings at the Cathedral altar with her own special holy water made of a tar mixture. Throughout her life, for this and other offenses, she suffered imprisonment in places such as Bedlam and the Tower of London.[34]

Although it is certain that she had some knowledge of Latin, using it in her prophecies to emphasize her claims of supernatural powers, there is no evidence of the extent or the quality of her training. In this regard, it is interesting to note that her only surviving child, Lucy Davies, the wife of the sixth Earl of Huntingdon, and her granddaughter, Lady Elizabeth Langham, the scholar lauded by Samuel Clarke, the Puritan minister, were both classicists. While Lady Eleanor did use Latin phrases in her prophecies, all of her books were written in English. In 1625 she published her first tract, *A Warning To The Dragon And All His Angels,* and in 1633 and 1641, she had three more treatises printed. During the succeeding years until her death in 1652, she authored an additional forty-nine books and broadsides, most of which were printed privately.[35]

Because learning to pray in Latin was as important to some members of the Roman faith as learning to read the scriptures in the vernacular was to members of the reformed religions, Latin training began early in many Catholic households, often directed by mothers who taught their children simple vocabulary in the nursery. Since a knowledge of this language facilitated their spiritual meditations, a few members of the Roman faith did encourage intelligent young women to study more advanced Latin, but even with this support, only eight Catholic women, one of them of noble birth, can be specifically identified as having any fluency in this language. The noblewoman who was able to read extensively in Latin was Elizabeth Howard, the child of the Countess of Arundel, but her knowledge was limited, for there is no evidence that she was taught composition or rhetoric, and it is not likely that she was permitted to study the pagan authors.[36]

While only seven Catholic women of the lesser aristocracy can be definitely identified as classicists, one of them, Mary Ward, did attempt to give members of her sex this training in schools that she founded. Unfortunately, it is impossible to estimate the number of women of the fourth generation who studied grammar at her Institute of the Blessed Virgin Mary. Of the five compatriots who traveled with her to St. Omer in 1609 to begin this new order, only Winifred Wigmore, born in 1585, was reputed to be a classicist, but as one of the complaints raised against Ward as early as 1621 was that those who presented themselves to her were trained to give public exhortations in Latin, it is likely that most of her novices received some advanced instruction in that language. Even more interesting is the information that Ward, herself, referred to her day schools for poor students in Munich as Latin schools. In a letter of 1627 to Winifred Bedingfield, who was in charge of the Munich establishments, Ward congratulated her on the quality of the Latin themes of her students and then commented: "All such as are capable invite them to it, no talent is to be so much regarded in them as the Latin tongue."[37]

While the members of the Institute probably read few, if any, pagan works, there were at least four Catholic women who may have had the Latin training advocated by Sir Thomas More: Jane Owen, Elizabeth Jane Weston, and Mary and Helen Copley. Jane Owen is best known for her book, *An Antidote Against Purgatory,* which was published posthumously, probably on the continent, in 1634. Its title page described her as the "Honour of her Sexe for learning in England" and identified her residence as Godstow, Oxfordshire. In the work, itself, Owen indicated that her sources were several Latin books that she had personally translated, including those of the Church Fathers and of Cardinal Roberto Bellarmine. As there were many Owens who resided in Stuart Oxfordshire, her exact identification cannot be ascertained, but it can be suggested that she was a grandchild of Dr. George Owen of Godstow, an eminent physician to both King Henry VIII and Queen Mary. Some of his descendants were recusants, for it was noted in 1615 that his grandson was in trouble with the authorities because of his stated desire to implement the Papal Bull of deposition against King James. She may also have had a distant kinship to John Owen, the Latin epigrammist. In one of his verses published in 1607, he praised as an erudite and capable Latin poet, a woman named Jane Owen, who was his relative, the eldest of six daughters, and a resident of Oxford.[38]

Outside religious circles, the most well-known female classicist was Elizabeth Jane Weston. A few years after her birth in London in 1582, her family fled to Bohemia, an exile that was probably caused by her father's Roman Catholicism. After his death in 1597 that left his family in desperate financial straits, his daughter dedicated some Latin poems to a number of Bohemian patrons. In 1602 a Silesian nobleman, Georg Marten von Baldhoven, collected some of her scattered poems and published them at his own cost at Frankfurt under the title of *Poemata.* Four years later he had another volume, *Parthenicon,* printed at Prague. While some of her verses are of a personal nature and indicate her friendships, others are addressed to royalty, including James I, and a few are translations of Aesop. She had a fine education, for she wrote wih a careful meter and exceptional diction in the style of the "pure Latin of Cicero," and even Thomas Farnaby, a classical scholar and a friend of Ben Jonson, compared her work favorably to that of Sir Thomas More. Besides Latin, English, and German, the tongue in which she was most fluent, she also knew Greek, Italian, and Czech. In about 1602 she married Johann Leon, an agent at the Imperial court of the Duke of Brunswick and Prince of Aphalt, and gave birth to seven children before her death in 1612.[39]

It is only by chance that information has survived of the education of the two Copley sisters, who were the daughters of Magdalen Pridieux and William

Copley; the granddaughters of Helen Clement Pridieux, and the great-grand-daughters of Margaret Gigs Clement. The only evidence of the learning of Mary and Helen Copley is a contemporary statement that when they joined the convent of St. Ursula's at Louvain, they took along with them their copy of Virgil. As, unfortunately, there is no extant information about their training, it can only be assumed that Sir Thomas More's program of study was extended to them. It seems rather fitting to end a review of the classical instruction of Catholic women with the Copleys, the descendants of Margaret Gigs, one of the female humanists of the More circle, where both the movement for the advanced education of women and this book began.[40]

The female classicists of the fourth generation belonged to three different groups, the court as well as less-fashionable Protestant and Catholic circles. As it was no longer an acceptable pastime for women at court to study the classics, the learned Lady Falkland, who was self-taught in several languages, was viewed as somewhat eccentric. By the standards of Sir Thomas More, Lady Falkland's humanism was a failure because it did not contribute to a pleasant marital relationship with her husband, although the great martyr would have approved of her conversion to Roman Catholicism. Her Protestant associates could well have cited her experiences to support their arguments that well-educated women were certain to lose all respect for husbandly authority.

Turning to the other six Protestant scholars, no information about the training of Legge, Armyne, and Rainbowe can be discovered other than the report of their linguistic abilities. While the fourth woman, Lady Eleanor Audley, did make public utterances in this language, it is not definite that she had any language training other than an elementary acquaintance with a few words and phrases. There is no doubt that the final two scholars, Jocelin and Speght, were well grounded in Latin, both having studied a few pagan authors as well as the Church Fathers. Unlike Lady Falkland, their approach to their learning was one of gratitude that they had been given the opportunity to acquire knowledge not normally available to women. Their humble attitude prevented their readers from accusing them of eccentricity.

Although the reformers had adopted Sir Thomas More's familial concepts, they had generally ignored his advocacy of classical training for women, viewing this education as a hindrance rather than a help to marital harmony. While the adherents of the Counter Reformation, in contrast to the Protestants, rejected the religious patriarchalism of More because it was based on anti-clerical attitudes, some did display more sympathy for his educational philosophy. The result was that there were a few outstanding classicists among the Catholic women of the fourth generation, for two women became Latin poets and one founded a teaching order dedicated to training young girls in that language. Because of the perse-cution, the poems of Weston were published in foreign lands and the girls' schools of Ward generally had to be founded abroad. Before condemning the short-sightedness of the English Protestants for causing the exodus of some excellent female talent, it is well to note that without the religious conflict and its accompanying human suffering, it is unlikely that Ward and Weston and perhaps Owen, would have made the intellectual commitments that led to their accomplishments.

While the Protestant women had studied Latin as an aid to learning English, to understanding the vernacular Bible, or to making their utterances and writings appear more erudite by sprinkling them with classical phrases, the Catholic female scholars showed an appreciation for the innate beauty and structure of this ancient language. Considered exceptional by their contemporaries, Ward, Owen, and Weston all achieved their impressive literary goals while they were single. In fact, the only one of the three to marry was Weston, but unfortunately, there is no evidence about the influence of her education on her family relationships partly because, unlike Lady Falkland, she was unable to survive her childbearing years. It is indicative of the failure of Sir Thomas More to popularize this instruction for Tudor women as a preparation for matrimony that in the fourth generation the Protestants came to view it as a marital handicap, a majority of the women classicists of the Catholic faith remained unmarried, and of the female descendants of his own circle, only Magdalen Pridieux Copley, the granddaughter of Margaret Gigs Clement, remained faithful to his program, educating her two Copley children, as she had been taught by her mother, to read classical literature.

NOTES

1. S. J. Houston, *James I* (London, 1973), pp. 3-9; *The Private Correspondence of Jane, Lady Cornwallis, 1613-1644* (London, 1842), p. 125; Sir John Haringon, *A Tract on the Succession to the Crown* (London, 1880), p. xi; John Oglander, *A Royalist Notebook: the Commonplace Book of Sir John Oglander of Nunwell, 1585-1655,* ed. Francis Bamford (London, 1936), p. 192.

2. Ivor John Carnegie Brown, *The Women in Shakespeare's Life* (New York, 1969), p. 159; Mervyn James, "English Politics and the Concept of Honour, 1485-1642," *Past and Present Supplements,* No. 3, (1978), p. 73; C. T. Onions, *Shakespeare's England,* 2 vols. (Oxford, 1917), II, 311-317; although women did not perform on the public stage in England, there were women actresses in both France and Spain and in 1629 some French actresses performed in England. See Oscar G. Brockett, *History of the Theatre,* 3rd ed. (Boston, 1977), p. 106; Alfred Horatio Upham, *The French Influence in English Literature* (Reprint, 1965), p. 370; and Mary Elizabeth Perry, "Acresses, Singers, and Dancers in Early Modern Seville," paper given at the West Coast Conference of Women Historians, April, 1978; for the connection of prostitution and the theatre, see E. J. Burford, *In The Clink: The Story of England's Oldest Prison* (London, 1978), p. 95 and Gamini Salgado, *The Elizabethan Underworld* (London, 1977), p. 58; George C. Williamson, *Lady Anne Clifford,* 2nd ed. (London, 1967), p. 75.

3. Jeremiah Holmes Wiffen, *Historical Memoirs of the House of Russell,* 2 vols. (London, 1833), II, 66-120; Ian Grimble, *The Harington Family* (London, 1957), pp. 152-166.

4. For a few of the works dedicated to her, see Michael Drayton, *Endiminon and Phoebe Ideas Latmus* (London, 1595); John Donne, *With Elegies On the Author's Death* (London, 1633); Samuel Daniel, *The Vision of Twelve Goddesses* (London, 1604); William Perkins, *A salve for a sicke man* (Cambridge, 1597); *The Letters of John Chamberlain,* ed. Norman Egbert McClure, 2 vols. (Philadelphia, 1939), I, 306 and II, 55, 245, and

250; Jeremiah Holmes Wiffen, II, 109-120; Ian Grimble, pp. 165-170; Bernard H. New-digate, *Michael Drayton and his Circle* (Oxford, 1941), p. 66; Pearl Hogrefe, *Tudor Women: Commoners and Queens* (Ames, Ia., 1975), pp. 136 and 141; Lady Jane Corn-wallis, pp. 28 and 40; for the quote, see John Florio, *A worlde of wordes or dictionaries in Italian and English* (London, 1598), dedication.

5. Charlotte Kohler, "The Elizabethan Woman of Letters," Ph.D. dissertation, University of Virginia, 1936, publication charts.

6. *The Lady Falkland: Her Life from a MS in the Imperial Archives at Lille,* ed. Richard Simpson (London, 1861), pp. 1-9; Kenneth B. Murdock, *The Sun at Noon: Three Biographical Sketches* (New York, 1939), p. 10; Kurt Weber, *Lucius Cary, Second Viscount Falkland* (Reprint, 1967), pp. 3 and 11; Bernard H. Newdigate, pp. 77-78; John Bodenham, *England's Helicon* (London, 1899), p. xii; see also Lady Georgiana Fullerton, *The Life of Elizabeth Lady Falkland, 1585-1639,* quarterly series, vol. 43 (London, 1872).

7. *The Lady Falkland,* pp. 1-9.

8. *Ibid.,* pp. 8-10; Lady Elizabeth Cary, *The Tragedy of Mariam,* ed. A. C. Dunstan, (Oxford, 1914), pp. v-xiii; Sir John Davies of Hereford, *Muses Sacrifice, or Divine Meditations* (London, 1612), dedication.

9. Alexander M. Witherspoon, *The Influence of Robert Garnier on Elizabethan Drama* (New Haven, 1924), pp. 84 and 152-154; Virginia W. Beauchamp, "Sidney's Sister as Translator of Garnier," *Renaissance News,* X (1957), 12-13; see also Chapter 7 of this book.

10. Arthur C. Dunstan, *Examination of two English Dramas* (Königsberg, Germany, 1908), p. 4; Charlotte Kohler, p. 195; Nancy Cotton Pearse, "Elizabeth Cary, Renaissance Playwright," *Texas Studies in Literature and Language,* XVIII (Winter, 1977), 601-608.

11. *The Lady Falkland,* p. 9; Lady Elizabeth Cary, pp. ix-xix; Charlotte Kohler, pp. 183 and 195; Nancy Cotton Pearse, p. 606.

12. Nancy Cotton Pearse, pp. 601-608; *The Lady Falkland,* pp. 18, 23-36, 43-45, and 184-188; see also J.A.R. Marriott, *The Life and Times of Lucius Cary, Viscount Falkland* (London, 1908).

13. *The Lady Falkland,* p. 113; D. A. Stauffer, "A Deep and Sad Passion," *The Parrott Presentation Volume,* ed. Hardin Craig (Reprint, 1967), pp. 291-314.

14. *The Lady Falkland,* pp. 39 and 108.

15. Ibid., p. 31.

16. *Dictionary of National Biography*; John Marston, *The Workes of Mr. J. Marston, Being tragedies and comedies, collected into one volume* (London, 1633), dedicatory letter by William Sheares.

17. Ibid.

18. *The Poetical Works of William Basse,* ed. R. W. Bond (London, 1893), p. 155; Douglas Bush, *English Literature in the Earlier Seventeenth Century, 1600-1660* (Oxford, 1962), p. 53; John Buxton, *Elizabethan Taste* (New York, 1965), p. 246.

19. *Report on the Manuscripts of Lord De L'Isle & Dudley Preserved at Penshurst Place,* H.M.C., 6 vols. (London, 1934), II, 164, 268, and 424; John Chamberlain, II, 16; Bridget MacCarthy, *Women Writers: their Contribution to the English Novel, 1621-1744* (New York, 1948), pp. 54-77; F. P. Wilson, "Some Notes on Authors and Patrons in Tudor and Stuart Times," *John Quincy Adams Memorial Studies,* ed. James G. McManaway, Giles E. Dawson, and Edwin E. Willoughby (Washington, D.C., 1948), p. 555; Margaret Anne Witten-Hannah, "Lady Mary Wroth's Urania: The Work and the Tradition," Ph.D. dissertation, University of Auckland, 1978, pp. 66-69; see also W. C. Waller, "An Extinct County Family: Wroth of Loughton Hall," *Transactions of the Essex*

Archaeological Society, N.S. 8 (1903), 156-186; and Graham Parry, "Lady Mary Wroth's Urania," *Proceedings of the Leeds Philosophical and Literary Society: Literary and History Section*, XVI (1976), 51-60.

20. Bridget MacCarthy, p. 59-77; Charlotte Kohler, p. 221.

21. Charlotte Kohler, pp. 205-221, Bridget MacCarthy, pp. 55-77; *Report on the Manuscripts of the Earl of Denbigh Preserved at Newnham Paddox, Warwickshire*, part V, H.M.C. (London, 1911), p. 3; *Calendar of the Manuscripts of the Most Honourable the Marquis of Salisbury Preserved at Hatfield House, Hertfordshire*, H.M.C., 24 vols. (London, 1971), XII, pp. 160-162; Margaret Anne Witten-Hannah, pp. 68-70; two of these books may have been written anonymously by men. See the discussion later in this Chapter; John Chamberlain, II, 427; Josephine A. Roberts, "An Unpublished Literary Quarrel Concerning the Supression of Lady Mary Wroth's "Urania' (1621)," *Notes and Queries*, XXIV (1977), 534-535; see also J. J. O'Connor, "James Hay and 'The Countess of Montgomeries' Urania,' " *Notes and Queries*, II (1955), 150-152; Paul Salzman, "Notes: Contemporary References in Mary Wroth's Urania," *Review of English Studies*, XXIX (1977), 177-181; it was nine years before another woman published a non-religious work on a topic that was not associated with domestic matters. In 1630 Diana Primrose published *A Chaine of Pearle*, a book of verses honoring Queen Elizabeth.

22. Katherine Duncan-Jones and Jan Van Dorsten, eds., *Miscellaneous Prose of Sir Philip Sidney* (Oxford, 1973), pp. 216-217; Ben Jonson, *The Complete Poetry* (New York, 1963), pp. 33, 81, and 166; for a discussion of the *Arcadia*, see Chapter 7; *The Works of Edmund Spenser*, 8 vols. (Baltimore, Md., 1947), VII-ii, 161.

23. Lady Mary Wroth, *Pamphilia to Amphilanthus*, ed. G. F. Waller (Salzburg, Austria, 1977), pp. 3, 6, 8-9, and 19-20; Charlotte Kohler, p. 202; Josephine A. Roberts, "Lady Mary Wroth's Sonnets: A Labryrinth of the Mind," *Journal of Women's Studies in Literature*, I (Autumn, 1979), 319-329.

24. For the verse see, Lady Mary Wroth, *The Countess of Mountgomeries Urania* (London, 1621), p. 13; see also G. F. Waller, pp. 5, 14, 41, and 87; James L. Sanderson, *Sir John Davies* (Boston, 1975), p. 38; she died in 1668. See Margaret Anne Witten-Hannah, p. 46.

25. Roger Thomson, *Women in Stuart England and America: A Comparative Study* (London, 1974), p. 4; Charlotte Kohler, p. 234.

26. Douglas Bush, p. 26; Dorothy Gardiner, *English Girlhood at School* (Oxford, 1929), p. 232, note 4, quoted by Ruth Hughey, "Cultural Interests of Women in England from 1524 to 1640 Indicated in the Writings of Women," Ph.D. dissertation, Cornell University, 1932, p. 61; Katherine Rogers, *The Troublesome Helpmate, A History of Misogyny in Literature* (Seattle, 1966), p. 129.

27. Mary A. E. Green, *Lives of the Princesses of England from the Norman Conquest*, 6 vols. (London, 1857), V, 155; see also Josephine Ross, *The Winter Queen: The Story of Elizabeth Stuart* (New York,1979); P. M. Handover, *Arbella Stuart: Royal Lady of Hardwick* (London, 1957), p. 198.

28. John Florio, *The Essayes or Morall Politike discourses of Lo: Michaell Montaigne* (London, 1603), dedication; *The Lady Falkland*, pp. 4 and 10; Francis R. Johnson, "Shakespearian Imagery and Senecan Imitation," *John Quincy Adams Memorial Studies*, p. 40; D. A. Stauffer, p. 305.

29. Margo Todd, "Humanists, Puritans and the Spiritualized Household," *Church History*, XLIX (March, 1980), 18-34; Dorothy Leigh, *The Mothers Blessing*, 7th ed. (London, 1621), pp. 49-50; Richard Mulcaster, *Positions (1581)* (New York, 1971), p. 30; *The Works of John Taylor, the Water Poet*, Spenser Society, No. 7 (Reprint,

1967), p. 30; Thomas Salter, *A Mirrhor mete for all Mothers, Matrones, and Maidens, intitled the Mirrhor of Modestie* (London, 1579); *The Lady Falkland,* p. 35; Samuel Clarke, *The Lives of Sundry Eminent People in this Later Age,* 2 vols. (London, 1683), II, 197; Elizabeth Joceline, *The Mothers Legacie to her unborne Childe* (London, 1624), dedication; see also Chapters 8 and 9 of this book.

30. George Ballard, *Memoirs of British Ladies* (London, 1752), p. 361; *Dictionary of National Biography*; Doris Mary Stenton, *The English Woman in History,* (Reprint, 1977), pp. 136-137.

31. Samuel Clarke, *The Lives of Sundry,* II, 192 and 197 and *The Lives of Thirty-two English Divines,* third ed. (London, 1677), pp. 415-418; for a discussion of the tutor of Lady Langham and her mother, see J. R. Brink, "Bathsua Makin: Educator and Linguist (English, 1608?-1675?)," *Female Scholars: A Tradition of Learned Women* (Montreal, 1980), p. 90.

32. Joseph Swetnam, *Araignment of Lewd, Idle, Froward, and unconstant women* (London, 1615), p. 1; Charlotte Kohler, pp. 245 and 340; Rachel Speght, *A Mouzell for Melastomus* (London, 1617), dedication, and pp. 4 and 10; and bound with the *Mouzell, Certaine Quaeres to the bayter of Women* (London, 1617), dedication; and *Mortalities, Memorandum* (London, 1621), dedication; Ester Sowernam, *Ester hath hanged Haman* (London 1617); Constantia Munda, *The Worming of a mad Dogge* (London, 1617); *Dictionary of National Biography*.

33. *Dictionary of National Biography*; Elizabeth Jocelin, preface; Samuel Clarke, *The Lives of Sundry,* II, 197.

34. *The Poems of Sir John Davies* (Oxford, 1975), pp. xlvi-xlvii; C. J. Hindle, *A Bibliography of the Printed Pamphlets and Broadsides of Lady Eleanor Douglas, The Seventeenth Century Prophetess* (Edinburgh, 1936), pp. 5-12; George Ballard, pp. 271-280; Theodore Spencer, "The History of an Unfortunate Lady," *Harvard Studies and Notes in Philology and Literature,* XX (1938), 47-61; Charlotte Kohler, p. 319; see also J. R. Brink, p. 90.

35. Norma McMullen, "The Education of English Gentlewomen, 1540-1640," *History of Education,* VI (1977), p. 96.

36. Henry Foley, ed., *Records of the English Province of the Society of Jesus,* 7 vols. (London, 1875-1880), II, 445; Henry Graville Howard, fourteenth Duke of Norfolk, *The Lives of Philip Howard, Earl of Arundel and of Anne Dacre, His Wife* (London, 1857), p. 224; see also Chapter 9.

37. Mary C. E. Chambers, *Life of Mary Ward,* 2 vols. (London, 1882), I, 236 and II, 45 and 193; see also Chapter 9; Ward did have sisters, but no information about their education has been discovered.

38. Jane Owen, *An Antidote Against Purgatory,* English Recusant Literature, Vol. 166 (Menston, Yorkshire, 1973), title page and p. 8; *Dictionary of National Biography; Joannis Audoeni Epigrammatum,* ed. John R. C. Martyn, 2 vols. (Leiden, 1976), I, 146.

39. Douglas Bush, p. 663; J. C. Kalckhoff, ed., *Elisabetha Joannae Westoniae Opuscula* (Frankfort, 1723); Antonin Kolar, *Humanisticka Basnirka Vestonia* (Bratislave, 1926); see also Thomas Fuller, *The History of the Worthies of England,* 3 vols. (Reprint, 1965), III, 217.

40. Catherine S. Durrant, *A Link between Flemish Mystics and English Martyrs* (London, 1925), pp. 208 and 420; Dom Adam Hamilton, *The Chronicle of the English Augustinian Canonesses Regular of the Lateran at St. Monica's in Louvain,* 2 vols. (London, 1904), I, 88-89.

11

Summary and Conclusion

By using a generational structure to maintain chronological integrity and by analyzing female achievements within the context of the impact of humanist ideas and religious reform, this book has provided the first historical account of scholarly accomplishments of Tudor women. All such studies must begin with the Christian humanism of Sir Thomas More. He argued that instruction in the pagan classics combined with a study of Christian thought would produce a moral and enlightened governing class of men committed to reform of the Church and to eradication of social ills. These men were to function as heads of households in which nuclear family relationships were to be strengthened by the extension of classical instruction to women, for More believed that the female humanist would not only be an attractive and desirable wife but also a loving and caring mother. Although he remained loyal to the doctrines of his Church, his philosophy was strongly anti-clerical in that one of its many aims was to remove women from the influence of the ill-educated clergy by insisting that wives look to their husbands for spiritual guidance. In this first generation, More was unable to convince the English aristocracy to accept his educational ideas partly because most women of this elite group were not then fully literate in English. In his lifetime, only one woman outside his circle, the Princess Mary, became a humanist.

Events in England soon led to the martyrdom of this great Christian humanist. Because More was unable to support the lay supremacy, Henry VIII had him executed and turned to scholars like Sir Thomas Elyot for assistance in convincing the aristocracy to extend classical training to their sons. While continuing to promote many of More's educational goals, the royal family also patronized scholars who wrote verses in which Petrarchan and chivalric themes were blended to honor poetic suffering for unobtainable loves rather than domestic tranquility. The native poetry of the Earl of Surrey and of Sir Thomas Wyatt in which they introduced Italian literary forms has earned their authors as much if not more fame than their translations.

By appointing classical tutors for the Princess Elizabeth and her half-brother, Prince Edward, the King prompted four esteemed and ambitious noble families, all with a child named after Queen Jane, the mother of the young Prince, to offer similar instruction to their daughters in the hope that advantageous royal marriages might be arranged for them. In this second generation, the women were given a variety of programs of study. Influenced by both Christian and court humanists, Elizabeth and her Howard relatives, for example, learned to appreciate the Italian language as well as the ancient ones. Some of the most intelligent women humanists of this generation were the Cooke sisters, one of whom, Lady Bacon, completed a translation of Bishop Jewel's *Apologia* that still gives testimony to her superb Latin skills. In addition, the work of More's granddaughter, Mary Clarke Basset, has been greatly admired.

Having survived the Marian persecution, the Protestants of Elizabeth's reign were determined to prevent any future resurrection of Roman power. Although they adopted many of More's familial concepts, they attempted to suppress the classical instruction in the household that he had advocated, for fear that even an elementary knowledge of Latin would encourage clandestine Catholic devotions. While, after first learning their religious lessons in English, increasing numbers of young men were able to study grammar at public schools, most women lacked similar academic opportunities, largely because no secondary schools for them were founded. Despite this neglect of advanced female education, two important reformed women of the third generation did become Latinists: Anne Cecil, a daughter of the learned Mildred Cooke, and Arbella Stuart, a royal claimant. Because Arbella was never recognized as the royal heir and because the Queen lacked children of her own to instruct, the court ceased to offer educational leadership to the nobility as it had done during the reign of Henry VIII.

While the men who were inspired by the presence of the Virgin Queen to write the esteemed poetry of her reign had a classical education, they chose to express many of their ideas and feelings in English. It was Sir Philip Sidney's tragic and chivalric death that provided an excuse and an opportunity for his sister, Lady Pembroke, to pursue his poetic goals in a public forum. The result was that a woman without classical skills was able to win recognition for her great literary accomplishments.

An outburst of female creativity occurred in the next generation. Although there had been women classicists in the first and second generations with superb skills, it was an impoverished young woman, Elizabeth Jane Weston, born in 1582, who wrote secular verses which won the international praise of disinterested scholars. Despite the prevailing assumption that Englishwomen should be educated in the home, a Catholic woman, Mary Ward, attempted to found a new religious order dedicated to teaching girls the Latin tongue in free day schools. Among the Protestants there were also outstanding scholars. Lady Falkland and Lady Wroth turned from translating the work of eminent men, as most of their predecessors had done, to the challenge of reinterpreting classical values to meet the needs of their society in their own words and from their own personal points of view.

Finally, even among the religious radicals, this originality could be noted. Although in the 1530s, the Maid of Kent had dared to suggest that she had been visited in trances by Our Lady, she remained a victim and perhaps a puppet of well-educated clergymen. Her Protestant counterpart of the fourth generation, Lady Eleanor Audley, seems to have functioned independently of the advice of her family and Church. Even her persecution was less savage than that of the Maid of Kent, for Lady Audley suffered imprisonment rather than capital punishment. After her release from custody, she not only continued to make prophecies but to publish broadsides and treatises about them.

One important question raised in this book was whether, as has been asserted, the Protestant Reformation elevated the social esteem of women in England above that of members of their sex in Catholic countries. While a definitive answer was not attempted, the suggestion was made that the legalization of clerical marriage had a far less positive impact on community attitudes toward Englishwomen than has previously been claimed. At least until the end of Elizabeth's reign, even bishops' wives failed to win the respect that their husbands' office would ordinarily have bestowed upon them. Closely related to this issue is the comparison that was made of the practical results of the Reformation on the domestic roles of both Protestant and Catholic women in England. Although they failed to encourage secondary education for women, the reformers did favor strengthening nuclear family relationships as More had suggested. They argued that women should be instructed in their native tongue not only to enable them to read the scriptures in translation but also to assist their husbands with the moral and Godly training of household members. As part of the Protestant program to expand lay participation in religious matters, it was also expected that wives would seek spiritual advice from their husbands rather than from clergymen.

Had Protestants successfully implemented the spiritualized household, the status of women would have undergone a demotion rather than a promotion, but from the beginning of the Reformation, there were factors that hindered its widespread acceptance. While many men were nothing more than indifferent conformists, even those who were genuine reformers found these family responsibilities extraordinarily difficult if not impossible to fulfill. The defeat of the clerical elite also made it possible for some women to assume pastoral roles, which Protestants had expected laymen to perform, and by the middle of the seventeenth century, a few of their sex were even gathering churches in defiance of male authority. If, indeed, the standing of women was enhanced in the kingdom, it was because reformed theology was not implemented successfully by a monopoly state church.

While in theory the clerical position remained strong in the Catholic religion, its faithful women in England found themselves in a position similar to that of their Protestant counterparts. Because of the persecution, the household had to function as a parish, a development that presented women with many opportunities to assume pastoral duties. It may even have been Mary Ward's upbringing among these assertive women that emboldened her to challenge the male hierarchy of her Church. While her efforts to combat the secondary status of her sex within her religion make her an attractive figure for modern study, her immediate failure to accomplish her goals symbolizes the unwillingness of the Church leaders to permit women to participate equally with men in the Counter Reformation. Although a few English women could live respectably in nunneries and convents on the continent, it is unlikely that in England single women of this faith had any great social advantage over their Protestant counterparts. Even if within some pious Catholic families, the esteem for privately professed females, like Anne Vaux, was high, the hostility evinced by the majority culture to unmarried women surely served to undermine that positive tone.

It was not the theology or practice of any particular variety of Christianity that gave birth to vigorous and exciting work on the part of women. What happened in the sixteenth century was that a religion which had been struggling with heresies from its origin split asunder not just into two different factions but into a variety of splinters. Attacked first by More and the other Christian humanists who proposed reform of its outward medieval trappings and of its clerical elite, the Church was next assaulted by Protestants who denied its essential doctrine but who also paused to argue among themselves over non-essential matters. The prolonged conflict among kaleidoscopic Christian views created opportunities for both men and women to perform in unexpected and unusual ways. The result was the wonderful Latin translations of Margaret Roper, Anne Bacon, and Mary Clarke Basset, the majestic symbolism of the court of Elizabeth, the intricate Psalms imitations of the Countess of Pembroke, and the outpouring of accomplishments in classical and native literature of the fourth generation.

While it was suggested in the introduction to this book and in Chapter 10 that of the four generations under review, the Jacobean was most deserving of the epithet of "golden," it also must be recognized that if the literary efforts of these women are examined within the context of contemporary religious, social, and economic conditions, it is impossible to argue that any of them lived in a "golden age." Not only was an extremely small percentage of women ever offered an advanced classical or vernacular education but even by the end of Elizabeth's reign, less than five percent of them knew enough about writing to sign their names. In addition, the same dynamic process that gave rise to a variety of scholarly achievements also produced death and deprivation. Some contemporaries of Margaret Roper were expelled from their convents; of Lady Bacon were burned in the Marian fires; and of Lady Pembroke were executed and imprisoned for aiding priests. Although the suffering of women for their faith was lessened in its severity by the Jacobean period, the serious scholarship of the fourth-generation women was greeted with greater public and private scorn. Among pious Protestants, there was a pervasive fear that the advanced education of a woman would make her too proud to humble herself properly to her husband. By not extending classical instruction to Princess Elizabeth, King James also set the tone at court that disparaged learned females.[1]

While a few aristocratic women struggled to overcome social hostility to their advanced scholarship, their lower-class counterparts were confronted with far more severe liabilities including persecution as witches. All women were oppressed by the privilege extended to literate men of benefit of clergy and by the discriminatory laws that regulated marriage and domestic affairs. In addition, there were social and economic problems that profoundly diminished the living standards of both sexes, for the country's famine, inflation, underemployment, and vagabondage are a reminder that, as the historian Penry Williams recently asserted: "The glamour and brilliance of the Tudor court and the Elizabethan theatre shine against a backdrop of dark suffering for the majority of the population."[2]

NOTES

1. For suggestions about a "golden age," see Pearl Hogrefe, *Tudor Women: Commoners and Queens* (Ames, Ia., 1975), p. 97.

2. Penry Williams, *The Tudor Regime* (Oxford, 1979), p. 214.

Bibliographical Essay

One major problem in writing women's history is that of finding proper documentation, for there is reason to believe that many of their records have been selectively destroyed because they were deemed of little value.[1] Thus, although it is true that far more evidence has survived about Tudor women than about their predecessors, much information about them must still be culled from the works of men: their publications, wills, letters, diaries, and public records. Even when women took advantage of the new printing industry, their publications were too often only translations, however brilliant, of male creativity. Given these qualifications, a surprising number of women's records are available: letters, both private and public, several translations and compositions, three journals, a few monastic chronicles, and a biographical study. Some of their writings have been printed in two useful modern volumes: *The Female Spectator: English Women Writers Before 1800,* ed. Mary R. Mahl and Helene Koon (1977); and *the Paradise of Women: Writings by Englishwomen of the Renaissance,* ed. Betty Travisky (1981).

In addition to the primary sources, there are a number of secondary works on women. Although historians have made frequent reference to women humanists and reformers, no entire book has previously been devoted to them. Four recent bibliographies will be of great assistance to future researchers of this topic. In 1974 Norma Greco and Ronalle Novotny published "Bibliography of Women in the English Renaissance," in the *University of Michigan Papers in Women's Studies*; in 1977 Patricia Gartenberg and Nena Thames Whittemore had their article "A Checklist of English Women in Print, 1475-1640," printed in the *Bulletin of Bibliography and Magazine Notes*; in 1979 Rosemary Masek included her essay, "Women in an Age of Transition: 1485-1714," in *The Women of England: From Anglo-Saxon Times to the Present: Interpretive Bibliographical Essays,* ed. Barbara Kanner; and in 1982 Suzanne Hull published *Chaste, Obedient, and Silent.*

A few general works are available on Tudor women. Pearl Hogrefe included information on well-educated women and a few references to religious victims in her book, *Tudor Women: Commoners and Queens* (1975). In her work published in 1979 under a similar title, *Tudor Women: Queens and Commoners,* Alison Plowden gave a brief study of the life and times of Henry VIII and his family. In addition, two articles in the *International Journal of Women Studies* are helpful. The first, Minna F. Weinstein's "Reconstructing our Past, Reflections on Tudor Women" (1978), suggested researching topics, such as childbirth and female organizations, which are especially relevant to women. In 1981

Caroline Andre's article, "Some Selected Aspects of the Role of Women in Sixteenth Century England," also provided some valuable approaches to women's history.

There are a variety of other books which contain some information about Tudor women. Many are outdated but are still useful sources. They include: Willam Alexander, *The History of Women from the Earliest Antiquity,* 2 vols. (1779); Thomas Wright, *Womankind in Western Europe from the Earliest Times to the 17th Century* (1869); Georgiana Hill, *Women in English Life from Medieval to Modern Times,* 2 vols. (1896); two works by Violet Wilson, *Queen Elizabeth's Maids of Honour* (1922) and *Society Women of Shakespeare's Time* (1924); Lucy Hunter Murray, *The Ideal of the Court Lady in England, 1558-1625* (1938); Carroll Camden, *The Elizabethan Woman: A Panorama of English Womanhood, 1540-1640* (1951); Wallace Notestein, "The English Woman, 1580-1650," *Studies in Social History,* ed. J. Plumb (1955); Ruth Kelso, *Doctrine for the Lady of the Renaissance* (1956); and Doris Mary Stenton, *The English Woman in History* (1957), which is still the standard work on this topic. Especially good are three recent books: Julia O'Faolain and Lauro Martines, eds., *Not in God's Image* (1973); Susan G. Bell, ed., *Women from the Greeks to the French Revolution* (1973); and Renate Bridenthal and Claudia Koonz, eds., *Becoming Visible: Women in European History* (1977).

Space does not permit a comprehensive listing of all the biographies and articles devoted to specific women. For some of these works the reader is invited to explore the notes of this present study. A few general biographical collections have been included here. They are: George Ballard, *Memoirs of British Ladies* (1752), an often quoted and helpful source; Louisa Costello, *Memoirs of Eminent English Women,* 4 vols. (1844); J. G. Nichols, "Female Biographies of English History," *Gentleman's Magazine* (1845), a surprisingly informative and sympathetic series of articles; Agnes Strickland, *Lives of the Queens of England,* 12 vols. (1840-1848); Emily Sarah Holt, *Memoirs of Royal Ladies,* 2 vols. (1861); Mary A. E. Green, *Lives of the Princesses of England from the Norman Conquest,* 6 vols. (1857); the most recent collection is Pearl Hogrefe, *Women of Action in Tudor England* (1977).

There are a variety of books dealing with the Christian view of women. Two of the most interesting are Matilda Gage, *Women, Church, and State* (1900) and Rosemary Ruether, ed., *Religion and Sexism* (1974). Although several historians have included references to Protestant women in their works on religion, none has attempted a comprehensive study of those of the Tudor period. Besides the books of James Anderson, *Ladies of the Reformation,* 2 vols. (1855) and *Memorable Women of Puritan Times,* 2 vols. (1862), there is one recent collection of biographies: Roland Bainton, *Women of the Reformation in France and England* (1975). In 1981 Carol Levin's well-received article, "Women in the Book of Martyrs as Models of Behavior in Tudor England," appeared in *International Journal of Women's Studies.* Although there are several separate studies of women's convents, this, too, is a topic that needs modern investigation. Among the works available, although sadly outdated, are Thomas Hugo, *The Medieval Nunneries of the County of Somerset and Diocese of Bath and Wells* (1867); Lina Eckenstein, *Women Under Monasticism* (1896); Eileen Power, *Medieval English Nunneries* (1922), and A.F.C. Bourdillon, *The Order of Minoresses in England* (1926).

As the women of Tudor England were often restricted to household activities, studies of the family and the home are especially relevant. Although somewhat outdated, Chilton Powell, *English Domestic Relations, 1487-1653* (1917) and Lu Emily Pearson, *Elizabethans at Home* (1957), are good sources. The most controversial work, and one that must be examined, is Lawrence Stone, *The Family, Sex and Marriage in England, 1500-*

1800 (1977); Margo Todd in "Humanists, Puritans, and the Spiritualized Household," *Church History* (1980) offered an interesting response to part of Stone's thesis on the Puritan family.

As it is impossible to refer to all of the books devoted to the literary accomplishments of women, only a few surveys will be included here. Three Ph.D. dissertations of the 1930s are extraordinarily helpful in introducing new students to the literature of this period: Ruth Hughey, "Cultural Interests of Women in England from 1524 to 1640 Indicated in the Writing of Women," Cornell University (1932); Traugott L. Richter, "Anti-feminism in English Literature, 1500-1660," Northwestern University (1934); and Charlotte Kohler, "The Elizabethan Women of Letters," University of Virginia (1936). Among several general publications on this topic are two older ones: Jane Williams, *The Literary Women of England* (1861); and Myra Reynolds, *The Learned Lady in England, 1650-1760* (1920). Three useful modern studies are: Katherine Rogers, *The Troublesome Helpmate, A History of Misogyny in Literature* (1966); J. R. Brink, ed., *Female Scholars: A Tradition of Learned Women* (1980); and Roland H. Bainton, "Learned Women in the Europe of the Sixteenth Century," *Beyond Their Sex,* ed. Patricia Labalme. For a study of the activities of women as patrons, see David M. Bergeron, "Women as Patrons of English Renaissance Drama," *Patronage in the Renaissance,* ed. Guy Fitch Lytle and Stephen Orgel (1981).

Because many works have been written on education, only those dealing specifically with women can be listed here. They are: Foster Watson, *Vives and the Renascence Education of Women* (1912); Mary Cannon, *The Education of Women During the Renaissance* (1916); Dorothy Gardiner, *English Girlhood at School* (1929); Ada Wallas, *Before the Bluestockings* (1929); Josephine Kamm, *Hope Deferred: Girls' Education in English History* (1965); and Phyllis Stock, *Better than Rubies: A History of Women's Education* (1978). A recent summary can be found in Norma McMullen, "The Education of English Gentlewomen, 1540-1640," *History of Education* (1977). In addition, a thesis by Dorothy Meads, "An Account of the Education of Women and Girls in England in the Time of the Tudors," London University (1928) is still useful.

Most of the information about the succession of women to the throne must be found in general studies on that issue. The two best books for this research are by Mortimer Levine, *The Early Elizabethan Succession Question, 1558-1568* (1966) and *Tudor Dynastic Problems* (1973). Louise Scalingi also has a perceptive article on this topic, "The Scepter or the Distaff: The Question of Female Sovereignty, 1516-1570," *Historian* (1978).

NOTE

1. Eleanor Shipley Duckett, *Women and Their Letters in the Early Middle Ages* (Baltimore, Md., 1965), pp. 3-4.

Index

About the Author

RETHA M. WARNICKE is currently an Associate Professor of History at Arizona State University, Phoenix. She received her Ph.D. from Harvard University, and is the author of *William Lambarde, Elizabethan Antiquary* and of articles in *Guildhall Studies in London History, English Language Notes, The British Library Journal, Rendezvous,* and *Moreana.*